CHI

MIDNIGHT SUN

A Journey with Heart

Maud Steinberg

Cover Art by Chrissy Shamas

ISBN:10 1547177896
ISBN:13 978-1547177899

Printed in the United States of America

Library of Congress Control Number: 2018902614

To my Mother

This book is dedicated to my mother, Maj, who has been my inspiration and support on this journey. She is my best friend and confidante, and I love her with all my heart. We are mother and daughter, but also sisters.

A Memoir

This is a true story. Memories are imperfect and flawed at times, but I have been painfully honest about what happened so many years ago. I have relied in part on memories and family lore but mostly on my journal entries, letters, and my mother's journals. Some peoples' names have been changed to protect their privacy.

Chapter 1

When we are old and failing, it is the memories of childhood which can be summoned most clearly.
—Dan Simmons

When my mind wanders back to my early childhood, the memories I recall are mostly from the bright summer months in northern Sweden.

The area I come from is called Jämtland, located high in the mountains, toward the northwestern parts of Sweden and Norway. My family lived in a small town called Undersåker, and the beautiful city of Trondheim in Norway is only two hours away. The land over the mountains between Undersåker and Trondheim looks barren, due to the high altitude and cold temperatures.

I was born during the war in the spring of 1943, and I was a "virgin child." My mother, Maj, became pregnant at the age of sixteen. She was seduced by a dark-haired, handsome twenty-five-year-old soldier who was also a musician and a singer. I am sure she didn't know exactly what had happened, but there I was anyway, and she was still a virgin. Sören, the young man, told Maj that he didn't want to take her virginity, so there was no intercourse involved.

The pregnancy was a disgrace. Maj didn't know that she was pregnant until the day she felt something move inside her belly. When the news hit Undersåker, Maj was immediately sent away to give birth somewhere else.

Those were dark days for a young, intelligent student. Maj had always been a quiet, industrious girl. From the time, she was nine years old she was always busy knitting, and she started sewing when she was twelve. Maj made all her own clothes and some for her sisters and brother as well.

Maj's small, petite frame and her beautiful, bright face with the dark, shiny hair and blue-green eyes stirred protective feelings in the town's males. They were outraged and wanted to kill the musician-soldier for what he had done, but he was long gone. Nobody knew that Maj was still a virgin.

After I was born, my grandparents brought my mother and me home, and I became another addition to their family of five children. When the new school year started, Maj was allowed to go back to school. That was unheard of back then, but she was, after all, the best student the school had. Maj received her high school diploma the following summer. After graduation, Maj left to take a job in another town several hours away, and Karin, my grandmother (*mormor* in Swedish), whom I called *Momma*, became my mother for the next eight years of my life. *Mor* means "mother" in Swedish, so *mormor* means "mother's mother."

We truly lived during the summer months, engaging in many outdoor activities. We worked the fields, had picnics and family gatherings, went hiking high in snow-covered mountains, and swam in icy cold mountain streams. The midnight sun was an aphrodisiac, seducing us to stay up late and be more active than we were during the winter. The bewitching sun never really set. Around midnight, the sky became slightly caliginous, with a dim haze; the birds would stop singing for a couple of hours, and then the ball of fire was lit anew. It was wonderfully romantic and beguiling—probably the reason for the Scandinavians' obsession with the sun. In the winter, unfortunately, we only saw the sun for a few hours each day, but the snow brightened the landscape with a luminescent glow.

My grandparents' colorful house sat on a hill above town with sturdy, tall pine trees scattered around and a few birch trees here and there. On the south end of the house, the basement door faced a neatly cultivated garden with flowers; bushes of gooseberries, raspberries, and blackberries; a variety of vegetables; and lush rhubarb. In the garden was a hammock with a green awning, a picnic table, and several wooden chairs with brightly colored cushions. The garden was surrounded by a tall, neatly manicured hedge, which provided protection from the cows grazing around the house.

Across the misty blue-green river below was a mountain called Vällista, towering like a big black boulder, and I frequently saw large moose grazing along the river's edge. August, my grandfather, was the chief moose hunter in Undersåker. I called him *Morfar* in Swedish, which means "mother's father," as *far* means "father."

During the month of August, he and every other grown male left for tiny, rustic cabins in the woods to hunt these impressive creatures. Every year, Morfar shot at least one moose, sometimes more. Whatever the men killed was shared among all the families, prepared by the women, and eaten during the long, cold winter. Moose meatballs are the best meatballs in the world, and with the creamy gravy my grandmother made, complemented by lingonberries and new potatoes, it was the best meal in town.

There were mountains all around us, big and small, but the tallest was Åreskutan to the west, large and majestic with snow-covered peaks. That's where most of the tourists went skiing and where the Winter Olympics were held one year when I was young, and again in later years. To the east of us lived my grandfather's brother Jöns with his family, in a similar square wooden house, three stories tall with plenty of windows for the sun to peek in. The only difference was the color—our house was bright yellow, and Jöns's house was fire red.

Houses in northern Sweden are made of timber from the large tracts of forest covering the region. Wood is not only readily available but also very warm. Initially, wooden houses were not considered attractive, so people started to paint them red, to look like bricks, or yellow, to resemble stone. Today, most houses, from the smallest hut to the grandest building, are built from timber and painted in all sorts of vibrant colors all over Sweden.

Our house had numerous windows with wide, sturdy windowsills, which attested to the formidable insulation, and they were home to many houseplants and flowers that brightened the rooms.

Every house had a special entrance to shield the interior from the cold. First, you entered a separate hallway where you removed your shoes and outer clothing, and then you stepped into the house itself through another door.

In our house, we stepped into the kitchen, which was the central meeting place. The kitchen was the gathering place, the eating place, the place where you bathed in a big galvanized tub every Friday night, the place where you worked on projects or sewed, and even the place where one family member would sleep, in a wooden sofa box with a lid. The bedding was inside the sofa during the day, and the lid was closed, and at night it was opened into a bed. It was a hard, uncomfortable bed, but nobody complained. In the corner of the kitchen was a large black cast-iron wood-burning cook stove. Hanging above it on the wall was the switch. The switch, an impressive birch branch, was a constant reminder to be good, or else. I was never punished with it; the threat was enough.

Next to the stove was a door leading down to a cellar, which was used for food storage, as we had no refrigeration back in the forties. It was a large walk-in cellar located below ground, with walls lined with shelves for easy storage. Morfar kept a stash of Rio Cola bottles for himself in a cubbyhole in the far-right corner of the cellar. Sometimes he would give me a cola, which I thought was the most amazing taste I had ever experienced in my young life.

Our house, like Jöns's, had three stories, for practical reasons. During the winter, we lived in the middle of the house on the second floor, as that was warmer, and every spring we moved to the cooler basement, which was the ground floor. Moving every six months was exhilarating. Every surface was cleaned from top to bottom, and then we moved all our belongings, including the silverware and dishes, from one floor to the other. The top floor was either rented or used by visiting family members. Whatever floor was not lived on was rented to tourists year-round. It was a busy house, with people coming and going all day long and the smell of food, coffee, and baked goods always filling the air.

Morfar August was a farmer, a carpenter, and a bit of a medicine man. There was no doctor in town, so he took care of medical emergencies until a doctor could be reached and also tended to everyday medical problems. He was a jack-of-all-trades. Morfar was also a very handsome man, a Paul Newman look-alike with black hair and deep, dark-blue eyes. His build was athletic, and he was as strong as an ox. I remember clearly that he could do somersaults in his sixties.

Most men built their own houses and even some of the furniture. There was no running water in our house back in the forties and therefore no bathrooms. The indoor plumbing was installed later, in the early fifties. We saved rainwater in big galvanized barrels for washing our hair, making it soft and shiny. My grandmother, Momma, carried many heavy buckets of water from the well into the house daily.

The outhouse was behind the barn, close to the cow-dung heap, which made those visits even more unpleasant. In temperatures of negative thirty to forty degrees Celsius equivalent to negative twenty-two to forty degrees Fahrenheit, it was a rather unpleasant experience. At night, we had the old standard potty under the bed.

Family members helped each other with carpentry, farming, and slaughtering of moose and calves at the end of each summer. Every year, my pet calf disappeared, and for several years I wondered why, until one sunny summer day I walked in on the slaughter. I ran out with a horrified scream. I had caught Morfar in the act of cutting the calf's throat, and I saw the blood flow into a bucket. On the farm, you had to learn that your life depended on the food the farm provided. I was deeply saddened for my pet calf, but I learned not to get too attached when a new calf was born each spring.

The women traveled around from house to house, helping each other with the cooking and canning of moose and calf meat as well as making the thin, crisp bread called *tunnbröd*, which means "thin bread." This bread was baked in a large brick oven, comparable to a pizza oven; the bread was about two feet in diameter. The still-warm bread was folded three times and then stored in the attic for the winter. As a special treat, the women also baked *mjukbröd*. Mjukbröd means "soft bread," and it was baked the same way as tunnbröd but did not have the same long shelf life. When the mjukbröd was freshly made, it was soft and sweet, and the smell made my mouth water. It was my favorite.

August had four brothers and two sisters. One of the brothers, Olle, married Karin's sister Olga. Karin had two brothers and five sisters, so we had a large family with many cousins. It was a little confusing for me, though, to figure out where I fit in. My mother, whom I called *Mamma*, breastfed me for almost a year while going to school, but she was young and did not have the patience and understanding that my grandmother did. So, at the very beginning, I had two mothers, and when one left, it wasn't such a big loss.

Momma was the light in my life, and I was hers. She called me her *guldklump* (golden nugget), and I was very spoiled. Momma had a round, sweet face with soft light-blue-green eyes, but she was already wrinkled and gray in her forties. Her laughter was light and infectious. She loved to sing and play the mandolin, and she hummed and sang hymns while working. Jesus Christ was her lord and savior, and she believed more strongly in salvation than anyone I have ever known, without forcing her beliefs on anyone. We went to church every Sunday, and Momma would speak in tongues. I loved listening to the Bible stories at Sunday school, but as the indoctrination became more serious and the sins were explained in more detail, I started having misgivings at the age of seven.

Everything seemed to be a sin, at least the things that were fun, such as dancing, going to the movies, and using lipstick. It was even a sin to cut your hair. Therefore, I decided when I was seven that I would just live a sinful life, as I couldn't fathom living a life without dancing. I figured I would ask God for forgiveness just before I died. That way I wouldn't miss anything that might be fun. Of course, I never told Momma about any of these thoughts, as I knew that would hurt her. Momma was true "love", in everything she did or said. She knew forgiveness in the most real sense of the word, and she was never harsh or cruel, just loving and kind. Because of her, I learned to love, and that is what has carried me through all the difficulties of my life. She instilled in me the values I have today—to always be honest and treat others how you want to be treated.

We had two cows, and every morning at 4:30, Momma milked them and again in the afternoon at about the same time. One afternoon when I was about six, I was being hyperactive and making the cows antsy while my grandmother was milking them. Instead of yelling at me about my behavior, Momma gently suggested that I go to the cellar and cut myself a piece of her newly baked yellow pound cake. I ran to the cellar, cut myself a very generous piece, and sat down on the wooden stoop in front of the house, while I enjoyed every tiny, moist morsel of this heavenly cake. I couldn't resist; I had to have another piece. I went back several times until I realized that I had eaten half of the cake. What would Momma say now? I knew I had to confess and tell her the truth, and I did. Instead of getting angry, Momma explained to me how totally selfish I had been and that now the rest of the family would have less. That made a deep impression on me.

Another lesson in honesty happened during that same period. I had been playing with my cousin Lennart, Jöns's grandson, at his house. When I came home, I noticed that I had accidentally brought a safety pin home with me.

I became worried because Momma always said, "It starts with a safety pin and ends with a silver bowl."

I was afraid that I had become a thief, so I ran back to Lennart's house, through the dark thicket of hovering trees filled with trolls, to return the pin. While I was running my heart was beating so hard that I thought I would drop dead any minute. I knew then that I could never be a thief.

My grandmother had other children to raise, but I was the youngest, so I got to lick the bowl, and I got the extra attention.

"You are like my own child," Momma always said.

I was "Miss Sunshine," always ready for laughter and play, but also quick to break into tears and tantrums.

My uncle Herbert was eight years older than I, quiet and reserved, but was a little annoyed at all the attention I was getting. Next in line was Dagmar, who was ten years older and she had Down syndrome. Dagmar was my protector and equal for a long while, and I used her as my bodyguard against the bullies in town. She was very stout with a loud voice and a menacing look. Ruth, a motherly, loving, sweet girl, was thirteen years older; she was Momma's helper and "right-hand man."

After Mamma Maj left, Ruth served as another mother figure in my life. Mamma's oldest sister, Britt, had left the nest by the time I arrived, but she would enter my life years later.

Chapter 2

They say that abandonment is a wound that never heals.
I say only that an abandoned child never forgets.
—Mario Balotelli

It is interesting how some memories can be clear and others so fuzzy, but I guess some things make a deeper impression on you than others. My earliest childhood memory, though, is not a happy one. I remember waking up crying in a dark, strange room, and the person who entered upon my crying was not my grandmother. I was hysterical and full of fear. I later learned what that unpleasant memory was all about.

When I was about two and a half years old, my mother, Mamma Maj, wanted me closer to where she lived and worked so that she could see me more often. Therefore, I was placed with a friend of hers, Ingrid. Ingrid was married, and she was a good, sweet person, but she was not Momma. Ingrid had not been able to conceive any children, and Mamma figured she could lend me for a while, so I was taken from Momma and placed with Ingrid and her husband, Vidar. When I woke up in that strange, dark room, I was sick with the measles, and not having Momma's loving arms to comfort me, I was in total despair.

After about nine months, Ingrid said that she could no longer take care of me unless she could adopt me. Of course, that was out of the question. Momma, my loving, sweet grandmother, had been heartbroken since my departure, and even Morfar, who usually didn't show much emotion, must have missed me, as he eagerly joined Momma to bring me back home as quickly as possible. It is surprising that one can remember so far back in time with such clarity.

The next memory is connected to this one, as it had to do with the fear I experienced lying alone in that strange place where I didn't belong.

Momma went to the washhouse by the river to do the laundry every week, and I would usually accompany her. I loved running around and chatting with all the women and playing in the grass outside. But most of all, I loved having a new adventure away from home.

One summer morning, when I was about five years old, Momma wanted me to stay with the Jönssons, who rented the top floor of our house, while she did the weekly wash. The Jönssons had two daughters, Kristina and Ulla. Kristina was one year younger than I, and she was tall and pretty, with dark hair and piercing blue eyes. Ulla was two years younger. Ulla was sweet, soft, and round, with golden baby skin, curly yellow hair like an angel, and soft light-blue eyes. They were good friends, and we played together often; I knew them very well. However, when I found out what the plan was for the day, I panicked. I had not been apart from my grandmother since that last fateful time when I had lived with Ingrid, and seeing Momma leave the house without me put my mind in a rage. I was disconsolate all day. Momma was gone from early morning until late afternoon. I stood by the kitchen window on the third floor crying the entire day, while looking toward the beautiful flowing river below. I did not play, nor did I eat, and by the time Momma came back, my eyes were red and swollen, and my face still wet with my many tears. I felt betrayed and abandoned. The fear was indescribable.

Life went on, and I forgot this unfortunate separation until later in life. I was, overall, a very independent and adventurous little girl by nature and quite a tomboy.

My best friend was Lennart, my second cousin. Lennart's mother, Elsa, who was Jöns's daughter, had become pregnant out of wedlock, about the same time my mother had during a long summer night under that seductive midnight sun. I was ten days older than Lennart, which I always managed to remind him and others of whenever there was a dispute.

Lennart's home was not a happy home like mine, though. His mother had quickly married a suitable man and moved away, leaving Lennart behind with her brother, Holger, and his wife, Ruth. Ruth was unable to bear children, so Lennart was adopted by Holger and Ruth and never became part of his own mother's family. We were both, for a while, not wanted by our mothers, but the difference was that I had a grandmother who loved me, Momma, and of that I was certain. Ruth treated Lennart very differently and was quite cruel and strict at times. We were both very much afraid of her. When we saw her coming with a stern expression on her face and hands on her hips, it never boded well, so we would disappear for a while until the storm passed. Holger, on the other hand, was a gentle, kind soul and a child at heart. He spent many hours playing hide-and-seek with us until Ruth put a stop to it. Even to this day, I haven't figured out where his hiding place was.

Lennart and I were two peas in a pod. We did everything together. We even planned to marry when we grew up. I was often the director of our plays and adventures, and I had many ideas. I was a little taller than Lennart, but I blamed it on the fact that I was ten days older, as I knew it bothered him a lot. Lennart's face was pixie-like with sharp, chiseled features, even as a child, and he was lean and wiry with mousy blond hair and ears that were a little crooked, but I loved him with all my heart, and we shared all our fears and frustrations with each other.

Sometimes strangers would stop on the road and ask who we were, as we looked like two little orphans in our plaid shirts, overalls, and dirty bare feet. My answer would proudly be that I had three mothers: Momma, Mamma Maj, and Mamma Ingrid. Even though I didn't want to live with Ingrid, she had been very loving and kind to me, and I regarded her as one of my many mothers. People were a little perplexed by my answer, but to me it was the most natural thing in the world. I knew my real mother was Maj, but the mother of my heart was Momma. Morfar was a distant, stern, authoritative figure (who, nevertheless, loved me in his own way). I knew he wasn't my father, and I also knew that I didn't have a father.

Mamma Maj would visit twice a year, once in the summer and then during Christmas. I would get very excited, but also nervous when she visited. Her presence was a little intimidating, as she looked like a model in her handmade fashions, fancy shoes, and lovely hair. I was free as a bird with Momma, but with Mamma Maj, I was always reprimanded and corrected. Mamma Maj wanted me to be a perfect little girl.

When I was six, we had a large family gathering at my great-grandmother's farm in Romo Höjden. Everybody was asking who that cute little girl was, and I noticed people whispering to each other.

I heard one person exclaim, "Oh, she is Maj's daughter!"

Then they rolled their eyes and looked away. My heart sank. What was wrong with me? What had I done? I felt awkward and out of place, and I just wanted to go home. I felt judged somehow, but I didn't understand why. I did understand one important thing; I was different from the other children. I came home that night feeling that some of my inner light and joy had been dimmed. There was a sadness in my heart that I would carry with me for a long time. I desperately wanted to be like everyone else.

But life continued, and I was happy and content for the most part, except for some minor childhood fears, like fear of the dark, fear of the trolls, fear of separation from Momma, and fear of death.

Shortly after my sixth birthday, my great-grandmother died. Everyone was crying hysterically, including Momma, and the wailing continued all day in full force. I was bewildered by all this grief and sadness. It scared me. Everyone seemed to have lost their senses, and a deep fear of death engulfed me. I sensed that death was a very bad thing.

Something unexpected happened during the summer of 1949. My mother married a man named Axel, from Bornholm, Denmark, a small island southeast of Sweden in the Eastern Sea. I was excited about this exotic creature with the foreign voice because he spoke Swedish with a Danish accent. That made me smirk and giggle because it sounded so ridiculous. Axel was very friendly and full of laughter, jokes, and stories. He could easily entertain a hundred people; he was a great speaker and storyteller. Axel loved the spotlight and the attention. Children loved him, and I fell in love with him too. My mother was beaming because she was his "Queen."

Axel had a head full of unruly curls, mischievous hazel eyes, and a constant smile on his handsome face. His body was muscular, and his legs were very well proportioned and beautiful. He was only twenty-five-years-old. Axel's parents had come along for the big celebration of their son's marriage and to meet their new in-laws.

I understood, then, that I now had a father and a new set of grandparents, and they talked funny as well. It took more effort to understand what they said, as they spoke Bornholmsk. But, that didn't stop me from engaging my new, slightly plump, jolly grandfather in play, and I chased him around, whenever I could, with stinging nettles in my hand.

The summer was full of adventures and sightseeing trips to the mountains for the benefit of the guests, and I received loads of attention from my new family. It all ended too soon, though, and they all left to go back to their jobs and responsibilities.

My mother had met Axel through work, and he had proposed to her on their first date. A year later, they were married. It's a romantic story, and my father never got tired of telling it. He worshiped my mother and put her on a pedestal, and that is where she stayed until the day he died.

Axel and Mamma Maj visited again during the Christmas holidays, confirming that Axel was real and that he was my new father. He was amazing, so loving, kind, and full of fun, even though he couldn't speak proper Swedish. Also, my mother seemed more relaxed with Axel around.

December was full of lights and candles, to make up for the overwhelming darkness. The town of Undersåker put up a tall, bright Christmas tree by the train station, which was the unofficial town center. On the twenty-third, "Little Christmas Eve," as we called it, we danced around the tree and sang Christmas songs in anticipation of the great day, the twenty-fourth, when Santa Claus, or *Jultomten*, would arrive. Every child received a bag of goodies, and even though it was usually quite cold, we celebrated for hours, dancing, singing, and eating candy, chocolate, and cookies.

On Christmas Eve, Momma was busy cooking with everyone's help. It was an elaborate meal with many courses. The first course was an open-faced sandwich (*smörgåsar*) with homemade ham, mustard, and other trimmings. The main meal was *lutfisk* (a fermented fish that only Swedes and Norwegians like), which was served with potatoes, vegetables, and a dill gravy. For dessert, we had rice pudding, with sprinkles of cinnamon and sugar, and finally, coffee with cake and half a dozen different cookies.

After the dishes were done, which seemed like an eternity to me, Morfar went out to get Jultomten. Morfar explained that he had to help babysit Jultomten's children while he was gone, and therefore he had to leave. I bought this story until 1949, when I accidentally walked in on Morfar and Aunt Ruth in the hall. Ruth was helping Morfar get into Jultomten's clothes. They didn't see me, as I quickly slipped back out unnoticed. I was in shock. Morfar was Jultomten, and I had been lied to all these years! I was more than angry;

I was furious. I decided not to say anything, but to play their little game because apparently, all the grown-ups were in on this at my expense.

After the Christmas dinner, we gathered in the living room—*finrummet*, which means "the fine room"—for coffee and cake and then waited for Jultomten to arrive and knock on the door. The excitement, of course, was gone, and I felt grief and disappointment all at the same time. As I waited on the living room couch, I was fuming, sitting with my arms crossed and my lips pressed together in a thin line of anger.

Finally, the knock came, and everybody hollered, "Come on in!"

Everyone smiled and looked at me to see my expression, which this year was stern, yet neutral. Santa came in with a big smile and a huge, bulky bag across his shoulders. I looked closely at my grandfather's face under the fake beard and then into his dark-blue eyes, and I thought how stupid I had been not to have seen through this sham before.

In a roaring, deep voice he said, "Ho, ho, ho, are there any good girls or boys here?"

I didn't answer.

Everybody looked at me and poked me in the side to make me speak up, but I remained silent.

"What is wrong, Maud? Have you lost your tongue?"

Everybody laughed, but I didn't utter a word or move from my seat.

Jultomten moved toward me and said, "Well, here is a sweet little girl."

I still did not answer.

Everybody looked perplexed, but Jultomten continued, "I think I have something for you here in my bag. I know your name is Maud because I know all the children," and then he reached far into his bag to give me my first present.

I remained quiet and just stared, transfixed by his face. I reached out my hand and accepted my present, but I didn't thank Jultomten.

"Maud, say thank you," Momma chimed. I quietly squeaked out a thank-you and lowered my eyes to avoid revealing what I knew was the truth.

By the end of the evening, I had received all my presents, but the excitement of Christmas was gone forever. I never told anyone that I knew Jultomten was not real. Nobody really noticed the change in my attitude. Maybe they were all so busy with the newcomer, Axel the Dane, that my quietness eluded them.

Early on Christmas morning, we went to *Julotta* (Christmas morning service) at the local church to celebrate the birth of Christ. A farmer friend and neighbor came to pick us up in a large horse-drawn sleigh that could accommodate about eight people. The morning was dark, but the road was illuminated by diamond-like stars in the sky and the translucent moon hanging overhead. The sleigh had a burning torch at each corner to help with the visibility. I was snuggly seated between Momma and Mamma under a thick warm reindeer skin. It was extremely cold with temperatures many degrees below zero, but I was warm and felt happy and safe in the bosom of my family. It was an extraordinary Christmas morning filled with sights and sounds that permeated my senses, and I managed to push away the sadness that Jultomten was not real.

Axel and Mamma Maj left soon after to go back to work in Kristinehamn, and I stayed on with Momma and Morfar.

Chapter 3

Our trials, our sorrows, and our grieves develop us.
—Orison Marden

During the dark, cold winter days, the only activities we could do outside were skiing or sledding. We only had a few hours of sunlight, so it was precious. Sometimes the temperatures were so low that we couldn't go outside at all. Lennart and I loved skiing. We received our first cross-country skis when we were three years old. By the time we were six, we were quite proficient in doing all kinds of tricks on our skis, including slalom runs and jumps. We had to ski to school. It was uphill the entire way, which was tough, but going home was pure joy, and it was both challenging and exhilarating.

Spring came to Undersåker in April with a gush of melting snow running down the roads. It took about a month for the three feet of packed snow to melt, and it was so exciting finally to see the bare ground and green grass. That's how I knew that my birthday was near. There was a celebration in the air for many reasons—the sun was beginning to shine brighter and higher in the sky, and birthdays were arriving.

The big celebration on April 30, which is called Walburgis Night, or *Valborgmässoafton*, was the night we celebrated the end of winter with a big bonfire to chase it away. Witches on broomsticks were another symbol of this passing. There was a ton of candy for the children and, of course, singing and dancing around the bonfire.

Easter was also celebrated during this time by bringing tree branches into the house for blooming. The branches were decorated with eggs and toy baby chicks, another symbol that spring was near, even though there was still plenty of snow on the ground.

I loved candy, like all children, but didn't get much of it, since it was a waste of money, according to Morfar. However, Momma made many kinds of delicious cakes and cookies in all shapes and sizes. The cookies were stored in large metal jars, and I knew the hiding place. It was a custom to get cookies and milk (or coffee, for grown-ups) in bed on special occasions such as Sundays or birthdays.

I don't remember owning a toothbrush, and even if I did, Momma probably didn't have the strength to enforce its use. My teeth were therefore in terrible shape. By the summer of 1950, my rotten teeth were finally replaced by my permanent teeth. One day I developed a terrible toothache in a molar, and Morfar could not help me. We had pulled out several of my baby teeth with the door method before. Morfar would tie one end of a string to my rotten loose tooth and the other end to the doorknob. Suddenly, someone would open the door with a quick jerk, and the tooth would fly out with a scream. This time, the molar had to be taken out by a dentist, so we made the trip into the town of Järpen. I had no idea what was going to happen.

Morfar and Aunt Ruth accompanied me, but Momma was busy with the farm, animals, and cooking. When we arrived at the dentist, and this was my first visit, I was placed in a big gray dental chair. I was lying there, very apprehensive and scared, holding Ruth's hand, while Morfar and the dentist talked. The dentist approached me slowly, smiling, and told me to open my mouth so that he could see the tooth. I complied. Suddenly, everybody grabbed my arms and legs and held me down, while the dentist miraculously managed to fit a big pair of pliers around my tooth and started pulling with all his might. I felt this incredible sharp, searing pain going through my jaw, and I screamed at the top of my lungs and started kicking.

It felt like the tooth took a long time to come out, and I wailed louder as the pain increased in intensity. I couldn't get away from my attackers; everybody just held on harder to my limbs with their iron grips. When it was finally over, I was in severe shock and sobbed the whole way home, holding my sore, throbbing jaw in my hand. I had received no anesthetic or numbing medication to help with the pain. I realized that I could never trust grown-ups, except Momma, of course. The hole in my mouth healed without any problems, but I didn't like dentists after that, and I hoped I would never see one again.

When school started at the end of the summer, I was ready for a new adventure and eager for learning. The small red schoolhouse had only one big room. The first-and-second-grade classes shared it, with an invisible division down the middle. Sturdy wooden desks filled the room, one for each student.

Ms. Maja, who taught both classes, was a small woman, but her serious attitude, closed-off spinster look, and tight hair knot made her seem very impressive and intimidating. As I walked into the classroom on my first day, I was proud and confident because I knew who I was and who my parents were. That had been clearly demonstrated over the last year.

I stepped up in front of the class and announced as loudly as I could, "I have a father now, his name is Axel, and he is from Denmark."

A deep silence descended on the room. Ms. Maja immediately came up to me with a stern look on her face, grabbed me by the arm, pulled me aside, and said, "We don't speak about these things here. Be quiet!"

I looked up at her angry face and into her hard, blue eyes in confusion and wondered, "What did I do wrong?" I realized that there was something wrong with what I had said, but I didn't understand. My heart had been so filled with love and joy the entire summer because of my new family, and just like that, it was squashed.

A feeling of shame swept over me, but as the tears welled up in my eyes, I defiantly responded, "But, he is my father now!"

Ms. Maja became angrier and shoved me into a corner and said with a quiet hiss, "You will stand here for the entire lesson as punishment for your behavior!"

I was crushed. I felt totally misunderstood. Did this mean that I was wrong? Did this mean that I didn't have a father after all? I was very confused and embarrassed, but I managed to control my developing tears.

I was too ashamed to mention the incident to Momma, and I didn't want any more punishment, so I kept it to myself. I never mentioned my father again in school, and school became a mixed blessing. Even though I enjoyed learning new things, my unbending teacher took much of the joy out of my school experience. There was no levity in her spirit. I continued to feel like an outsider from that first day of school, and I never really felt comfortable around Ms. Maja. I despised her from that day on.

My first year of school was not what I had hoped it would be, but I had learned how to read and write, and my favorite book was *Pippi Longstocking* by Astrid Lindgren. I wished I were Pippi because she was my hero. I read that book over and over. Pippi was precocious, adventurous, and independent, and I wanted to be like her. Pippi lived in her own house with her horse and monkey, and her father was a pirate. The book was my bible, and I still have it in my possession.

Despite these unfortunate experiences, I was still a very trusting and loving child. I have always been slightly naive and somewhat gullible, which must be a personality trait that I inherited from my mother.

There were fascinating stories about scary trolls living deep within the dark woods and nearby hills. Trolls were menacing and evil. They were bigger than a child, stocky, hairy, ugly, and strong, and they liked to kidnap little children. I used to see them as I sat in my Sunday school class and looked out the window toward the dark, enormous hill across the street from the church. I was so convinced that they were there that I saw them in my mind's eye.

Because of these scary stories, whenever I had to run over to Lennart's house at night, it was torture. My grandfather shared the daily newspaper with his brother Jöns, and Lennart and I took turns running the newspaper over every night. The gravel road between our houses was not that long, but it went over a small creek and through a thick section of tall, dense pine trees. To a seven-year-old, it seemed like running through the dark for miles, with threatening tree branches hovering above, potentially hiding a hundred trolls. I lived with this constant fear every day, but out of embarrassment, I never mentioned it to anybody. I sucked it up and ran as fast as I could, but fear of the dark stayed with me into early adulthood.

In the spring of 1951, my brother, Hans-Peter, was born. Shortly after Hans-Peter's birth, Axel proposed to Mamma that I come and live with them. After all, I was her daughter. There was much discussion back and forth between Mamma and Axel because my mother was not certain that it was right to uproot me. I had lived with Momma and Morfar all my life, except for a short period with Ingrid and Vidar. But my stepfather, whom I called *Pappa*, was a very persuasive man, and Mamma eventually gave in. My big move was planned very quickly, and there was no transition period. It was a shock for me to be taken away so abruptly and without warning, especially since nothing was discussed with me.

Just like that, one day, I was dressed in my finest clothes—a red coat, white leggings, and a homemade white dress. I had braids on top of my head and a big white ribbon.

All my earthly belongings fit into one small suitcase, and I was put on the train with my grandmother's sister, Olga, who was traveling in the same direction. Momma didn't even come to the train station to say good-bye. She couldn't bear it. I remember looking at Momma's sad, teary-eyed face when I said good-bye. We hugged for a long time, and Momma was trying hard not to cry. I didn't understand the magnitude of it all at that moment. At first, it was exciting to go somewhere new, traveling on the train and experiencing new things. The fear of losing my grandmother again was too painful for tears, so I pushed them away. I was a big girl now, and I could not cry, as that would make it worse for Momma. I understood that much; so, I showed her how strong I was and kept the tears inside. My heart ached, and I felt very lonely when I walked out the door of my childhood home.

My grandmother was devastated, and I found out later in adulthood that she had had a nervous breakdown when I was taken away. She was never the same, and neither was I. I missed her all my life. I wrote Momma a letter after I left:

> *Dear Momma,*
> *Please don't be sad or cry. I have all the food I can eat, and I have my own bed. I miss you.*
> *Love, Maud.*

I didn't just lose Momma; I lost a whole family—Dagmar, Herbert, Morfar, my best friend Lennart, and a whole way of life.

I still miss those years of my childhood, living on a farm in the mountains of Jämtland with a large loving family and my many friends around me.

Chapter 4

Don't handicap your children by making their lives easy.
—Robert A. Heinlein

When I arrived in Kristinehamn, Mamma Maj, Pappa Axel, and my little brother, Hans-Peter, who was then three months old, picked me up at the train station.

Everything looked different; there were large buildings and streets with sidewalks. During the first week, it was an adventure, and I forgot the pain in my heart for a while. It was all so exciting. I had my first ice-cream cone, and I never knew something could taste that good, except Morfar's cola. My parents bought me a light-blue cowgirl outfit, a jacket, and a pair of jeans. I felt like a model and a special little girl. Then I was taken to the hairdresser, and my long braids were cut off. I now felt like a modern girl. My life seemed wonderful until the daily routine started.

We lived in a one-room apartment with the tiniest kitchen I had ever seen and a small bathroom. There was only one window. The room was dark and furnished with only the essentials, like a bed for my parents, a crib for my brother, and a small bed for me in one of the corners. We had a modest dining table and some chairs, and that was all. This living condition was a stark contrast to the bright and spacious home of my grandparents.

Mamma was busy with my brother, whom we called Peter. She was breastfeeding him and working part-time as a bookkeeper in an office, downstairs in our building. While Mamma worked, she put Peter in a stroller in the gloomy backyard, and I was given the responsibility of watching over him after school.

The backyard was all concrete with a wire fence around it, and the surrounding buildings blocked it from the sun. At first, I had no one to play with, so I kept myself occupied with my brother. I was very conscientious about taking care of him and giving him his tomato juice, which my mother had prepared ahead of time. I would feed Peter the tomato juice with a spoon while holding his head up like Mamma had shown me. By then, my brother was a healthy four-month-old baby with chubby red cheeks, blue-green eyes, and a happy smile. I loved him as most big sisters would, and I was proud that he was my brother.

There were plenty of other children at the farther end of the backyard playing handball, but I was ignored for the first two weeks. I watched them play, day after day, hoping for an opportunity to join them. Finally, one day the ball rolled my way. I picked it up and threw it back.

They looked at me and then looked at each other and nodded, and one of them asked, "Do you want to play?"

That was the day I had been hoping for, and I happily shouted, "Yes!"

I was in the game, and another life had started. Now I had something to look forward to each day—playing ball with my new friends.

When I came to live with Mamma, Pappa, and Peter, I was the one who didn't belong. They were the family unit, and I was the one on the outside. I felt that way during most of my childhood, yearning to be accepted and to be like everyone else.

Mamma was totally absorbed in taking care of Peter and working, so Pappa, now twenty-seven-years-old, became my main caregiver. Pappa had no idea how to raise a child.

One minute he was all fun and games, and the next minute he would suddenly turn serious and strict. He was trying very hard, I think, but often things were blown out of proportion, and I would be accused and punished for things I hadn't done. I tried hard to be the perfect little girl, but, of course, that was impossible. I stayed outside as much as possible, playing with my new friends, and only came in for food and sleep.

One day, Mamma decided that I needed to see a dentist, as my front teeth were growing in very crooked. She did not know about my first dental experience, and neither did Pappa, who had to bring me to the appointment. Fear rose in me when I heard about the planned dental visit, but I didn't say anything. I was trying to be good and not complain.

We were greeted with smiling, happy faces, as before, and I was told to sit in the scary dental chair. I was frightened, and my posture was defensive, with arms crossed tightly across my chest. The dentist asked me to open my mouth, but I refused. Pappa was perplexed and embarrassed by my behavior and tried to reason with me, but to no avail. The dentist tried all kinds of sweet-talking, but I knew I couldn't trust him, so I kept my mouth tightly shut. Finally, the dentist tried to poke his fingers through my teeth by force, and this was when it happened. It was not premeditated, but rather an instinctual reaction. I opened my mouth just enough to let one finger in, and then I bit down as hard as I could. The dentist screamed at the top of his lungs, while cursing some obscene words, as he pulled his finger out of my mouth. He jumped around the room for a while, holding his injured finger. I don't remember if he was bleeding or not because we were quickly thrown out of the dental office and told never to come back.

Once outside the dental office, Pappa grabbed me by my shoulders and yelled at me, "How could you do such a thing?"

I started crying. I didn't have an answer because I couldn't articulate all the fears that were inside me. I just knew I was scared to death of dentists. I was scolded severely, but my parents gave up on any more dental visits for the time being. My attack on the dentist's finger was never discussed again. I had stood up for myself the only way I knew how at eight years old.

We only lived in Kristinehamn for two months, and then my father was offered a job as store manager of a co-op store in Hässleholm. There were no apartments available in Hässleholm, so we had to settle for another one-room apartment, in Vinslöv. My father commuted an hour each way by train because we didn't have a car. The apartment in Vinslöv was even smaller than the one in Kristinehamn. Pappa and I slept on a thin mattress in the cramped closet, and Mamma and Peter slept on the bed. Luckily, an agreeable one-bedroom apartment became available in Hässleholm a couple of months later. Besides the bedroom, we now had an official living room, a dining room, a bigger kitchen, and a bathroom. It was pure luxury compared to how we had lived before, but still not what I had had in Undersåker.

Mamma needed to work full-time to make ends meet, so Peter and I needed a babysitter. Aunt Britt was the first choice, and that worked out well, except for the tight quarters. My parents, Peter, and I slept in the bedroom, and Britt got a bed in the dining room.

Britt was an extremely religious woman, demure and self-effacing. She spoke with a low voice, careful not to offend anyone, and the only real opinion she had was about Jesus. He was her lord and savior and her only reason for living. It was almost as if she were married to him. She had the same strong beliefs, like Momma, but more fanatical in a way. She prayed for our souls every night, and she rarely looked happy or content. Britt lived a torturous life, always worrying about all the people who would end up in hell unless they were saved. I had already made up my mind about all this dogma and sin, and I dismissed her concerns with carefree resistance.

For the third time in one year, I had to change to a new school when we moved to Hässleholm. Since each school only lasted a few months, my memories easily blend into one another. However, the December 13 celebration of *Sankta Lucia* (Saint Lucia), at the Hässleholm primary school, became etched in my mind.

The Sankta Lucia celebration is an exotic Swedish custom that became universally popular in the 1900s. Saint Lucia can be traced back to a mythical figure who died as a martyr in the third century. According to the old Almanac, Saint Lucia Night is the longest and darkest night of the year, so the celebration of Saint Lucia coincides with the Winter Solstice. Saint Lucia symbolizes bringing the light of Christianity into the darkness of the world, and the celebration also signals the arrival of Christmas. Every town of any significance picks their own Lucia every year, and the competition can get fierce among the young Swedish girls.

According to the Saint Lucia tradition, the girl who was chosen to be Lucia in my school was dressed in a full-length white robe, signifying her purity, and she had a red sash around her waist symbolizing the red blood of her martyrdom. She carried a candle-lit wreath on her head, and all her handmaidens, like me, wore the same white robes and red sashes and we carried lit candles in our hands. We walked in a procession while we sang the Swedish Lucia song, and then Saint Lucia handed out gingerbread cookies to everyone.

Saint Lucia is celebrated with saffron flavored buns and ginger cookies together with coffee or *glögg*. Glögg is a Swedish mulled wine made from spices, raisins, and almonds cooked in sugar water, and then the wine and brandy are added.

I was very proud to be part of this celebration and be chosen to sing in front of the entire school.

Life improved drastically in Hässleholm. I had better surroundings—fields of green grass, woods nearby, playgrounds, and many children to play with. Since I was such an active child, I gravitated toward the boys. The girls would sit on the stoop outside the building and play with dolls, which had no appeal at all for me. I tried hard to befriend the boys because I wanted to play catch and cowboys and Indians with them. Before that could happen, I was required to go through some tests.

The boys organized running races in which I would compete with different boys. I was still only eight years old, so my first opponents were the same age. I found out then that I was very fast. I beat everyone my age by a wide margin, which surprised everybody, including myself. Older and older boys were added to the competition. The oldest boy that I beat was twelve years old, but he was probably the least athletic kid on the block. Anyway, that was the tipping point of acceptance and total respect, and I was allowed into the exclusive league of the Boys' Club. I was the only girl ever allowed into this group, and I felt honored. I was more than an equal. They called me *Flygmaskin*, which translates directly as "flying machine," but it means "airplane." Flygmaskin became my nickname, and I wore it proudly. This group of delightful boys became my best friends and comrades. We played hard and rough into the late evening, running and jumping over fences while playing. Mamma learned very quickly, as Momma had, not to dress me in skirts or dresses after I tore one of her beautiful creations to shreds on a wire fence.

One afternoon after school, my friends told me that they had a surprise for me, and they wanted me to come with them to the woods nearby. I was excited, and I trusted them completely, so I obliged. Once we arrived at a clearing in the woods, they told me to sit down on the grass. All eight boys sat down in a circle around me. They started giggling a little, and then as if they had rehearsed a play, they got up, one by one, crawled up to me, and planted a firm kiss on my cheek. At that moment, which seemed to last a long time, I felt like a princess, surrounded by love. I was floating on air when I left the forest that day. I felt happier than I had in a long time. Mamma never hugged or kissed me, and I missed Momma terribly, but these boys were giving me a lot of love, and I felt happy. I lived for those afternoons and early evenings with all my boyfriends as we had so much fun together.

Sometimes, I was a wild little girl, looking for excitement and adventure, so when the gypsies arrived in town, I was fascinated. The gypsies lived in campers and had set up a small carnival not far from where we lived. They were dark-skinned and mysterious. Their fashions were colorful and bright, and they had many children of all ages.

I had to check these visitors out, so I set out on my own one afternoon after school. The gypsies quickly noticed the young blond girl snooping around, and they befriended me. All my life I had been surrounded by my family, but now I was on foreign ground. I was totally ignorant, and it was an alien concept to me that people might harm me. I was asked to babysit for a gypsy family with a small baby. I was nine years old by then and was proud to be asked to babysit. I felt confident that I could do it because I had helped take care of my little brother many times. I was lured into a camper where there were a baby and a big, ferocious-looking German shepherd dog. But I was not afraid of dogs and took everything in stride. The parents left me alone with the baby and the dog and told me to stay there until they got back.

Hours passed, and I started to get a little concerned because the sun had gone down, and it was now dark outside. I was afraid of the dark and wondered how I would make it back home, but I felt obliged to stay until the parents came back, as I had given my word.

Suddenly, there was a knock on the door. It frightened me, but when I opened the door, I found to my surprise that it was Pappa. When I saw his stern, angry face, I knew I had messed up.

"What do you think you are doing?" Pappa asked in a very controlled but angry voice.

I stammered something about babysitting, but before I could finish explaining, my father yanked me out of there, while at the same time preventing the dog from attacking him through the open door. My father pushed the dog back and closed the door behind us, and then we ran.

"Don't you know that these people could have kidnapped you, and we would never have seen you again?" Pappa asked.

He was so angry that he scared me, and he talked incessantly the entire way home as if he were trying to calm himself down.

Mamma and Pappa had been terribly worried when I hadn't come home for dinner. Pappa had combed the whole neighborhood, and knowing my adventurous nature, he had figured out where I must have gone. He had talked to some people and got a lead from someone who had seen me get into the camper. I was a very lucky girl that night even though I was in big trouble.

There was another experience that taught me that not all people are good. The superintendent in our building was a middle-aged man with gray, thinning hair and pale skin. He was very friendly with the children; he talked and joked with us. I was usually busy playing with my boyfriends, but on this afternoon, I was hanging out with a group of kids outside the apartment building by the basement door.

The super came out from the basement and asked in a loud voice, "Who wants to earn some money by helping me sweep?"

Everybody raised his or her hand, so I did, too.

He pointed directly at me with his right index finger and asked, "What's your name?"

I answered, "My name is Maud!"

"Come here, Maud," he said, beckoning to me with his big hand.

I walked quickly toward him, thinking how lucky I was to be picked. The superintendent put his arm around my shoulders and led me into the basement, closing the door behind him. I saw the broom and grabbed it, eager to fulfill my obligation, and started sweeping the floor. After a while, he told me to put the broom away and to come and sit on his lap. I instantly felt uneasy but reluctantly complied. Slowly, he started caressing my leg with his calloused hand while his bad breath poured over my cheek.

"Have boys ever touched you this way?" he asked.

I shook my head in denial and wanted to run.

He moved his hand up my leg and into my panties and said to me, "This is our secret. You better not tell anybody about this, or you will be in big trouble."

I sat there for what seemed like an eternity while his rough hand touched me in strange ways and his beady light-blue eyes hovered over me. Finally, he let me down and warned me again to not tell anyone. I ran out of the basement door as fast as I could. From that day on, I made sure I was as far away from him as possible. Out of fear of the consequences, I never said anything to my parents.

Chapter 5

Life is an adventure, not a package tour.
—Eckhart Tolle

We lived in Hässleholm, Sweden for almost a year from November 1951 to October 1952. My father was then presented with the challenge of starting a co-op store in the Faroe Islands.

The Faroe Islands are a self-governing territory within the Kingdom of Denmark. This archipelago of eighteen islands is located between the Atlantic Ocean and the Norwegian Sea, southeast of Iceland and northwest of Scotland.

The Danish firm Brugsen had tried to start a co-op store in Torshavn, the capital of the Faroe Islands, but had failed several times, and money was lost.

My father was young, adventurous, and idealistic, and he accepted the challenge with enthusiasm, but this meant uprooting our small family from Sweden. We packed what little furniture and personal belongings we had into a large crate, which was loaded onto the same ship we sailed on for three days and three nights, over some very rough seas. There was a terrible storm with high winds, and the waves were so monstrous that they seemed likely to engulf the entire ship. The continuous twenty-foot rise and fall of the ship took its toll on everybody.

Pappa and I were the only ones on deck and in the dining room every day. The cook looked quite annoyed when we showed up expecting some food to eat, as nobody else cared to eat anything. Mamma and Peter stayed in the cabin during the whole voyage because my mother was quite seasick. I had a constant queasy feeling in my stomach, and I was terrified of the high waves. It felt like the ship was at the mercy of the ocean, but my father reassured me by pointing out the adventure of it all. Pappa kept dragging me out of the cabin to prevent me from getting seasick, and we would walk the slippery decks day and night, watching the tall, frothy waves come and go. We got cold and wet, but the fresh sea air and constant wind kept us in the moment, preventing us from suffering the same fate as Mamma.

The Faroe Islands are made of volcanic rock and rise out of the ocean like huge, dark boulders. As we approached, we could see the lush bright-green carpet of grass that covered all the rocks like a blanket. The air was amazingly clean and fresh, but there was a gray mist hanging over the islands, keeping the air moist and cool. Despite the latitude, the climate was mild, with warm winters and cool summers, due to the Gulf Stream, and, as in Sweden, the summers had extended daylight.

Most of the people lived in the capital of Torshavn. There were several other towns scattered around, which were only reachable by sea back in the 1950s. Today, things have changed, and most of the islands can be reached by car, due to tunnels and bridges that connect them. The more remote islands can be reached by ferries or boats.

The language of the Faroe Islands is Faroese. It descends from the Old Norse language that was spoken during the Viking age. When I arrived, I had to learn Faroese as well as Danish. By the age of nine, I could speak three languages. Of course, Danish and Swedish have some morphological similarities, but those are difficult to discern, as the pronunciation of the words is entirely different. Danes speak with a guttural sound, at the back of the tongue, and Swedes speak more at the front end of the tongue, with a musical tone. My mother would try to speak Danish with her lyrical Swedish accent, and my father spoke Swedish with a thick Danish accent. On the Faroe Islands, though, they both spoke mainly Danish. My mother's singing Danish accent threw me off, and this confusion caused me to make up a Swedish-Danish hybrid language, which is uniquely my own. It's a strange mixture of both. Whenever I talk to my mother today, her singing Danish accent still makes me go into this mixture of Swedish and Danish. When I speak to my brother, it is in real Danish, and I speak Swedish to my family in Sweden. It is only my mother who causes this language confusion.

The Faroese economy is dependent on the unstable fishing industry, which makes it very vulnerable. The Danish government has often bailed them out with financial support, which has been a hard pill to swallow for the proud, stoic Faroese.

For centuries, sheepherding has been a big part of Faroese culture, as well as bird hunting and whaling. There are twice as many sheep on the islands as people, and there is plenty of grass for the almost one hundred thousand sheep. The sheep provide food and wool for clothing. There are also innumerable birds living on the cliffs over the ocean. Hunting these cliff-dwelling birds provides quite a challenge for the Faroese men. The Faroese do not consider whaling a sport, but a way of survival. Today they are still holding on to this tradition.

When our ship finally docked in the Torshavn harbor, I was happy that our harrowing journey was over. We were tired, and our bodies were still swaying from the motion of the sea. It took a couple of days to get grounded. We rented a two-story house not far from the harbor. There was a small backyard, where my brother would sometimes be locked in, to prevent him from running to the harbor and drowning. That was always a big worry, and I was carefully instructed about the possible danger. At the tender age of nine, I felt that responsibility strongly. Peter managed to get out a few times, and where did he go? To the harbor, of course.

The harbor was a fascinating place, with big ships, small ships, and fishing boats. One day, Pappa showed me a fifty-foot-long whale that had been caught and was tied to a large ship. It was a sad but impressive sight.

The town of Torshavn was not built for cars. The streets were narrow and made of cobblestone and had numerous small alleys. Most of the houses back then were either made of stone or tar-coated wood, and the roofs were often covered with grass. Today the scene has changed, and people have started painting their houses in colors even more brilliant than in Sweden.

The weather was very unpredictable, and storms could develop at a moment's notice. The winds would get so strong at times that they could topple a small child in a second. It was foggy and rainy most of the time, but I never noticed that too much. I had so many things to explore and new friends to get to know.

My parents had heard that the Catholic school had a better reputation than the public school, so they enrolled me. However, when I started making the sign of the cross before eating my dinner, Pappa changed his mind.

I hated the Catholic school; the nuns were cruel and strict. We had to remove our shoes when we entered the school, and I had lace-up boots. After each class, we had a break during which we could go outside. It took me almost the entire break to put my boots back on, so I rarely got to play. This break was essential for me because I needed some physical activity. When I finally made it out into the yard one day, I found out that running wasn't allowed. I felt like a prisoner. So, when Pappa announced that he was taking me out of the Catholic school, I couldn't have been happier.

The public school was in town, close to the harbor and a beach where the fishermen would sit, talk, and drink beer during the day. There were also small shops with candy and other goodies. During the breaks, I found a way to creep out through a hedge behind the school, and I always headed to the candy store. I was careful to stay clear of my father's co-op store, which was nearby. I sneaked out of school regularly, but one day a teacher was waiting for me inside the hedge. He caught me by the collar and put me in detention. I was punished with detention often, but I begged my aunt Britt, who had joined us a few months earlier, to not tell my parents, and she didn't, to my surprise. I got in trouble a lot, and I rarely did my homework because I was too busy playing and roller-skating with my friends. I had a grand time, and I had tons of freedom. My parents were so busy working that I rarely saw them except on weekends.

One day when I was in class, I heard fire-engine horns in the distance, and it sounded like several of them. A fire was a rare occurrence on the island, and the sirens were so loud that everyone took notice. Out of curiosity, we all went outside to see what was going on. I heard someone say that the Catholic school was burning. I knew I had to see that, so I took off running in that direction. The desire was so strong that I didn't think of the consequences of my actions.

The Catholic school was on the outskirts of town, quite a distance from my new school. I was breathless when I got there. What a sight! The whole school was ablaze with red and yellow flames billowing out of all the windows. I could feel the searing heat on my face, and I felt a curious glee in the excitement of seeing the school burn. I knew that everybody was safe, which made it possible for me to enjoy this incredible moment fully. I stood there for a long time watching the magnificent fire engulf the entire building. There were not much the firefighters could do but let it burn. Time stood still, and I was immersed in the violent, yet beautiful spectacle.

When I returned to my school, so much time had passed that everyone knew I was missing, and there was no way to sneak back in. I was punished severely for my infraction with more detention, but it was worth it. I have never seen a fire like that since; I don't regret a thing.

On Sundays, Pappa would take Peter and me for early-morning walks to Torshavn's barren park, to let my mother sleep. The park was nothing more than some grassy hills with a few gnarled trees that had been imported from Denmark. There were no native trees on the islands, and the ones that had been planted looked like crooked dwarfs suffering from malnutrition. The walks were kind of boring, but Pappa's stories made up for it. Pappa was a great storyteller; he made them all up himself. He could make me laugh and cry all at the same time.

We walked until we figured Mamma was out of bed, and it was safe to go home and make noise. Pappa was always very considerate of my mother. She was, after all, his queen.

One night, at three in the morning, we were all awakened by yelling in the streets: "The whales are coming; the whales are coming!"

People, young and old, emerged excitedly from their homes and ran down to the harbor. The sky had a slight dusky haze, but since it was summertime, the midnight sun still dominated the sky. I didn't know what to expect, as nobody had told me anything.

When we reached the harbor, we went to the bridge, where we would have the best view of the ocean. The harbor was built with a bay area, and at the outer end of it, the water was deep, and the ships could dock. As you got closer to the bridge at the bottom of the bay, the water was very shallow.

As time passed, the sun surfaced a little brighter behind the haze, and I could see many rowboats in the distance, surrounding a school of pilot whales in a semicircle and forcing them toward the harbor. The dark-gray pilot whales were trapped and had only one way to go, and that was toward the shallows. Unknowingly, these peaceful, innocent creatures swam right into the trap. When they reached the shallow water, they were helplessly stuck in the sand.

Young, strong Faroese men jumped out of their boats and punched hooks into the blowholes of the whales and dragged them farther ashore. Once a whale was totally beached, a cut was made near its blowhole to sever its head. I watched in horror when a young man of about twenty sliced open the chest of a beautiful, dark, shiny whale. He cut out its heart with his knife, yanked it out with his left hand, and let out a victorious scream while taking a big bite out of the heart. The whale's fresh red blood was running down his face, and I looked at him in shock! I felt sick but was transfixed by the horrible massacre. Everyone seemed jubilant about what was happening. How could something so ghastly be so celebrated? The entire harbor was filled with blood. I was fascinated and disgusted all at the same time. I had a sad feeling in my heart for all those whales that lost their lives that day.

When the killing was over, the whales were lifted from the water by cranes and butchered. Every citizen got his or her fair share of whale meat to take home, whether he or she had taken part in the kill or not. That was the custom. I understood then that this meant food for the entire town for a long while.

We received two buckets full of whale meat that we had to learn how to cook and eat. It was quite an unpleasant experience. The fishy stench permeated everything, and the meat tasted just as bad as it smelled. The Faroese considered it a delicacy, and everything was eaten, including the blubber, which was the worst part. The whale meat that wasn't eaten immediately was hung out to dry under the eaves. The high salt content of the air made it possible to preserve the meat for a year or more. The whale meat dried into a jerky, and the same thing was done with the fish. You either caught whales and fish yourselves, or the meat was given to you. Whaling and fishing were not a business among the citizens of the islands but part of their culture.

After the business of killing, butchering, and dividing the catch was over, the entire town celebrated by dancing through the streets for the rest of the night and into the morning. The children, like me, had to go back to bed, but the men and women danced a traditional dance holding each other's hands in long lines and singing victorious songs from centuries ago.

This night was a night I will never forget. I understood why the Faroese did what they did, but I question now their need to continue this tradition, as they certainly don't need to kill these beautiful, intelligent mammals for survival anymore.

I had many friends. Most of them were boys, but I had two strange female friends. One was fat and ate candy all the time. Since she liked me, she often shared her stash with me. The other girl was a short chubby one, and she became famous among us because she ate earthworms. One day, when we dared her, she pulled a squiggly worm out of her pocket, lifted it up into the air for us all to see, and then lowered it slowly into her mouth, chewed it, and swallowed it. We were all in shock over what we had just witnessed. I gagged, then screamed, and jumped around in a circle with flailing arms trying to collect myself.

"That's worse than whale blubber," I thought.

Not everybody on the Faroe Islands was that strange, however. The brother of our first babysitter fell in love with me. Olaf was a cute ten-year-old, with black curly hair and dark-blue eyes; he always tried to impress me. One day he brought me a beautiful gold ring with a big fancy stone. He asked me if I would be his girlfriend and handed me the ring. I accepted it graciously with a shy smile. The ring was too big for my finger, so I put it in my pocket. We were now engaged! That evening I proudly pulled the ring out of my pocket and showed it to my mother, who immediately recognized that it was very expensive.

She asked me, "Where did you get such a beautiful ring?"

I told her about Olaf. I was quite disappointed when Mamma told me that I had to give it back. We found out later from Olaf's mother that he had stolen it from her. The engagement was over, and I pretty much ignored him after that. I had no more respect for him. I hadn't given any thought to how he could possibly afford a ring. I had no clue about the value of such things. What did I know at the age of ten anyway?

My parents were friends with the Haroldsons, and we saw them often. Mr. Haroldson was the principal of the local high school and the president of the co-op union. My father was the manager of the store and its operations, and my mother was the bookkeeper.

The Haroldsons had two sons—Erik, who was a couple of years younger than I, and Finn, who was fifteen. Erik was a handsome boy with a dark complexion, nearly black hair, and deep-brown eyes. He resembled his mother, who was a good-looking woman with the same dark, attractive skin color and a radiant smile. Finn, on the other hand, was tall, thin, and pale faced, with watery blue eyes, glasses, and a nerdy look, just like his father. I liked Erik, but he was a little too young for me to play with, as he provided little competition in the various games we played. Finn, on the other hand, was too old; he was a teenager with strange ideas. He wanted to play doctor, and he wanted me to be his patient. He worked on this idea for a few weeks, but he was mostly talking about it in the beginning, and then, slowly, Erik was excluded from the game.

One afternoon, Finn pushed me into the bathroom and locked the door behind him. He wanted to show me how a doctor would examine me. Finn cornered me, forced himself on me, and tried to take my panties off. An intense fear came over me, and my heart was beating very fast while he pawed me. I was trapped in the tiny bathroom with a boy who was a foot taller than I was and most certainly stronger. My mind was racing, thinking of how to get out of this situation without making him angry. At the same time, I was embarrassed and therefore I didn't want to cry out for help. I stubbornly resisted his attempts to investigate my private parts further, and he finally gave up and let me out. I felt dirty, angry, and used, and I was close to tears. I collected myself the best I could and went to sit by my mother on the couch in the living room. Mamma looked surprised but was clueless about what was going on.

The next time we were invited to the Haroldsons for afternoon coffee and cake, I started to cry and told my mother that I didn't want to go. I was almost hysterical, but Mamma did not grasp that something was seriously wrong.

I begged, "Please let me stay at home. I don't want to play with Finn."

Mamma answered, "If you don't want to play, then come and sit with us on the sofa."

I was a very active ten-year-old with too much energy, so for me to sit still for four hours was pure torture. But, that is what I did. After that day, I managed to stay clear of Finn and kept close to Erik; that way I couldn't be drawn into a compromising position with him. Shortly after this disturbing incident, we moved to Denmark, and I was safe.

Five years later, Finn came to Denmark to visit us. I was fifteen by then, and he was almost twenty-one years old. He was even uglier than I remembered. I felt sick and embarrassed just looking at his pale face and sleazy, light-blue eyes that followed me around like a predator. I felt he was mentally undressing me as soon as he arrived through the front door. It made me feel physically ill. More than that, I felt humiliated by this pervert who had taken advantage of my youth and innocence. I couldn't look him in the eye, and I avoided him the whole time he was visiting. I hoped that I would never have to set my eyes on him again and fortunately that came true.

I never told my parents about this incident because it was embarrassing, and I thought it might have been my fault somehow. I always tried to please people. Most of my life, I have had a great need to be accepted, so I rarely spoke up for myself, except on rare occasions when I felt I had no choice.

Aside from this unfortunate experience with Finn and the gruesome whale killings, my time on the Faroe Islands was happy, and all the good memories overshadowed the bad. It was a unique and different way of life, and I enjoyed my freedom and carefree life. My schooling was questionable and inadequate, but I caught up later when we moved to Denmark.

Chapter 6

Every parting is a form of death,
as every reunion is a type of heaven.
—Tryon Edwards

In the summer of 1954, we left the Faroe Islands, as my father's job was done. The Brugsen store was up and running and doing well, with profits to boot. My father had only promised the co-op two years, and my parents needed a vacation after all their hard work. We were going back to Sweden to see my grand-parents and the rest of the family.

Britt, Peter, and I left in June, a month earlier than my parents, as they had loose ends to wrap up at the store. My father didn't seem worried about not having a job, as he figured that FDB (Foreningen for Danske Brugsforeninger—the firm that regulated the co-ops) would come forth with an offer soon.

The excitement of seeing Momma again gave me butterflies, and I was also a little anxious about seeing my cousin Lennart after all this time. What would he be like, and how would he look?

I also visualized the moment when I would enter the doorway and see Momma, whom I hadn't seen for three years. Would Momma be the same loving, caring, warm person I had always known? We had corresponded over the years and kept in contact but talking on the phone was not possible back then. I longed for her voice, her wonderful melodious laughter, and her loving arms. There were painful expectations and urgent longings for this final moment of reunion, and the days seemed longer and slower until we finally arrived at Undersåker's train station. As usual, Momma didn't come to meet us, but waited at home in her own anticipation.

The moment I walked through the door, Momma cried out, joyous and childlike, and ran to hug me, my brother, and Britt. I was finally home again, and it felt like heaven to me. The love that surrounded me felt like a warm, comforting cocoon. Momma wept with happiness, and there was laughter and chatter throughout the day and into the night. I ran through the house and checked everything out, examining every corner and every cookie jar with an eagle's eye. I took in every smell, sight, and sound with a deep hunger in my heart. Everything was there just like before, so I settled down to enjoy all the different foods that I had missed for so long. No more dried fish or whale blubber for me; moose meatballs, lingonberries, and wild strawberries with fresh raw cream were what I was longing for, and Momma had it all waiting for me, as I knew she would.

My parents arrived a month later to enjoy their much-needed vacation. Shortly after arriving in Undersåker, Pappa received a phone call from FDB in Copenhagen. He was offered a consultant job in Esbjerg on the west coast of Jutland (Jylland) in Denmark.

For six weeks, Jämtland warmed my heart. It was not just the glorious, constant sun but also being at my childhood home with my family, and especially my momma—it was all I needed.

Momma looked the same, except for some extra wrinkles around her eyes. Her tears and delightful laughter were easily interchangeable, and her love made me feel whole and safe. The sadness of our separation was gone for a while, but

I knew it was short-lived. I would leave again, and that ache and longing in my heart would return.

To my surprise and great disappointment, Lennart did not come knocking on my door, even though he knew I was back. Everybody else came to see us, but he didn't. I was hurt. I realized after a few days that I would have to walk through the thicket of pine trees on the narrow gravel road between our houses if I wanted to see him. I was a little anxious, but I figured he was still shy and insecure and needed me to make the first move, as always. We were ten days apart in birth order, but as different as earth and fire. I was the fire, and I always had to take the lead somehow.

When Lennart opened the door, he stood there like a statue, just staring at me. He seemed at a loss for words.

He never talked that much anyway, so I broke the silence with my excited greeting, "Hi, Lennart, I am back!"

He smiled sheepishly, not uttering a word.

Ruth came to the door and shouted with her exuberant, loud voice, "Oh my God! Maud is here!"

She hugged me with her strong manly arms and pressed me into her expansive bosom, giving me an extra squeeze before inviting me in for cookies and milk.

While Ruth chatted incessantly like a machine on an automatic setting, Lennart kept at a distance with his quiet shyness and timid smile. He finally sat down at the table to partake in the feast that was offered. I tried to get a conversation going, but Lennart was tongue-tied. I realized that I had some work ahead of me to get him warmed up to me again.

After a few days of constant badgering, though, Lennart began to relax, and we started talking. We were finally able to play, but after three years apart, the closeness we'd once had was gone. The relationship never revived completely, and I felt the distance between us. I had left once, and I would leave again. Intuitively, I felt, I had lost my best friend forever. Even then I knew I had outgrown him because I had been out in the world and had seen and experienced different things than he had.

Lennart lived a sheltered life in Undersåker, and I envied him for that. I had changed. I wanted to see more of the world, and I was eager to experience it all, despite the risks.

Even though our close connection was gone, Lennart and I played every day. We built forts and made up imaginary characters that we acted out in long, drawn-out dramas that fulfilled our childish fantasies of heroism and danger. Peter was occasionally included if he served a purpose in our games.

Before long, however, the summer was gone, and it was time to leave for the real world. Pappa left for Esbjerg in Denmark to start his new job and to look for an apartment for us. Apartments were scarce, and the search took months, so Mamma, Peter, and I moved to Bornholm, the small idyllic island in the Baltic Sea east of Denmark where Pappa was born and where most of his family lived.

Denmark consists of many islands, about 406, excluding the territories of the Faroe Islands and Greenland. Only about seventy of the biggest islands are inhabited. The number of islands changes from time to time depending on weather and sedimentation. Denmark is flat, and the highest point is only 561 feet tall and located in Jutland.

Bornholm is considered the best island in Denmark because it has the sunniest days in all of Denmark. It is therefore called *Solskinsøen* (the Sunshine Island). Bornholm's topography consists of steep, rocky granite cliffs to the north, lush farmlands in the middle, and sandy white beaches to the south. The largest towns are situated on the coast, and they all have harbors.

Bornholm has many interesting sights and landmarks. At the northernmost tip is Northern Europe's oldest ruin, Hammershus Slot (which means Hammershus Castle), built in the thirteenth century. It remains a popular tourist attraction. There are numerous windmills on the island, but an unusual sight is the round churches. They were built around 1200 when pirate attacks were a constant threat. The round churches are dedicated to different saints and built like forts, with seven-foot-thick granite walls. The top level was used for surveillance. Small holes in the walls allowed the inhabitants to shoot arrows or throw stones at invaders. These impressive churches are painted white, with black or red roofs, and have gorgeous Gothic wall paintings on the inside.

The main industries on Bornholm are farming, tourism, fishing, glass production, and pottery. Bornholm is especially known for its smoked fish and art.

After leaving the Faroe Islands, Britt took a job in Sweden working in a nursing home. Mamma and Peter went to live with my father's uncle Axel in Hasle, one of Bornholm's oldest towns on the west coast. He was a relatively wealthy man with a big house on a cliff overlooking the ocean.

I went to live with Pappa's sister Grethe and her husband, Kaj, in Rønne, the largest town on Bornholm. They had four children—Ole was the oldest, at sixteen, and Jytte was fourteen—she became my mentor regarding teenage behavior and boys. Dorthe was a couple of years younger than I, at nine years of age, but I felt she was too young for me to play with, and Hans was only eight.

It was a very busy family, and Grethe was the quintessential mother, ever loving and giving, and she ran the household in a laid-back manner. I immediately felt at home, and my cousins became instant brothers and sisters. I developed a slight crush on Ole, but, of course, he barely noticed the skinny, undeveloped eleven-year-old kid who looked longingly at his handsome face with the blue eyes and gorgeous mop of blond hair. I knew he was beyond my reach, so I clung to Jytte, who had just become interested in boys. She took me walking into Rønne, down its winding cobblestone streets, past quaint stores and ice-cream shops. She knew everybody, and we always ran into some interesting kids her age and older. I was automatically accepted as Jytte's appendage. I was a little exotic because I was from Sweden.

At first, I had trouble with the Bornholmsk language, which was a dialect of Danish. The old Bornholmsk was impossible to understand, but I started to learn the new Bornholmsk very quickly, because of my previous education in Danish in the Faroe Islands.

There were many boys aged fourteen to seventeen, and I was part of this group. I felt very flattered and privileged to be included in the group, protected by Jytte's sweet, accepting nature. She counseled me on what to do and not do and was sometimes like a mother and sometimes like a big sister. It didn't matter to me, as long as she took me along for the ride. I loved the excitement of whatever was going on. I wanted to be where the action was, and that has never changed.

On some afternoons with a group of friends, Jytte and I would ride our bikes to a beautiful beach with surprisingly white sand south of Rønne. The gorgeous blue ocean water was ice cold. That was the summer I learned how to swim with the help of Jytte's friends. We brought drinks and sandwiches and lazed leisurely on the beach for hours after swimming. The bike ride was long and arduous but worth it. Riding back seemed harder, but we chatted and laughed the whole time, which helped pass the time. There were bike paths on the side of the roads, and the land was relatively flat around Rønne.

Pappa thought I was better off living with Grethe and her family in Rønne than in the small town of Hasle, where nothing ever happened, and he was right. I visited Mamma, Peter, Uncle Axel, and his wife, Anna, occasionally, but I also had school to attend in Rønne. I don't remember doing anything of importance in school or taking my schooling seriously.

We only lived on Bornholm for three months, as my father managed to get us an apartment in Esbjerg. I loved Bornholm and was sorry to leave this sunny, beautiful island.

Esbjerg felt like it was on the other side of the world. It was also a fishing town, like Torshavn and Rønne, but much bigger, with a large harbor. The first thing I noticed when we arrived in Esbjerg was the awful stench of fish. It penetrated everything. Over time, the fishy, stinky smell became part of our lives, and we got used to it.

As far as apartments go, we were moving up in the world. I had my own bedroom, and we lived in a large apartment complex built in a square, with a courtyard in the middle, grass to play on, swings, and a sandbox for the little kids.

There were many children, and I found a group of boys to play with again. I also met my first crush, and his name was Rickard. He was a great runner, and I let him catch me behind a door one day. When he caught me, he put his hand on the wall slightly above my right shoulder and leaned his face close to mine without touching me. It was an intense moment. We looked deeply into each other's eyes for a long time, and I held my breath in anticipation of his next move. Then he let go and smiled, and just as quickly as he had come, he ran away, quietly. Years later, I heard that he became an Olympic athlete.

Chapter 7

One's first love is always perfect until one's second love.
—Elizabeth Aston

A big love affair happened when I entered middle school. The moment I saw Helena I immediately fell in love. I just knew I wanted her for my friend; I felt as if it was the most important thing in the world.

I was again, like so many other times before, walking into a classroom full of new faces. Everyone was staring at me, but I was getting good at putting on an air of confidence and nonchalance. I was cool on the outside and scared shitless on the inside. It was always difficult, but I had to try to fit in and make new friends among children who already had a history together.

Helena looked at me with her warm blue eyes and gave me a gorgeous smile. That's when I fell in love. What kind of love it was I didn't know at the time. It gripped my heart with a ferocity that surprised me, as I had never felt this for another human being before, except for Momma.

A couple of weeks after I arrived, I wrote Helena a letter. I told her that I liked her and that I wanted her to be my friend. Helena looked surprised when she received the letter and gave me an intense stare as if she was trying to read my thoughts. After a day or so, I received a note back. I had been on pins and needles; I was so afraid of being rejected because she was the person for me somehow. I adored everything about her: her smile, her beauty, and her petite frame. Helena's note said something like this:

> *I already have a friend, Birthe, so if you want to be my friend, you will have to include her as well.*

Wow, she was loyal, too. I didn't like the idea of sharing her with anyone, but I accepted it. It was better than not having her as a friend at all.

We became a threesome, which was annoying at times, but Helena was fiercely loyal. As time passed, we became closer, and I had increasingly more opportunities to spend quality time with her alone.

Helena lived on a lovely farm on the outskirts of Esbjerg. It was a large working farm with many farmhands. The farm mainly grew potatoes, but there were also cows, pigs, horses, and chickens, along with all the cats and dogs.

Helena was part of a wonderful, close-knit family, with two brothers and two sisters. I was frequently invited there on weekends, which was heaven to me, as living in the country with animals was something I related to completely.

We were put to work doing chores such as cleaning the chicken coop, feeding the pigs, peeling potatoes, and washing vegetables. I took it upon myself to clean the dirty floors in the kitchen, and the stairs. Everybody laughed at my futile efforts to keep the farmhouse clean, as there were about twenty people coming and going three times a day for meals. I was a hard worker, which surprised Helena's mother, and I received many compliments for my persistence and effort.

We had playtime as well, collecting tadpoles and fishing worms and climbing the huge oak tree in the front yard with Helena's two brothers, who were just a couple of years younger than we were. Her sisters were three and five years older, and I rarely had any interactions with them. They were teenagers and were involved with school and other things.

Helena and I bonded completely during the one and a half years I lived in Esbjerg, and we were together as a twosome more often than with Birthe.

Sometimes Helena would visit me at our apartment after school. We were often alone, which was when we would play house. We made a dwelling by covering the dining table with blankets. Helena was my wife, and I was her husband. We pretended to make love, and Helena would become pregnant. I would place a doll under her clothes to make her look pregnant. We would have a fictitious birth, and I would help pull the baby out. Afterward, we would take care of the baby, and I would pretend to go to work or do whatever a man does. There was an excitement in this love game. It was all so innocent and sweet. We had all our clothes on, and there was no touching except for hugging. I had no knowledge of sexuality or homosexuality. I just knew it felt good.

We were only twelve years old, with hormones surging. We were both showing small buds of developing breasts and growing pubic hair. Though I didn't realize it then, our game was sexual and experimental. After a while it ended, as all things do when the excitement wears off. Helena has remained a lifelong friend, no matter where in the world I have gone to live. I love her as a friend and nothing more, as I discovered boys and their effect on me later. I attribute my feelings during our game to hormones, growing up, and becoming a woman.

Helena was a smart little girl as well, with a good amount of common sense, and I admired her tremendously. She wasn't as spontaneous or as energetic as I was; she seemed to have things more under control. I was a fire on wheels, going in many different directions. But I was often insecure inside, and I never had anyone to talk to about my life. I held in whatever hurt I experienced; I didn't know any other way. I was still trying to be a perfect little girl, which I thought was what was expected of me. So, I kept most things to myself, no matter how painful they were.

A perfect example of this was my experience with the school dentist. The school dentist was free because of the socialized medicine in Denmark. Every student went to the dentist to be checked once a year. I hadn't seen a dentist in four years, since that fateful day in Kristinehamn when I was eight.

I was petrified when I was told what was coming down the pike—another visit to the dentist. I couldn't sleep the night before my appointment. When I saw the dentist was a woman, I thought maybe everything would be all right.

The first visit was just a check-up, and there was no pain involved, just a tremendous amount of fear. The dentist told me that I needed three root canals on my front teeth. I didn't know what would be involved, but I knew the dentist wasn't going to pull any teeth, so I figured it would be fine.

At the next visit, the dentist started drilling into one of my top central incisors until she reached the root. When she hit the root with the drill, the pain felt like an electric shock going through my head with such power that I almost blacked out. I had not been given any local anesthetic. I put my hand up to my mouth and started crying loudly in pain. The dentist looked coldly at me and told me to shut up. She continued drilling, while I continued crying. At one point she stopped drilling, shouted at me again, and slapped me hard across my face. I tried to think of something else to stop myself from crying, but the tears just kept flowing as the pain only increased with the continued drilling.

These procedures went on for several sessions since I needed three root canals. I suffered silently, with quiet tears streaming down my face every time. Before each visit, I was a nervous wreck, and I could barely sleep the night before. I never said a word to my parents, though, as I thought that this was the way it was.

Years later, when I told Helena about my dental experience, I found out that she had complained to her parents about the mistreatment. Her parents then sent her to a private dentist. Helena avoided all that torture because she spoke up.

Why didn't I speak up? Why couldn't I see that it was wrong to treat me like this?

I wasn't secure within myself, and I wasn't secure within my family. I didn't want to cause any trouble. I just wanted to be a good little girl at any cost.

At school, I was finally trying to apply myself, as I wanted Helena and the others to respect me. After living in Denmark for only one year, I had to take a major examination for my age group, the sixth graders. The examination determined whether students were suited for higher learning or whether they should take up a more practical vocation.

It was an important milestone in our lives, as it determined our future. But I had the disadvantage of only having lived in Denmark for a short time. I don't think anyone expected me to make it, but I did much better than average. I passed successfully, which made me proud, and I got some confidence back in my insecure mind.

Chapter 8

Don't trust anybody who looks back on the years from fourteen to eighteen with any enjoyment. If you liked being a teenager, there is something wrong with you.
—Stephen King

During the summer of 1956, we were uprooted again, and this time we moved to Odense, on the island of Funen (Fyn), where Hans Christian Andersen was born. It is yet another idyllic island, with rolling hills to the south and marshland in the north.

Funen is known as the "Garden of Denmark," due to its bounty of fruits and vegetables. It has an extensive coastline with some beautiful beaches. Like everywhere else in Scandinavia, the water was too cold for me, but since I now knew how to swim, I braved the chill. Most Scandinavians, however, have no problem with the icy temperatures.

Odense is Denmark's third-largest city and one of the oldest. It is a university town with a large hospital and a prestigious nursing school. The name is derived from the Nordic god Odin, who was worshiped by the Vikings. Odense has many beautiful, aristocratic mansions, well-preserved historic buildings, and castles. There is also a rich, bustling cultural life.

Funen has its own dialect, just as Jutland and Bornholm do. The island is situated in between the largest island, Zealand (Sjælland), where the capital of Copenhagen is located, and the peninsula Jutland (Jylland), which extends up, from Germany.

To my surprise and great joy, we found a modern apartment in a newly built apartment complex called Odinsparken on the outskirts of Odense. For only the second time in my life at the age of thirteen, I got my own modern bedroom, and it had a huge window. The apartment had three bedrooms, a kitchen, bath, and a combined dining room and living room. We had moved a little further up in the world, and it felt good.

My mother started a job as a full-time bookkeeper, as Peter had now entered first grade in a public school nearby. Unfortunately, there was no room for me at the local high school, so I was admitted to a school for girls called *Pigerealen* in the center of Odense. Pigerealen (meaning "girls' high school") used to be a private school for the wealthy, and now it had become a public school. I was devastated by the news that I had to go to a girls' school, as my friends had always been boys, except for Helena, whom I missed terribly.

Many of the pupils in the school were from the wealthiest families in town. Then, there were the rest of us and the ones from the wrong side of the track, who were poor and just faded into the woodwork. It was a very unpleasant experience, and it lasted for four agonizing years.

Since my mother made most of my clothes, I was teased daily. My clothes were stylish and of high quality, but because they were not bought from a prestigious department store, with a high price tag, I was a target for cruel, degrading comments during those four years. I was teased about other things as well—the way I walked, wore my hair, my small breasts, and my hairy legs (which were not worse than anyone else's). I was miserable, and I had no real friends.

I often felt like running away to Momma but could never get the money together that I knew I needed. It was a struggle every day to get up, get on my bike, and ride for thirty minutes into town through the cold, windy, wet weather. In the wintertime, I could take the bus, which helped, but I was always racing to the bus. I didn't want to go, and when I missed the bus, I had to ride the bike anyway.

One day, the bus driver wanted to teach me a lesson. When he saw me sprinting toward the bus, he pulled out just as I arrived, and even though he had to stop at the corner before taking the right turn, he refused to open the door. I saw the grin on his face through the windshield, and I realized that he was tired of my arriving at the last minute. I didn't ride the bus again for months but biked to school in all kinds of weather. The bus driver had managed to humiliate me thoroughly, and it stung for a long time.

Pappa noticed that my grades were quite poor, and he knew that I could do better, so we made a deal that if I could get my grades up to mostly A's, he would buy me a dog. I was inspired and started applying myself. Within a few months, my grades were even higher than expected. I was now third in my class of thirty-six students. Pappa had been right. I had not worked up to my potential at all.

Life at school changed a bit after that, and I received a fluffy white Maltese dog, whom I called Grock. Grock slept in my bed, and he was my responsibility and comfort.

I now received more respect from my fellow students, but that came with a measure of jealousy. I was good academically as well as athletically, and I looked like a model in my mom's handmade fashions, so the teasing continued, though to a lesser degree. Once I had shown my potential, I couldn't lose my third place in class, so my studying continued, and I did very well. Despite these successes, I was not a happy teenager. I was moody and depressed, and I still missed Momma.

School was miserable—just something to get through daily. But when I arrived home after school, a whole new life was waiting for me. I did homework for three hours every evening until bedtime, but in the afternoon right after school, I played with the neighborhood kids.

I met a girl who lived in a house next to our apartment complex. Her name was Birgit. She had two brothers and two sisters, but she was the oldest. Her father had Parkinson's disease and looked very frail. Birgit had a sweet mother who always had cakes and cookies ready when I visited and even named one of her cakes after me since it was my favorite.

Birgit became my best friend while I lived in Odinsparken. She was a great runner, with long, shapely legs. She was a bit taller than I was and had delicate features, short brown hair, and serious blue eyes. We didn't have that much in common, except for our ability to run. We could never catch each other; it was always a draw. Therefore, there was mutual respect between us. I preferred spending time at her house rather than my own. It was a busy, exciting household, yet relaxed and comfortable. Birgit was a little shy and didn't say much. She couldn't replace Helena, but since she was the only girl available around my age, we became friends.

I had to form a gang with Birgit out of necessity. The kids in a neighboring apartment complex would attack us and our brothers and sisters regularly. We called the apartment complex *Rottereden* (the Rats' Nest), as there were so many kids living there.

We never started any fights, but we were not going to let them get away with abusing the smaller kids in our neighborhood. So, we fought back with the same weapons they used—sticks and stones and sometimes hand-to-hand combat. It was very scary, and someone could have gotten seriously hurt.

During a fight one day, my dress was torn to shreds, which was hard to explain to my mother. Mamma was ignorant, as usual, about what was going on, and she never asked too many questions. Peter, of course, knew, but I never told my parents about my difficulties, which I think made my life harder than it had to be.

At the age of thirteen, I was still quite a tomboy, and there were a few boys I could play with at Odinsparken. We made a raft, from some timber we found in a junk pile near the complex, for a small pond that was just a filled-up mud-hole from too much rain.

The large watery mudhole had formed in the center of the big lawn inside Odinsparken. We had so much fun and we pretended we were savage pirates sailing on a big ocean. One day, I fell off the raft into the muddy water. When I came home drenched from top to bottom and entered the apartment, my mother looked horrified and embarrassed as she was entertaining lady friends from work. I didn't look pretty or respectable, and my mother reprimanded me how a thirteen-year-old ought not to behave in that manner but be more ladylike. I felt two inches tall in front of all those ladies.

I kept up with my schoolwork and became a teacher's pet, which didn't help my popularity. To show that I had a more daring, courageous side, I would take orders from the other students for goodies from the bakery. I would sneak out of school during breaks and buy the cakes and cookies that they wanted. It didn't make me popular, but it earned me a bit of respect. I also found it exciting to break the rules a little. I was getting better at sneaking out of school and was only caught once at the girls' high school.

Even so, I hated school with a passion. I did my best to keep up my grades to maintain my status, but I felt more than ever that I was alone and an outsider at school and in my own family.

Sometimes at home, I would hide for hours in a far corner of the basement and weep out of desperation and loneliness. Pappa would notice that I was disappearing for extended periods of time, and nobody knew where I was. He searched for me many times. Eventually, I would show up and then I was scolded for being late, but I never said where I had been. Finally, Pappa found me in the basement one day, curled up in a fetal position, sobbing. I explained that I was missing Momma, but we never talked about it again.

We visited Undersåker every summer, and sometimes we drove the sixteen hours in the wintertime, too, to see my grandparents during Christmas. Those trips were the highlights of those years, as they were Momma time.

The grief of missing Momma was deep and painful. She was the light of my childhood and my life. I wrote a poem about her:

Momma

I am going home to the land of the midnight sun
where the rivers are flowing and the mountains a wonder
and where my mother is.
Let her fragile arms embrace me and hold me with love
because that is my reason for coming.
How still is the night and how quiet the need
of my only mother, who always followed
in thoughts and prayer
this child who grew up
as a stranger
away from the land of the midnight sun

Chapter 9

Love, like fortune, favors the bold.
—E. A. Bucchianeri

When I was fourteen, I fell in love with a boy a couple of years older than I. Børge lived two blocks from me, and I could hear him playing haunting classical pieces on the piano when passing by his house. I would stop and listen to the music that seeped through the window; it drew me back repeatedly.

Whenever Birgit and I would run into Børge and his best friend, Niels, I would observe them carefully. Niels was a handsome boy with dark hair and eyes, but Børge was more interesting and intriguing to me. He wasn't handsome like Niels; the attraction was that he played the piano so beautifully. Børge had a sharp, prominent nose and dark-blue eyes and wore nerdy glasses. His face was bright and open, with a timid smile, and he had a bit of an overbite. I could tell that he was shy, but he had a depth to him that was lacking in Niels, and I liked that.

We had an annual dance at my high school, and we had to invite boys. I wanted to ask Børge to accompany me, but I didn't know his name or how old he was. We knew each other by sight only. I knew where he lived, and that he played the piano.

I confided all this to my mother, and she thought that I should just go to his house, knock on the door, introduce myself, and ask him for a date. Danish girls didn't do that back then unless you already knew the family or each other through other people.

It took a lot of effort to figure out what to say and how to dress for this monumental occasion.

After a couple of weeks of preparation, I had mustered enough courage to walk to Børge's house. I dressed in a typical round fifties skirt, a sweater, and a brown suede leather jacket, with a belt at the waist to show off my slim waistline. I knocked on the door with a trembling hand and a fluttery, anxious heart. Børge opened the door and looked at me with surprise and suspicion. I nervously introduced myself, and then I popped the question and invited him to the dance. He was cool, really cool—not even a small smirk came across his face—as he studied my whole person with his penetrating blue eyes. He told me to wait a minute, and then he went inside, probably to get some counsel from his mother.

When he came back, he said, "I don't know who you are or where you live, and I will have to find that out before I can give you my answer!"

I didn't know if that meant that he didn't approve of me or if it was a complete rejection. I replied as confidently and calmly as I could that it was okay for him to check me out. I gave him my information and told him to call me with his decision. Børge gave me his name and closed the door behind me. As I walked down the steps, I felt quite uneasy. I didn't know if I were being dismissed without consideration or not. It certainly hadn't gone the way I had envisioned it. I felt disappointed and rejected. When I arrived home, I was disillusioned; I felt defeated and judged unfairly.

Mamma tried to console me and said, "I am sure that he will call in a few days and accept the invitation."

I had secretly had a crush on Børge for a while, so this defeat was a blow to my self-esteem, but I tried to heed my mother's words of encouragement and hoped for good news.

A few days later, Børge called, and I trembled when I heard his voice. He said very calmly, but with some warmth in his voice this time that he accepted my invitation to the dance. I was ecstatic and thanked him for calling. The dance was the beginning of an exciting two-year courtship.

Birgit and I would often hang out with Børge and Niels on weekends at my house when my parents were gone. We would play records, dance, kiss, and fondle a little. All this kissing and fondling stirred feelings in me that I hadn't known before. Birgit liked Niels, and it would have been wonderful if they could have had the same connection that Børge and I had, but that never happened, unfortunately. I think Birgit was a little jealous of my new relationship because I now spent much of my time with Børge.

We fell in love quickly, and the sexual tension rose. But I had decided not to have sex. I was not going to follow in my mother's footsteps. I was very firm on that. Børge respected my decision and never pushed past a certain point. We experimented with touching and kissing, but it was mostly Børge who touched me, and I would get very aroused. I was insatiable. It was intoxicating, and I often wished that I could let myself have the experience of sex, but I was too afraid of getting pregnant. Moreover, I didn't feel mature enough; I was only fourteen years old.

My relationship with Børge improved my outlook and mood in many ways. The teasing in school continued but having a boyfriend had earned me many points. I felt happier and more optimistic about life, but there was also turmoil in my mind when I wasn't with him. I felt insecure and longed for him and his touch when we were apart. So many hormones were flowing through my body; I was on an emotional roller coaster. At times I felt ecstatically happy, and other times I felt lonely and sad, just as I had before I met Børge. I put on a facade of confidence in public, but when I was alone, I was living with the insecurities of a teenager.

I spent many evenings alone in my room, fantasizing about sex, and masturbated for hours while doing my homework. I marveled at the incredible sensation it gave me. I couldn't wait to grow up and experience it all, but I had decided that sex would only happen with the man I would marry.

I went steady with Børge for two years, and we loved each other, whatever that means at that age. I guess it was puppy love, and it ended the second summer after we met. I had just turned sixteen, and I suddenly felt stifled.

My parents, Peter, and I were getting ready to go on our summer camping vacation through Sweden, on the way to visit my grandparents. I wanted to be free. I had romantic thoughts of meeting a handsome guy along the way.

The night before we left, I told Børge it was over, and I was quite flippant about it. Børge looked crushed, as he hadn't seen this coming. But Børge was slightly conservative and the novelty of him had worn off. Before we parted, though, I asked him for one last kiss. He was an excellent kisser, and I thought I would miss that a lot. To my surprise, he gave me a long, delicious kiss. It was a bittersweet parting, but I knew I had to move on.

The only notable highlight from that 1959 summer that remains clearly in my mind was meeting two gorgeous German boys from Köln. Pappa was always the person who reached out to people, wherever we went. He loved to talk to strangers and would strike up conversations with anyone who seemed receptive to his humor and stories. Pappa was the one who met the German boys and brought them over to our campsite. They had been riding their bikes through Denmark and Sweden and were now on their way back to Germany.

The tallest boy's name was Volker, and he was in fantastic athletic shape, which impressed me immediately. Moreover, he was an alpha dominant male, showing off his prowess with pride. Volker was blond with blue eyes but not as handsome as Heinrich, who was dark-skinned with brown eyes. Heinrich, however, was not prideful. He was sweet and sensitive, and he openly adored me. Volker was more reserved but vied for my attention by flaunting his physical superiority. I fell for his overpowering nature, even though Heinrich was sweeter and cuter. The competition for my attention increased in intensity as they followed us back to Denmark. It was an incredible position to be in, and I had a great time being adored by two handsome young men.

Volker started writing to me after he got back to Köln, and I was infatuated. Heinrich fell by the wayside, but I see now that I picked the wrong guy. I had one more year of high school to finish, and during Easter of 1960 Volker invited me for a visit. His mother was deceased, and he lived in a dark, dank apartment in the middle of Köln with his father. The weather was oppressive—a thick, wet fog hung over the city for the duration of my stay. I don't remember anything uplifting about that miserable trip. I found Volker to be unfeeling and uncommunicative, and when we kissed, there was not much of a sexual response from him. He was very restrained, which puzzled me. If he had pushed for sex, I might have broken down, because of his otherwise domineering personality, but fortunately he didn't. I know I would have regretted that later. So, I remained a virgin, and I finished high school at the top of my class. My teachers had high hopes for me.

Volker and I kept writing to each other in German, and frequently he would send my letters back corrected with red pencil marks, which hurt quite a bit. I admired his stoic sharpness, even though I couldn't comprehend his lack of passion. I wanted what he couldn't give me, I guess. For some reason, though, I kept corresponding with him for over a year.

When I finished high school in the summer of 1960, my parents decided that I should take an au pair position in Stockholm working for my mother's old friend, Ulla. It was a delightful family with two boys and two girls. The youngest boy was only a year old. He slept next to my room, so Ulla didn't have to get up in the middle of the night. At seventeen, I became the surrogate mother to those beautiful children, and I loved it. I also cooked, canned, baked, and cleaned. The only thing I didn't have to do was the laundry. I had my own modern bedroom and bathroom and a private entrance in a wing of their gorgeous home. I was treated very well; everything I did was appreciated. Ulla's husband was very fond of me and would take me to the horse races sometimes; he made me feel like a princess. On weekends, I would go dancing at Stockholm's Gröna Lund (Sweden's oldest amusement park) with some local teenagers. At these dances, I met foreigners from Africa and the Middle East for the first time. They seemed attracted to me for some reason, as they were the ones who most often asked me to dance. The Swedish men left me alone, and I wondered a lot about that, too.

One Saturday night, a Danish man, Jens, asked me to dance. We struck up a conversation in Danish. He was at least twenty-six years old, and I was trusting and naive enough to give him my name and address. He didn't feel like a stranger because he was Danish.

A few days later, Jens surprised me by coming for a visit. I had just had a shower and was wearing a bathrobe when I opened the door. I am sure that he assessed the situation with a male testosterone mind immediately. As soon as we sat down on the couch to talk, he pounced on me, opening my robe and pushing his face into my crotch. It happened so fast that it was impossible to avoid the contact of his tongue on my clitoris. I jumped up, surprised by the intense feeling he had caused. I had no idea what was happening, but I knew I needed to get away, as it felt too good, and it scared me. I ran to the bathroom and poured cold water on my genitals to cool off. When I re-entered my bedroom, Jens was furious and called me a tease, after which he left. I never heard from him again. I wondered for a long time—what had happened, and was that part of having sex?

When Christmas arrived, I went back to Odense, where my parents still lived in Odinsparken, and I continued corresponding with Volker. Apparently, Heinrich had shown up on my parents' doorstep, looking for me that summer. Unfortunately, I had already left for Sweden. I was very disappointed that I had missed him. I never saw him again. I guess our timing was always off, and our opportunity was lost forever.

Chapter 10

Love is like war; easy to begin but very hard to stop.
—Henry Louis Mencken

It was customary in the fifties and sixties for Scandinavian and European girls to go to England to attend college and then take an au pair position with an English family to earn some spending money while getting room and board. Pappa was always the one with the ideas, and he arranged for me to live with the Mr. and Mrs. Goldstein and their two children in Cardiff, Wales.

At the beginning of January 1961, my father drove me to Esbjerg, where I boarded a ship for England. It was cold, wet, and dark; the trip was miserable and lonely. I was anxious about my upcoming experiences in a foreign country. How I made it to Cardiff on my own was a miracle. I guess I must have had some savvy, even at the age of seventeen.

I arrived on a cold winter night at the Cardiff train station, where two short, stout, stern people picked me up. There was little conversation on the ride to my new home, where I was to live for the next six months.

By the time we reached the Goldstein's brick town house, I was exhausted. As we entered the house, two adorable, excited children greeted me with such warmth and innocence that I immediately forgot my weariness. Elaine, with her dark-brown eyes and hair and page haircut, was eight years old, and her smile lit up the hallway. Aron was a skinny, shy four-year-old with the same dark-brown eyes and black hair, but he had sharper features and a prominent nose. They walked right into my heart; it was love at first sight.

Mrs. Goldstein offered me cookies and milk, though I could have used something more substantial to eat. After finishing my meager meal, I dragged my heavy suitcase behind me up the steeply inclined stairs. I was told to leave it in my room and then commanded to put the children to bed with a story.

I asked, "Do you have any children's books for me to read from?"

"No, just make something up," Mrs. Goldstein curtly replied.

I felt panicky, as my English was only school English. I didn't have much experience with conversational English, and my vocabulary was limited.

When I entered the children's room, I saw two pairs of brown eyes looking at me with anticipation and eagerness. How could I possibly let them down? I relaxed, as I suddenly knew what kind of story I would tell. I remembered Pappa's stories, which could be about anything, even a small coin's adventures in the world. It was at that moment that I decided I was going to tell them about my dog and called my story "Grock and His Misadventures." I missed my little Maltese dog, whom I had had to leave behind. Grock and I had had some great experiences together exploring Odinsparken. The story was a hit, and Elaine and Aron wanted to hear more, but I told them they had to wait until the following evening.

There hadn't been any time to settle into my quarters, and I had never seen such a tiny room. It must have been a closet that had been converted into a bedroom, as it was only about four by eight feet. There was a narrow bed with a hard mattress, a bare wooden chair, and a banged-up old dresser. A small single-pane window provided a little light whenever the sun decided to shine. My room was incredibly cold, as there was no heat. I marveled at the difference between my Swedish accommodations at Ulla's and this deplorable situation. I had heard that England was behind, technologically, but I could never have imagined it to be this bad. In Scandinavia, we had oil heat and radiators throughout the house, so we never had to be cold.

That first night, I went into my tiny room and went to bed wearing most of my clothes, a cap on my head, and Mamma's knitted mittens and woolen socks. The room felt like an icebox. I could see my foggy breath, and the window was white with ice crystals.

In the morning, the children came banging on my door and climbed into bed with me for a few minutes before the day started. I realized that all the au pair girls who had come before me had been everything to Elaine and Aron. The Goldsteins rarely spent any quality time with their children.

My stories were a success, and I never ran out of topics. I had my father's stories to tap into, and my imagination grew, stimulated by the kids' enthusiasm. I was the first to see the children in the morning and the last to see them before bed. Those mornings and evenings were the best times of the day. The rest of the day I spent cooking, cleaning, ironing, polishing silver, and washing dishes and clothes.

I was kept busy from 6:00 a.m. until 10:00 p.m. almost every day. I had little time to myself, and I was treated like a mere servant. I dined alone in the kitchen, and then I sat there waiting for the dirty dishes to arrive. It was lonely, and I felt humiliated being treated as if I were of a lesser class. I felt the subordination acutely every day, and it made me quite homesick. In Sweden, I had been treated like one of the family, and I was appreciated as a human being.

On Tuesday and Thursday afternoons, from 2:00 to 5:00 p.m., I was supposed to go to an English class at the University of Cardiff. Mr. Goldstein offered to drive me to class, and I was surprised by the generous offer until I realized what was happening. By driving me to school on his way back to work, Mr. Goldstein could linger longer at home over lunch, and I had time to do more work.

But he was never able to get me to class on time. We were always at least thirty minutes late. I started getting increasingly more embarrassed, and after several late arrivals, I finally stopped going to class.

I spent my afternoons exploring Cardiff instead. I had paid for this class myself, and I felt bad about dropping out. But I didn't have any time to study anyway, due to the Goldstein's demanding schedule. The hours I worked were long and inhumane, but I never complained or asserted myself. The only other time I was off was on Sundays from 2:00 to 10:00 p.m. They obviously got a lot for the small pocket change they paid me.

One afternoon, while exploring the university area, I discovered the International Student Council, which was a club, where international students would meet to socialize. The stairs leading up to the club on the second floor were narrow and steep. I felt lots of apprehension walking up that staircase by myself and entering the club solo. Most of the students were male, of dark complexion, and came from the Middle East and Africa, but there were also some Scandinavian and European girls. Some men wore turbans and long robes, but most wore casual European clothes appropriate for the English weather.

As I entered the club, I received immediate attention, probably due to being young, female, white, and blond. It was hard to say no to an invitation for a date because some of the black men took it as an insult and claimed it was because they were black that I wouldn't go out with them. But it was not a matter of color for me, as I had not grown up with discrimination. I just didn't like any of them.

One young man from Ghana took my hand after he had been turned down and said, "Look at our hands, and tell me what you see?"

I looked at our hands, but I didn't understand what he was getting at, and I shook my head indicating my perplexity.

He then pointed to his and my hand separately and said, "Look at the difference in our colors. That is why you won't go out with me!"

Of course, I could not deny the marked difference in our color. His hands were charcoal black, and mine were snow white.

I remember thinking, "Wow, how white I am in comparison to him. And now, he thinks that is why I won't go out with him?"

The color had nothing to do with it. It was his attitude that repelled me. I had turned down several dates because I didn't like the young men, but nobody had made such a big deal of it. Now, I disliked him even more after his drama show. I pulled my hand away in disgust and quickly walked away.

One afternoon at the club, I was sitting on the couch with some Scandinavian and European girls chatting and talking about all the guys at the club. I was getting tips on who to watch out for when a good-looking young man came up to me and introduced himself.

He said, "My name is Afzal, and I am a medical student here at the university."

He was dressed well, in a pair of gray wool pants and a white shirt under a woolen sweater. Afzal asked my name and where I was from. Since he was a medical student with good manners, I relaxed and answered his questions. I found his dark golden-brown color exotic, and his big brown eyes warm and hypnotic. He was very handsome, with distinctive, chiseled features, a prominent nose that wasn't too big, and hair so black that it looked almost blue.

Afzal sat down on the armrest of the sofa while we talked, and I felt flustered having this handsome grown man give me all this attention.

I thought, "Gosh, he is the best-looking guy here!"

After all the formalities, Afzal asked me out for a date. He told me that his family was Pakistani Muslim and lived in

Uganda, where he had been born. I had no knowledge of what a Muslim was or what Muslim beliefs were. I knew it was a different religion, but, as always, I believed that we are all the same—human beings in different colors. I felt it was just like Momma used to sing:

Jesus loves the little children,
All the children in the world.
Black and yellow, red and white
They are all precious in his sight.
Jesus loves the little children
of the world.

We made a date for a sightseeing trip on his scooter on the following Sunday. The week crawled by slowly, and I had butterflies in my stomach, thinking about seeing Afzal again. I felt drawn to him, and my hand had felt good in his when we said good-bye at the club.

On Sunday, he came to pick me up on his scooter, and I remember his displeasure when he learned that I was living with a Jewish family. He was a gentleman, though, and we rode around Wales with its beautiful rolling hills as long as we could tolerate the cold. I had never received this much attention from a grown man before, and I felt flattered and giddy. Afzal was twenty-eight years old, and I was only seventeen.

When I met Afzal, I had been in England for two months and had only four months left before I had to return to Denmark and go back to school. Afzal was courting me seriously and fell head over heels in love with me. I was more cautious, as I didn't see this relationship going anywhere. We were too different—from different parts of the world with diverse cultures and religion. I didn't see any future for us, but Afzal was a romantic and very sentimental.

Afzal loved Elvis Presley. He would mimic Elvis and ask if I thought he looked like him. I thought he was more handsome than Elvis. Afzal told me all about his family in Uganda and that he had four brothers and five sisters. All of them, including the girls, were getting an English education. Two of his brothers, and one sister were also studying at the University of Cardiff.

On Sundays, I frequently joined Afzal, his brothers, and his sister at his apartment for spicy curried chicken dinners. My throat would burn for hours afterward, but I learned to like it after a while. It was a romantic and intense time for me. Afzal showered me with love and kisses, but I was barely eighteen and still a virgin. After a couple of months, Afzal declared his love for me and said he wanted to marry me. He was already engaged to a Pakistani girl for an arranged marriage. When he told his parents that the engagement was off, it caused quite a stir. The two families are probably still not speaking to each other to this day.

I wasn't sure what I wanted. It was all so overwhelming, but Afzal had made up his mind and pursued me with increased intensity. All through the spring we traveled on his scooter to many scenic spots and had picnics on the grass.

After three months of constant courting, I finally started to visit his flat alone, where he would kiss and caress me. I resisted his advances, though, because I was only going to make love to the man I would marry. However, after months of sweet, endless seduction, one evening I finally gave in. He had convinced me that we would marry when he finished his studies. I was sitting in an armchair in his room when he came over to me, bent down on his knees, and put his head in my lap. He kissed me on top of my dress, directly on my most tender, throbbing spot, and I gasped at the sensation. The Elvis Presley song "It's Now or Never" was playing in the background:

It's now or never,
Come hold me tight
Kiss me my darling,
Be mine tonight
Tomorrow will be too late
It's now or never
My love won't wait

I had no resistance left in me. Afzal picked me up and put me on his bed, and then he gently and tenderly made love to me. It was a wondrous experience, and I felt truly loved at that moment. We laid in bed for a long time, holding each other, before Afzal had to take me back to the Goldsteins.

When I walked through the door, I wondered if they could tell that I had "done it." I had gone against my long-held, strict principles, and I had broken a promise to myself. To my surprise, though, I didn't regret it, as it had been so beautiful and tender. I realized that I had fallen in love with Afzal.

A couple of weeks later, on one of our scooter trips, we stopped on the side of the road to have a bite to eat. When we were done eating, I started cleaning up the trash we had accumulated. Afzal asked what I was doing, and I explained that I had been taught to leave a place cleaner than I found it, and then I continued picking up our trash. Afzal told me angrily to leave it alone, as it wasn't important.

Annoyed, I replied that I couldn't do that and said, "We leave this place like we found it or better!"

That was the beginning of our culture clashes. Afzal couldn't understand how important it was to me, as he had not been raised that way, and I couldn't understand his ignorance. There was a great divide between us, and I still remember the hurt and disappointment I felt about him. I had difficulty understanding how he could be so selfish and thoughtless. I have a picture from that day, and I look so sad and unhappy after that fight. I knew I was right but making him understand this consideration for others and our planet was impossible.

When it was time to leave England, I thought Afzal would forget all the promises he had made once I was gone. I was wrong. Afzal started writing me letters every day, and they were full of love declarations and statements about how much he missed me.

Chapter 11

In school, you're taught a lesson and then given a test.
In life, you're given a test that teaches you a lesson.
—Tom Bodett

After returning to Denmark, I was accepted into a prestigious, competitive gymnasium school, which prepared students for admission to a university. High school students in Denmark cannot enter a university without completing this program, and it is equivalent to a bachelor's degree in America. It was normally a four-year program, but this school had a special curriculum that would allow us to finish in half the time. Universities in Denmark start at the graduate level. It was a tough program, and the students were carefully selected.

I was love struck, and I couldn't concentrate on my studies. Every day after school, I eagerly awaited Afzal's letters. I read them over and over and spent hours writing Afzal back, instead of doing my homework. I lived in a fantasy world where only Afzal and I existed. I daydreamed through classes, looking out the window, not hearing a word of what the teachers were saying. Reality and daily life were of no interest to me. I missed his affection and love. So, when Afzal told me that he wanted to come to see me for Christmas, I was ecstatic.

The school was not happy with my performance, and the principal called me in for a talk. Even though I had better grades than my best friend, who studied all the time, I was told that I was not working up to my potential. I knew the principal was right, but I thought I could get away with slacking off. He bluntly informed me that unless I shaped up, I would lose my spot at the school.

"Many students are eager for the opportunity to take your place," the principal said.

I didn't seem to care, and I didn't believe that he would do such a thing. I had passing grades, after all.

While living in England, I had been very homesick despite meeting Afzal, and therefore I had been eating a lot of English chocolate and Pakistani food with rich desserts. Upon my return to Denmark, I had gained quite a bit of weight. Pappa immediately commented on my increased body size, so, in a panic, I went on a strict diet of apples and yogurt for several months. I dropped from 128 pounds down to 105 pounds very quickly. My frame resembled Twiggy's, and I received many compliments. People told me that I looked like a model. I felt great about my skinny body until I became ill with a severe kidney infection. I was probably severely dehydrated and undernourished. The kidney infection brought me back to reality and scared me enough to stop my diet.

When Afzal arrived for the Christmas holidays in 1961, he was pleasantly surprised to see the skinny Maud, and he showered me with affection and love. My parents were gracious and invited him to stay in Peter's room. Afzal would sneak into my room every night, and we would make love, but he always made sure he was back in Peter's room before anyone woke up. It was like heaven to me to have this grown man adore me and tell me daily that he loved me. It was like a drug I couldn't get enough of.

After dinner, it was a customary to have tea or coffee with cookies and cake and sit in the living room talking for hours. Evenings were my favorite part of the day because my father always had something interesting and funny to tell us. I tried to translate the conversation as best I could for Afzal, but he was soon bored and wanted more excitement.

So, one evening, I was sitting on Afzal's lap in a lounge chair, dressed in a skirt and a blouse, when Afzal slowly slid his hand under my skirt and into my panties and started to caress me. I became flushed and tried to move his hand away, without any luck. Afzal had a smirk on his face as he continued his seduction until I could barely sit up straight. My parents were sitting right across from us, and I was at a loss as to what to do. I thought Afzal had a lot of nerve doing this in front of my parents. I felt embarrassed and victimized. I quietly whispered for him to stop, but he held on to me even tighter and continued with his little game. I couldn't even concentrate on the conversation anymore.

Finally, the evening was over, and everybody was ready to retire. Afzal gave me a victorious smile because he thought the foreplay had already been done. When he came into my room later, I expressed my anger, but Afzal just laughed it off. He was used to having his way, and it was only what Afzal wanted that mattered. Our opinions frequently clashed, and he showed little respect for me or my feelings. But I was so blinded by love that I repeatedly forgave him.

It became Afzal's responsibility to take care of the birth control, as I had little knowledge in this area. My parents were quite worried about our relationship but didn't say anything to me out of fear of sending me further into Afzal's arms. I was no match for this grown man. My mother had a talk with Afzal about my age versus his, and about protection. Pappa did not speak English and therefore could not communicate properly with Afzal, but he did not like or trust him, and he was worried about me. Mamma told me about Pappa's concerns years later.

Afzal told me that my mother had talked to him, and he respected her for that, but he was very critical of our Western culture. His world was the right one, and mine was all wrong. His parents had more love for their children than mine did for theirs, for instance, and gradually I started to believe him. Afzal also voiced his hatred for the Jewish family I had worked for and for Jews in general, and we had many fights about that as well. Even though the Goldsteins had treated me poorly, there was no reason to label all Jews as bad. That was my opinion.

Despite our clashes, we still had a wonderful Christmas with several feet of snow covering the ground that year. The Danish weather stayed typically cold, wet, and windy. My parents let us borrow their car, and I showed Afzal around Denmark. Afzal received many stares because of his dark complexion. He could be a charismatic and charming guy when he wanted to be, but he had some jealous tendencies. When we walked together on the street, I was not allowed to smile, especially at men—that would make him furious. By that time, though, I was too much in love to see the warning signs.

Afzal went back to the University of Cardiff to finish up his doctoral studies, and I went back to school. We corresponded daily, and Afzal planned to come back the following summer.

At the end of my first school year in the summer of 1962, I was kicked out of the gymnasium due to my poor performance, even though I had better grades than my girlfriend. The difference was that she worked so hard to hang in there, and I did nothing. I had shown that I didn't care, so the principal's action was justified. I walked out with an "I don't give a shit" attitude and decided to apply to nursing school instead. It was a blow to my self-esteem to be kicked out of school, but I would not admit that to myself or anybody else at the time.

Afzal arrived that summer for another visit, and my parents bent over backward again to accommodate him. They were still afraid to voice any concerns to me about my choice of a man, out of fear that I would cling to him even more. Differences of opinion kept popping up, which would make me very upset at times, but I was still in love. Afzal loved me with an intensity that I had never experienced before, and this overwhelming passion made my needy, insecure head spin.

One afternoon that summer, my parents took us for a picnic on a rocky beach. Afzal and I had another fight, which my parents didn't hear. Mamma only witnessed my angry reaction—throwing a paper plate at Afzal. She reprimanded me for my bad behavior.

Afzal responded with, "Don't worry; I will get that out of her!"

My mother looked puzzled and concerned. I can still remember the anger I felt because Afzal was trying to control me in subtle ways.

In the autumn of 1962, I started the three-and-a-half year nursing program at Odense Amts og Bys Sygehus. I lived on campus, and I was lucky to have Tove assigned as my roommate. Tove was shy, sweet, and calm—the opposite of me—so we got along famously. She was sometimes frustrated with me, though, because my crazy ideas and adventurous spirit got us in trouble more than once.

One evening, I persuaded Tove to hitchhike to Fredericia with me to go dancing. The trip to the dance worked out well, as we got a ride with a nice man. For the ride home, I accepted an offer from a young man I had met at the dance, with the understanding that Tove could come along. Halfway home, he stopped the car and told us that he was out of gas.

He said, in a reassuring voice, "You girls stay here with the car, and I will walk to the nearest gas station to fill this gas can."

It was about 3:00 a.m., so Tove and I tried to sleep as best we could in the cramped Volkswagen Beetle.

An hour later, a bright light pierced through the windshield, illuminating our groggy faces. Then the flashlight banged on the window, and a stern voice ordered us to open it. It was the police.

The policeman looked very grave. He asked us what we were doing in this vehicle, and I explained the situation.

"Do you know that this car is stolen?" the police officer asked.

Tove and I looked at each other in shock and shook our heads.

I felt responsible for getting us into this mess.

The police officer believed our story, and then he explained, "This is what car thieves do. They walk into a gas station to get gas with a can because the license plates of all the stolen cars are posted there."

The gas station had called the police because of the suspicious circumstances. We were obviously ignorant young girls, and we didn't drink or do drugs. The police officer said that he would drive us home if we promised that we would never do this again. The ride home to our dorm was pleasant in his Mercedes Benz car with the soft brown leather seats, but he lectured us the entire way. By the time we got back to our room, there was no time to get any sleep before we had to be back at work at the hospital at 7:00 a.m. I could never get Tove to hitchhike after that. We had to spend money on taxis if we wanted to go out dancing. I did hitchhike with other nursing students if I didn't have cab fare. On those nights, Tove stayed home.

We spent the first six months of the nursing program in the classroom. After that, we were sent out into "the field." Every three to four months, the students rotated between internships at various hospitals on the island of Funen to get practical experience in nursing. After each internship, we would go back to the classroom for three months of academic learning.

When we worked at the hospitals, we were paid a small wage. Our education was free, and so was the room and board. Even so, we were always broke, and I received no additional help from home. Fortunately, we each received a small monthly allowance from the nursing school, whether working or not. It was a great system and an affordable, quality education.

The nursing school was run by nuns, who were quite strict and critical. Being taught by nuns was not my preference, but I was determined to stick with the program and study well this time. I didn't want another failure. During the first six months, I made many friends, and we had a great time together.

Afzal and I kept the correspondence going, but he must have sensed something in my letters and started to worry about losing me. At the end of the year, he officially proposed and gave me an engagement ring. Our relationship was highly emotional, and I wasn't sure what I wanted, but felt I couldn't say no. I was flattered by his proposal and desperate for his love. Afzal was almost done with medical school, and I would be married to a doctor, which was every nurse's dream. My fellow nursing students were shocked that I was engaged to a Muslim. I had no clue what that entailed.

Afzal forbade me from going dancing because we were now engaged. I was not happy about having my dancing activities curtailed, but I tried to be a good girl and followed orders. The other restriction laid down by Afzal was for me to stop eating pork. I didn't care about this, as I had never really liked pork anyway, so that was easy.

The nuns liked control as well. All the students had their meals in a large dining hall with the nuns. We sat at long rectangular tables that accommodated ten students, with a nun at the head of each table. When the nuns found out that I was engaged to a Muslim and would not eat pork, all hell broke loose. I was ordered to sit next to one of the top nuns, Martha, dressed in her black nun outfit. She had a sizable behind hiding underneath all that holy cloth. Her beady blue eyes kept a sharp watch at dinnertime when the pork was served. I would pass the pork to Martha without taking any. She became increasingly infuriated with my stubbornness and kept putting pieces of pork on my plate, but I would return them promptly or just refuse to eat them.

Unfortunately, this problem entered the classroom as well. Martha frequently drilled me for the entire hour of class, looking for excuses to fail me. My friends knew what was coming whenever she called my name, and they looked fearful on my behalf. But I made sure that I was completely prepared for whatever Martha might throw at me.

I managed to keep my grades up and stayed at the top of my class. I was determined not to fail again, and I became a champion for myself—to have the freedom not to eat pork and to marry whomever I wanted. My friends admired my guts, but It was a daily battle that caused me much anxiety, stress, and further study. It would have been so easy to give in and have peace again, both in the classroom and the dining hall, but I just couldn't. It was the principle of the whole thing. I could easily just have eaten the pork, and Afzal would never have known. But, I had made him a promise, and I was going to keep it.

Chapter 12

Too young to know any better.
—Maud Steinberg

By early spring in 1963, I had finished my classes and started my first internship at a local hospital close to the dancing scene. I was feeling quite constrained by the restrictions being placed on me from all directions. I had always been a free spirit, and I had just turned twenty.

It was spring, with blooming flowers, brighter days, milder winds, and love in the air. The temptation to go dancing became too much. I threw caution to the wind and went dancing again. I felt alive for the first time in months. I wrote Afzal a letter telling him it was over and sent the ring back. It was a liberating feeling, and I was in high spirits. When I told my parents what I had done, they were greatly relieved that Maud was back.

Within a couple of months, I started dating a handsome young man, Hans, who was a fabulous dancer. He was tall, with dark-blue eyes and black hair. Hans was also mild mannered and sweet and quite infatuated with me because we danced perfectly together.

On my birthday, I received two bouquets of flowers at the nurse's station where I worked. One was from Afzal and the other from Hans. All the nurses and nursing students were impressed that I had two suitors. The bouquet from Afzal concerned me, as that meant he hadn't given up. Within a week, Afzal showed up on my doorstep as a complete surprise.

The week before Afzal arrived, Hans and I had had another date planned to go dancing that Saturday night. I was ready and waiting for him in my dorm room. Right before Hans was expected to arrive, I had to use the bathroom. The bathroom was at the end of the hall, but I left the door to my room open to indicate that I was home. It didn't occur to me to leave a note, as I would only be gone for a few minutes. When I got back to my room, I was surprised that Hans had not yet arrived. I waited for hours. I was crushed; I had been stood up, and it didn't make any sense to me.

After Afzal had arrived, I heard from a fellow student that a tall, dark-haired, gorgeous guy had been looking for me that Saturday night with flowers in his hand. Hans probably thought that he had been stood up, too. I have often thought about that incident, and years later I still wonder what would have happened if we had connected that night.

Once Afzal was in town, I was afraid to tell him about my dating. He smothered me with love and affection, and it was easy to give in to his advances. Afzal swept me off my feet again, and the relationship was re-established. He went back to England a happy man knowing that the ring was back on my finger. The plan was for Afzal to finish medical school and take his exams and board certification, and I would continue my nursing studies.

Afzal wanted to visit again for Christmas, and by this time I had a private room where he could stay incognito. However, nursing students were not allowed to have male visitors in their dorm rooms, but everyone had left during the holidays, so it was a perfect setup for us to be alone. My parents, who now lived in Copenhagen, had gone to see my grandparents.

What happened during Afzal's visit will be hard to explain, and my action has baffled me for years. My only excuse is that I was easily influenced back then, and I was young and naive. What I did, I think, was a last-ditch effort to get out of the relationship.

I asked Afzal, "Suppose I can't have children? Would that be something you could live with?"

Afzal answered very quickly, "No, that would be unacceptable. In that case, I would have to take a second wife."

I was appalled. If I couldn't have children, there was no point in marrying Afzal at all, I thought. Sharing my husband with another woman would be out of the question, too.

We started discussing doing an experiment to find out if I could get pregnant. I figured that if I didn't get pregnant, I would be home free. It was a crapshoot, but Afzal was very persuasive. Intuitively, I felt he was worried about losing me; if I got pregnant, he knew I would be bound to him forever. I don't know how I could have been so foolish as to agree to such an experiment. I remember that moment well. It was the night President John F. Kennedy was assassinated (daytime in America).

The decision I made that night changed my life forever. After all, I was my mother's daughter—very fertile—so, of course, I got pregnant. When I found out I was going to have a baby, I had mixed emotions. I had always wanted to have children someday, but I was too young and still in school. I still wasn't sure if I wanted to get married, but the baby needed a father.

When Afzal found out I was pregnant, he wanted to get married right away. Three months later, in March, we were married by the mayor of the Gladsaxe district, where my parents lived. Afzal's sister Sahar and his brothers Atif and Mahmoud came to the wedding. It was a civil ceremony with no fanfare or white dress.

My parents planned the wedding and paid for everyone's travel, accommodations, and food, including a very expensive dinner afterward at a fancy inn. But while they had serious concerns about our union, they felt helpless to stop it.

A couple of months later, upon Afzal's insistence, I traveled to England for a Muslim wedding, according to Muslim traditions. His brothers and sister were present during the ceremony. Afzal had warned me that I would not be able to speak for myself during the ceremony, which I thought was odd.

During the wedding, when the time came to ask the bride and the groom if we agreed to the union, Afzal's brother Mahmoud answered on my behalf. Even though I had been warned, I felt a rush of intense anger. My value as a person had been instantly diminished, and I felt an uncomfortable fear develop deep inside of me. I had become a Muslim's wife without a voice, and I was just beginning to comprehend what that meant.

I loved Afzal, and I knew he was a good man, but I worried about what I had done. Something was not right, because we fought all the time, and I was being controlled in many subtle and not-so-subtle ways. My personality started to change, and I felt I was losing my identity. I had no clue how to be a Muslim's wife.

Once I was back in Denmark and back in school, it all seemed like a surreal dream. I was living two lives. In Denmark, I was still considered a valued, independent person with intelligence, except by the nuns. Under Afzal's spell, I was a subservient, submissive person who was not allowed to have my own opinion.

When the nuns found out I was pregnant, all hell broke loose again. I was the first student ever to get pregnant and married while still in school. The principal called me to her office, and I felt very nervous. I was made to wait outside the principal's office for two hours, sitting on a hard, uncomfortable chair. I believe the waiting was done to try to break me down, but I kept my composure.

When I was finally let into the office, the principal asked in a stern voice, "So, what are you going to do with that black baby?"

I was dumbfounded and shocked by her question, so I was speechless for a while. I finally answered that I would, of course, keep my baby.

The principal then said, "You will never graduate. I will see to that!"

Fear swept over me, and at that moment I felt so discriminated against. How I wished Pappa could have been there by my side to protect me from this evil, prejudiced person.

Life at school did not become easier. I was constantly on trial in the classroom, and I could never let my guard down. I had to make sure always to be prepared, 110 percent. The stress was enormous, but I was determined not to fail, no matter what.

Afzal finished medical school and took his boards but decided to specialize in anesthesiology, so we were going to be apart for another year. I was on my own being pregnant, and with the difficulties at school, it was very lonely. My friends were distant, as I didn't have the freedom to go out anymore. There was no support and little money. I had to get help from social services to get a crib, baby clothes, and other necessities in preparation for the baby.

Two weeks before my due date, in September of 1964, the school allowed me to leave for England to give birth to my child. Asking me to travel to Wales to give birth while I was massively pregnant was crazy, but this was what Afzal wanted. He wanted to be present for the birth, and of course, I wanted that, too. Afzal also wanted the child to become a citizen of the United Kingdom.

During the first two weeks after I arrived in Wales, I tried everything, including running up and down hills, to get the birth going, but our child didn't come until the exact day he was due.

The labor lasted for twenty-one agonizing, lonely hours. I was doing natural childbirth, so I was in incredible pain without any medication, and there was nobody to hold my hand or comfort me in any way. Afzal would check on me periodically and tell the nurses to call him if anything happened. I had thought he would be there by my side during my labor pains, but apparently, he didn't think much of the period before the actual delivery. Afzal went home to bed instead of being with me, and the nurses left me alone during most of those grueling hours. My water hadn't yet broken despite the labor pains, which made me more uncomfortable. Because of the pressure on my bladder from all the amniotic fluid, I couldn't urinate, so I was catheterized several times.

After twenty-one hours, my water finally broke, and then the real labor started with such ferocity that I thought I was going to die. Everyone came running, and our baby boy was born at 1:05 a.m. I was exhausted but happy that the ordeal was over. I hadn't expected it to be that difficult, even though I had assisted with many deliveries as a nursing student. I knew some women had a harder time than others, but I had never thought that I would be one of them.

All this was forgotten when my baby was put in my arms. He was the most beautiful baby I had ever seen. He looked like a porcelain doll with gorgeous caramel skin, delicate features, dark eyes, and a mop of blue-black hair just like his Pappa's. We named him Tariq, and Afzal was a proud father, strutting around like a peacock and giving out cigars to all his male colleagues.

My allowed leave of absence was a total of two months, according to Danish law back then. Today maternity/paternity leave in Denmark is covered for a whole year by the government but not all of it at full pay. After the birth, I had six weeks left before I had to go back to Denmark and school.

Tariq was a ferocious eater. He never seemed to get enough, even though I had milk for two. The breast-feedings, which were truly a joy, had to be given every two hours around the clock. This schedule didn't give me much sleep, but I was young and healthy. I was so happy to be a mother that all my troubles vanished during those six weeks.

The day before I left to return to Denmark, Afzal presented me with some anti-lactation drugs to stop the milk. He thought it would be easier for me not to breastfeed. I objected strongly and assured him that I could continue to breastfeed whenever possible and otherwise express the milk with a pump so that Tariq would get the nutritional benefits of the breast milk. But Afzal insisted that I stop. I was heartbroken, but I didn't dare argue with him.

On the flight back to Denmark, Tariq developed terrible cramps and abdominal pain due to the abrupt interruption of the natural milk supply. He had become so constipated that he could not have a bowel movement. He screamed for most of the trip until I used my little finger to manually remove the obstruction from his tiny rectum. When Tariq finally fell asleep, I cried out of frustration over Afzal's ignorance and careless attitude. I was sad for myself for missing the wonderful experience of breastfeeding but also for my son, who would miss out on the nutritional breast milk and the bonding with me during feedings.

Coming back to Odense with my baby was a sad affair because I was not allowed to keep him with me in the dorm room. I had arranged before going to England for Tariq to live in a home for children about thirty minutes from the hospital. The children's home was mainly a place for children whose mothers had put them up for adoption. It broke my heart to leave Tariq in this strange place, but I was determined to see him every day, and this was the only way.

During that time, I was doing a dermatology internship at a hospital that was a thirty-minute bike ride away from my room and the main campus. After work, I rode my bike to the children's home, thirty minutes in a different direction. I visited for several hours every day and made sure I could give him at least two bottles of milk formula. Tariq was still demanding food every two hours. The staff at the children's home complained that my baby cried all the time, which tore at my heartstrings. Riding back in the dark and cold on my heavy bike, I cried buckets of tears every night. I missed my baby so much.

Even though it was against the rules to have Tariq in my room, I decided one day to take him home with me for the night, anyway. It was so painful not having my baby with me for more than a few hours at a time. I couldn't bring him on my bike because of the cold, so I paid for a taxi and left my bike at the children's home overnight. I spent most of my meager monthly income on taxis from then on and brought Tariq home with me several times a week. Nobody ever found out. Tariq continued being a ferocious eater, and I still had to feed him throughout the night, which gave me little sleep. I had to get up at 4:30 a.m. to get Tariq ready and back to the home and myself to work at 7:00 a.m. That was my life for several months.

One day, the director of the children's home told me that a couple was interested in adopting my baby. I was livid. I made sure she knew that my son was not there to be adopted. Tariq had been placed there only because of unfortunate circumstances, and I would take him when I could provide a home for him, which would be very soon, as it turned out.

At the end of February 1965, Afzal finally finished his anesthesiology education and was offered a position at Odense Amts og Bys Sygehus in the plastic surgery department. As an employed physician, he was provided with a small apartment on campus, and we were finally able to bring Tariq home and live as a family. Tariq was now five months old.

Since both Afzal and I were working, we needed a babysitter during the day. We found an older woman who lived only a few minutes away from campus. Afzal had an easy schedule, working from 8:00 a.m. until 2:00 p.m., whereas I had to get up at 5:00 a.m. to get Tariq fed and ready before leaving for work at 6:30 a.m. I worked until 3:00 p.m. and would be home half an hour later. Afzal picked up Tariq after he finished work and took care of him until I got home. Afzal would change his diaper and feed him, but all the work was piled up when I got home, such as dirty cloth diapers, clothes, and dishes. I came home every day to a mountain of chores, including cooking dinner and doing my homework late into the night.

For the first two months, we had no money coming in except for my meager salary, and we had to pay for a babysitter. Afzal's salary did not kick in until May, so it was very tough for a while. The only food we could afford was milk for Tariq, flour, salt, and butter. I would make *paratha*, a Middle Eastern flatbread, from the flour, salt, and butter, and then I fried it in a frying pan. That was all we ate until Afzal began receiving his salary.

In June, Afzal had to go back to England to take his boards in anesthesiology, and that was another expense. He passed successfully, as always. Afzal was intelligent and capable as a doctor, but as a husband, he was emotional and possessive. We still had many fights, and sometimes I had to leave the apartment to cool off.

I would walk the campus in the evening, crying about my sad situation. I had nobody to talk to about my problems, and Afzal made me feel that everything was my fault. If I would just do as he said, everything would be fine, according to him. He frequently accused me of being too independent, too European. I still loved him, but we were so far apart in understanding that it was impossible at times to come to terms with things.

One evening during an explosive fight, Afzal started throwing shoes at me, so I headed for the door.

When he saw that I was leaving, he shouted very angrily, "If you go out that door, you will never see your son again! I will lock the door and not let you back in!"

I feared he might do what he threatened, so I stayed. I was afraid to go for a walk after that, not knowing if Afzal would lock me out of my own home and take my son away. I felt like a prisoner; I was not free.

During another major argument, he threatened to put me in a mental institution if I didn't do as he ordered.

He said, "Who will believe you over me? I am the doctor here!"

I believed he had the power to do it. I tried to be a good wife and mother while working full-time as a student, but I was overextended in all departments. I became anxious and depressed, as I saw no way out of this dilemma. I had made my bed, and now I had to lie in it. That is how I perceived it. I was going to make the best that I could out of it.

The nursing school nuns let up on me a little after my husband started working at the hospital, which was enough of a relief to prevent me from crumbling under the enormous pressure.

My only friend was my diary, which I had kept since my teenage years. I would write down my troubles and thoughts at night after Afzal was asleep. Journaling gave me some comfort, but most of the time I felt alone and constrained. I couldn't complain to my parents, out of pride; I couldn't admit that I had made a colossal mistake. It was all my fault. I couldn't leave, as I couldn't risk losing my son, so I did what I could to keep peace in the home.

Chapter 13

I chose to forgive over and over,
because otherwise I felt my love was wasted.
—Maud Steinberg

During the summer of 1965, we traveled with Tariq to see my grandparents, as they had not seen him yet. Tariq was nine months old and already walking. He was a bundle of energy every minute he was awake. Afzal loved his son more than life itself, and he spent many hours playing with Tariq or just being with him. I was doing all the work and the chores that came with having a baby, so I missed out on most of the fun.

It was wonderful to be home again with Momma, but I couldn't tell her the truth about my marriage or how unhappy I was. There were moments during that summer vacation when things seemed better, and the love resurfaced between Afzal and me. We were both so proud of our energetic and smart little boy; it brought us together while we were in Undersåker.

Afzal was enchanted with Norrland (the northern part of Sweden, which includes Jämtland), and I think he sensed my grandmother's unconditional love. Momma told me several times to tell Afzal about Jesus. I didn't have the heart to tell her that Afzal would never believe in Jesus the way she did, so I just nodded.

During the warm summer afternoons, everybody gathered in the garden for coffee and cake while the stories flowed, and the laughter escalated and waned. It was quite healing for my fragile, sad heart to be home again, even for a short while. When the weather was warm, we poured water into a galvanized washtub for Tariq, so that he could play in the garden with his toys and splash as much as he wanted. Afzal would lie down in the soft green grass next to Tariq and watch him with proud eyes while smoking his beloved pipe.

We went for walks in the green hills around my grandparents' home and into town, with Tariq riding on his father's shoulders. Stares followed us everywhere we went because of Afzal's and Tariq's dark complexions. They were an unusual sight that far north in Sweden.

Shortly after arriving back in Odense to school and work, I started having morning sickness, and I suspected immediately that I must have become pregnant again, even though we had used protection. I was so sick on a couple of mornings that I had to stay home from work.

The principal called and wanted to know why I was not at work. I couldn't help but giggle a little bit out of embarrassment while telling her that I thought I was pregnant again.

She was furious and yelled, "I cannot understand why medical professionals like yourself and your husband can't figure out how to use birth control!"

Her last words before she hung up the phone were again, "You will never graduate!"

I thought to myself, with more determination than ever, "Don't ever tell me that I can't do something!"

Her venom inspired me to work even harder.

We didn't go out much, because of our busy life and having a baby, but one evening after we got back from Sweden, Afzal wanted to go out for a drink and some dancing. We were trying to maintain the romance that had been reignited in Sweden. We found a respectable romantic place with a live band.

When the band started playing a slow romantic love song, Afzal asked me to dance. I felt happy for a change and melted into my husband's arms, as he led me across the floor. We were the only couple dancing, and I noticed some sideways glances from the other patrons, but we were used to that by now.

At the end of the dance, Afzal embraced me closely in the middle of the dance floor and gave me a long, wonderful kiss on the lips.

The manager of the restaurant came running out, enraged, and shouted, "I want you two out of here immediately!"

Both Afzal and I were shocked at the commotion a little kiss had caused, but we realized it was because Afzal was of dark complexion. Would it have mattered if they had known he was a doctor, a plastic surgeon, and an anesthesiologist at the local hospital? I will never know, but it shouldn't have mattered anyway. It felt as if someone had dumped a cold bucket of water over our heads, and the romantic evening came to an abrupt halt. We were told never to return. I realized then that even the Danes were prejudiced. I had never felt so humiliated in all my life. I cried on the way home from what should have been a romantic evening out. We never went out dancing again in Denmark.

Our daily life at the hospital continued, and I struggled with my morning sickness for months, but I went to work no matter what, once the initial acute nausea had subsided. I had had a lot of nausea when I was pregnant with Tariq, so I realized that I would probably have to go through the same thing this time.

My baby was due at the end of April, and school was over in the middle of April. I was hoping that I could finish school and all the exams, including the boards, before my baby showed up. If the baby came early, it would create major problems and extend my schooling for several months.

One day, our babysitter accidentally burned Tariq's leg with hot water. It wasn't that terribly bad, but Afzal became so infuriated that he fired the poor woman on the spot. Now we had no babysitter. Afzal called my mom, who lived in Copenhagen, more than two hours away, and asked if she could take Tariq for a while. My mother was working, too, so she had to find a babysitter as well, which didn't make any sense. I was heartbroken to be without my son yet again.

I hated to uproot Tariq. I realized that Afzal had used the burn as an excuse. I was scheduled for another internship, at a mental hospital in Middlefart, less than an hour away. I was required to stay at that hospital, in a dorm room during the internship. Afzal would then be the main caregiver of Tariq, and he didn't want to do that.

It was very lonely in my small room at the mental hospital, so I traveled as often as I could to Odense to see Afzal, in the middle of winter with the miserable weather beating on my back. I was pregnant and tired, but I went home every chance I had. Afzal traveled only once to see me during the four months I spent there. He didn't seem to care that much or even miss me, and that hurt quite a bit.

This internship was the most depressing so far. How I managed to hold it all together, being a mom, a wife, and a student all at the same time, is amazing to me now. But I was young and healthy, both mentally and physically.

When I finished the internship, Tariq came back home with us after we visited my parents in Copenhagen during our Christmas break in 1965. I had looked forward to this vacation for months, but things went sour again between Afzal and me. We had another fight, and I stormed out of the apartment into the cold, snowy night to cool off. My parents were beside themselves and asked Afzal to go after me, but he ignored them. It was my father who went out looking for me and brought me back. I was deeply wounded by Afzal's indifference, the polar opposite of his behavior prior to our marriage.

After this incident, my father wrote a stern letter to Afzal, reprimanding him. My father had to write the letter in Danish, as he didn't know English very well, and then have someone translate it to English. Afzal never informed me about this letter, and I don't know what my father had written. I heard about it from my mother several years later. Mamma told me that Pappa was appalled at Afzal's lack of concern and his disrespect for me.

That night, Mamma and I had a woman-to-woman talk in the bedroom while Pappa, Afzal, and Peter were conversing in the living room. Mamma tried to make me understand that I didn't have to stay in this marriage and that I could get a divorce.

"We will help you with the children in every way possible," she said. "We are here for you, so please don't travel to Africa with Afzal."

Afzal had been planning for us to go to Uganda after I finished school and my boards. I knew my mother didn't fully understand the predicament I was in. Afzal would never agree to a divorce, and moreover he would never give up his children. Even if the courts in Denmark were on my side, he would probably kidnap them and take them to Africa, out of my reach.

I just shook my head, and said, "I am afraid to do anything to make Afzal angry, and I can't lose my children."

The one thing Afzal and I agreed upon was that I would finish my studies. I managed to finish my exams successfully, pass my boards, and get my certification as a nurse in Denmark just two weeks before my second child was born. I felt lucky, and I graduated at the top of my class.

When the graduation class picture was taken, however, I was not in it because nobody told me about it. The nuns did not want a nine-months-pregnant woman showing off her huge stomach in the class photograph. I found out about it after the fact, and it hurt quite a bit, but I was beginning to get used to all kinds of discrimination. I told myself that I didn't care, but of course that wasn't true. I would have loved to have had a picture with all my classmates, with whom I had shared so many turbulent yet fun times.

I had made an impression on the campus, though. I frequently had people come up to me and compliment me on my guts and perseverance in doing what I had done, despite all the opposition I had weathered. Strangers called me by name. I was proud of myself and hoped that maybe I had paved the way for others in the future.

On a sunny, blustery day at the end of April, my contractions started, and I needed to get to the hospital right away. Tariq had a babysitter already in place. I called Afzal to let him know that it was time and asked him to take me.

Afzal's response was curt. "You can walk there yourself, and I will see you when I can."

I felt abandoned. Since my first delivery had been so grueling, I was even more apprehensive this time. I had had nightmares in anticipation of this moment, and now I had to do it alone again, even though my husband worked right there in the hospital. I called my mother in Copenhagen, but she was at work. Mamma said she would be there as quickly as she could—she had to leave work, go home, and then travel two hours to get to Odense.

Battling through searing contractions that doubled me over in pain, I walked from our apartment to the hospital. It was several blocks away, and each time a contraction came, I hugged the nearest tree with both arms until it was over. When I reached the stairs to the obstetrics department, a couple of thoughtful nurses saw me and helped me into the building. The contractions were less than three minutes apart by this time, so I was immediately admitted to the delivery room.

This delivery was intensely painful but short, and my baby came out with a scream, that I thought could be heard for miles. All I saw was a big open mouth, a mass of thick blue-black hair, and, of course, caramel-colored skin. It was another boy, and he was named Afraz. He had chubby, soft cheeks and large, round dark eyes. He had more meat on his bones than Tariq did, and I could clearly see the resemblance to his father.

My mother arrived shortly after the birth but still before my husband, who came strolling in leisurely with a smile on his face. He had already received the news from the nurses.

The next day I went home with my baby, and now I had two children in diapers. Tariq was nineteen months old and still quite an energetic handful.

Afzal had planned for us to go to Uganda and join his family once I had finished school and given birth to our second child. It was Afzal's obligation, as the oldest son, to go home and take care of his family, who at this point needed him. His father was not well and could not provide for his family anymore. All their money was gone, mostly spent on education for the oldest children. It was now Afzal's duty to help the rest of the clan finish college, and to do that, he needed to make some money. Since Afzal was now the head of the family, he had all the power that entailed, as well as all the weighty responsibility.

We were planning to leave in July, and Afzal wanted his sons circumcised according to Muslim traditions before we left. Circumcision is usually done right after birth, but in Denmark, it is not a custom and therefore rarely done. Afzal wanted Tariq and Afraz to be circumcised by a plastic surgeon to make sure it was done well and under sedation—I was very relieved by that. Tariq still had a hard time after the surgery, because he was older and more active. It was distressing for me to see him suffer those first few days, but everything turned out well, thanks to Afzal's careful planning and my nursing care.

When we were packing our personal belongings to be sent to Uganda, Afzal found my diaries. They were written in Danish, of course, so Afzal could not understand what I had written. That made him quite annoyed, and he ordered me to throw them away. Afzal didn't see any point in saving such trivial stuff and spending money on shipping them.

My diaries were part of me—nine years of my life were written in them—so I flatly refused. Soon after, I discovered that my diaries were missing, and I confronted Afzal about it. He admitted that he had thrown them in the trash. By the time I found out, the garbage had already been picked up. They were lost forever. I was devastated that my husband could do such a thing. It was another dismissal of me as a person. My diaries would have been a great insight into my teenage years.

We had little money, but Afzal still found it important to buy an expensive camera, a fancy leather suitcase, and a pricey watch for himself. I found a small brown leather handbag that cost about twenty dollars. I just loved it, but Afzal refused to let me buy it. My mother was furious with Afzal for his selfishness and egotism, so she bought me that leather handbag. I cherished it for years. Afzal was not pleased.

As the day of our departure drew nearer, I became more uneasy about leaving everything and everybody I knew, especially my family. My parents were devastated and pleaded with me not to go. Mamma didn't understand how afraid I was of losing my children. I knew Afzal would never give up his sons. If I asked for a divorce, Afzal would probably take the boys from me and go to Uganda, and I would never see them again. I couldn't take such a chance, and my place was with my children. If that meant staying with Afzal, until death did us part, I was determined to make it work. After all, Afzal was the father of my children, and he loved them very much. I could not deprive them of a father who was so devoted. Our boys were the top priority for both of us.

When my small family and I were standing on the dusty platform of the gray train station in Odense to say our final good-byes to my parents, Mamma again whispered to me not to go. I just shook my head. I was completely void of emotion at this point. I felt numb. I felt I had no control over my life anymore. My face was frozen, and my eyes were dry. I couldn't even cry; I had already done so much crying. Now, it was time to be strong for my family. The sooner the goodbyes were over and done with, the better it would be for everyone concerned. I wondered when, or if, I would ever see my parents, Peter, or Momma again. I had no clue what kind of life I was going to have, and Africa was very far away. All I had was Afzal's word that everything would be fine.

Chapter 14

Uganda, an unknown country so far away.
—Maud Steinberg

The trip to Uganda was long and complicated. We had a stopover in Cairo for a night before flying to our next destination, Nairobi in Kenya. Cairo was a total culture shock for me. I didn't see any recognizable women anywhere, only a few black-robed figures with veils, walking along as if they were invisible. There were plenty of men dressed in pants and shirts. Everyone seemed very formal. I was dressed in European clothes—a simple cotton dress barely covering my knees. Even though the temperature was close to 100 degrees Fahrenheit, Cairo felt cold and uncomfortable.

Our hotel room had air conditioning, which I had never experienced before. There were no blankets on the bed—only thin Egyptian cotton sheets, which did not protect me from the cold conditioned air. I froze the whole night and could not wait to get out of Cairo. It was not a friendly place.

When we stepped off the plane in Nairobi, I was wearing a tie-dyed purple dress, with a large matching hat. I felt like a model, but that feeling was short-lived. My new in-laws glared at me with disapproval because my legs were showing. Afzal's sisters and the other women in the Khan family were dressed in bold, brightly colored saris, with part of their midriffs showing under all the yards of material that otherwise covered them from head to toe. They were not wearing hijabs or burqas, but their heads were loosely covered by scarves.

I acutely felt that I was a stranger in a very foreign land. I was white in a colored world, and my dress was inappropriate for the Muslim culture.

Afzal's oldest sister, Amira, lived in Nairobi with her husband and two children. We stayed with them overnight and then drove to Mbale, Uganda, which is in the eastern part of the country. Kampala, the capital of Uganda, is situated next to Lake Victoria (the largest lake in Africa) in the southern part. The equator runs right through Uganda with its mixture of swamplands, wooded hills, and desert regions.

On the way to Mbale, we drove through the countryside, which was mainly flat in this area, passing graceful antelopes and gazelles grazing in the fields. Crazy, energetic monkeys sprung from every tree, and ferocious crocodiles and corpulent hippopotamuses lounged in the muddy rivers. Intimidating rhinoceroses wallowed on the river banks, and regal giraffes nibbled meditatively at the highest branches of the trees. Noisy, colorful birds added a final bright touch to the landscape. It was a grand adventure to take all this in, and I was very excited.

We drove by little African villages composed of dirt huts and tiny shacks built of galvanized steel. The children were playing naked in the fields, and occasionally I would spot a white child among all the black ones. I realized they were albinos. They all looked happy and carefree, despite living in severe poverty.

My African journey had just started, and I had a lot to learn about Uganda and my new in-laws. I had only one protector, my husband, and he was part of this whole culture and different religion. Fortunately, the Khan family was not traditionalists but had rather modern views, which was lucky for me. Our culture clashes could have been many times worse.

We were greeted joyously by Afzal's parents; his thirteen-year-old sister, Sadia; and his eleven-year-old brother, Ashraf. Mahmoud was also there, with his wife. He had moved home to Uganda after finishing his engineering studies at the University of Cardiff and was now married to a Pakistani girl. The marriage had been arranged by the family, but Mahmoud did not look happy at all. He was not the same jolly, smiling, mischievous young man I used to know. He was working as an engineer in Mbale, and he and his pregnant wife lived with his parents. With our arrival, the family grew by another four people to a total of ten, and we all had to share the three-bedroom house located in the center of the dusty, hot town of Mbale.

It was a surprise to discover that Afzal's family home was far from being a palace, or even a decent place to live compared to the places where I had lived in Sweden and Denmark. The crudely made cinder-block building, which Afzal's parents owned and lived in on the top floor, had only basic living amenities. There was no real bathroom or shower. The bathroom was a square room with a waterspout in the wall located below waist height. It was difficult to wash efficiently due to the faucet placement, and the African water was amazingly cold. There was no hot water. The toilet was located at the end of the enclosed concrete backyard, in a small rectangular shed. The toilet was simply a hole in the floor feeding into an eight-inch-wide metal pipe. There was no flushing or toilet paper. I was instructed to bring water with me to the toilet and then rinse myself afterward. It was uncomfortable and primitive.

The kitchen was in the middle of the backyard and had a dirt floor. There were a wood-burning cook stove and a sink under a small window that opened to a back alley, where beggars would show up every day, looking for scraps of food. The walls were covered with crude wooden shelves, and a large table that could seat eight filled the cramped, primitive kitchen space.

The house had three bedrooms, a small, rectangular living room, and a larger square dining room for special occasions. The concrete floor had many holes in it, which frequently caused me to trip. The floor was the first thing I decided to fix, which I did by patching it with concrete to make it more level and not so hazardous.

The tiny living room had an old, hard olive-green vinyl couch; a small, dark-brown coffee table; and two matching wooden side tables. The two windows were dusty and dirty without curtains. I cleaned the windows and made curtains and pillows for the couch to make it look more like a home. As another touch of comfort, I bought a small lamp to read by. I made the corner of the couch my comfy spot for reading late at night after everyone had gone to bed; I needed solitude and quiet after a long day of hard work.

Our bedroom had a double bed with nightstands. There were no closets or dressers. We kept all our belongings in big suitcases under the bed, under lock and key, to prevent theft by the servants. The window in our bedroom was broken, so when it rained, the floor would be covered with water. The boys slept in a crib that was placed against the outer wall in the corner, barely shielded from the rain that came through the window.

One day after a nap, Tariq stood up in his crib and shouted, "Mamma, Mamma, *skål* is coming down!"

Afzal and I always said "skål" whenever we raised a glass of water to drink. It means "cheers" in Sweden. Tariq's expression was priceless—he thought that skål meant water.

Beyond the second door to our bedroom lived a family of sixteen, in only two rooms and a dirt-covered backyard. They were renters, and their cramped living quarters fueled a proliferation of bed bugs. The bugs eventually crawled under the door and contaminated our bed. This caused many problems for us. With tons of hard work and with the help of my mother-in-law, we got rid of the pests. We had to strip and clean everything thoroughly. My mother-in-law was ashamed, I could tell.

Downstairs from our living quarters were two vegetable stores, and they produced many mice. The mice frequently found their way up into our living quarters, and into our bed. I learned very quickly not to walk through the house in my bare feet at night on the way to the toilet. The first time I made my nightly run through the house, I heard crunching sounds under my feet. The next morning, I saw huge dead roaches where I had walked—a revolting sight.

There wasn't much time for me to acclimate to my surroundings before I was put to work by my mother-in-law. It was customary among Muslims that when the eldest son's wife moved in, she would take over the running of the household. My mother-in-law, whom I called *Amma*, immediately started teaching me everything I needed to know. She taught me how to cook Pakistani food—how to grind and mix the various spices for the curry and how to cook the meat.

I was instructed to boil the clothes in a large kettle on an open fire in the backyard until they were clean. I had boiled the clothes and diapers in Denmark, too, but on a stove in a modern kitchen. In Africa, I had to build a fire as well. It was very primitive compared to my previous life, but I never complained about it. I accepted that this was the way it was, and I adjusted, as always, very well.

The men in the family accompanied me to the market every day to buy meat and vegetables. I was not allowed to walk unescorted in the streets because it was not safe, I was told. The minute a white person showed up at the market, the prices would skyrocket. We bought live chickens, freshly slaughtered goat meat, and vegetables. The chickens were carried home, flailing, by a string tied around their necks. I flatly refused to kill or pluck the chickens. It was rare that I put my foot down, but this was one of those times.

Another time was when my father-in-law insisted I wear a sari at all times. He complained about having to see my bare legs showing under my short dress while I worked inside the house. I told him, without any excuses, that I could not run the household wearing a sari, as I would surely trip and fall with all that loose cloth around my legs. My movements have always been quick, and I was fast in my work, and I had little patience for such trivialities. I promised my father-in-law, whom we called *Babba*, that I would wear either a Punjabi dress with baggy pants or a sari whenever I ventured outside, and he reluctantly gave in. I liked Babba, and we respected one another, even though to him, I was "only" a woman. He felt my strength and straightforwardness, I think.

Babba had collected thirty years' worth of newspapers from Pakistan in the backyard, and they took up a lot of space. I like things tidy and clean, and moreover, my children needed a place to play. So, I set out to clean up the massive paper mess, but first I had to check with Babba. We had several heated discussions over the course of a week, but I emerged the victor. Eighty percent of the newspapers were removed, and the rest were organized and stored in a more appropriate place.

After a couple of weeks of tutelage under Amma on how to run their family household, I took over the overwhelming job. Amma was only forty-seven years old, but she was already worn out physically, having given birth to thirteen children. The first two children had died at birth. She had then given birth to Afzal when she was just fourteen. There had been six girls and five boys, and one of the little girls, Tahira, had died when she was only two.

When I married Afzal, I had to take a Muslim name. The family decided that my name would be Tahira. I liked the name, but it felt like I became another person. I was now Tahira Khan somebody I didn't know.

Babba had immigrated to Africa in the 1920s, due to the poor economic conditions in Pakistan. He came from the Punjab area of Pakistan. He started a maize and cotton business in Mbale and became quite wealthy until his arm was injured. Afzal used to tell me stories of how he would play with gold bars on the floor as a child. All the gold bars had now been spent on education for his children, including the girls, which said something about the quality of the man I was dealing with. Amma did not speak English, but Babba did, so I had more interactions with him. Babba had married Amma when she was only twelve and he was twenty-five.

It was customary then and still today among many Muslim families to arrange marriages for underage girls, sometimes as young as five years old. Muslim parents want to secure their daughters a good life and the husband wants a virgin at all cost. It was essential for Afzal that I had been a virgin, and he would not have married me if I hadn't been.

After Amma turned her duties over to me, she planted her short, plump body on the bed and never lifted a finger again, unless she was looking after her grandchildren. She seemed satisfied and happy that her job was done. I wondered when mine would end.

I rarely had time to think about the future or how my life would unfold for me in Africa. My days revolved around my husband and our two boys, and, of course, all my duties. I felt like an unpaid servant—a slave. Every day, I cooked three meals for ten people. My day started at six o'clock in the morning and ended at eleven o'clock at night. The hour from eleven to midnight I spent on the olive-green couch, reading, reflecting on my day, drinking English tea, and snacking on English cheddar cheese and crackers.

I was accepted into the Khan family as Afzal's wife and the mother of his sons. A son is worth more than a daughter in Muslim culture, and we had two adorable sons who had privileges. Afzal had grown up with the burden and the privilege of being the oldest son. One day when she was visiting from England, Afzal's sister Sahar told me what it meant to be a Muslim boy versus a Muslim girl, with this story:

> One day, Afzal wanted me to fetch him a box of crackers from the top of the refrigerator. I was just a little girl at the time, so I had to get a chair to be able to reach. When I finally got up on the chair and reached for the box, Afzal came and kicked the chair away from under my feet, and I fell to the floor, bruising my face very badly. Afzal's explanation for what he did was that I wasn't fast enough in getting him the box. Afzal was not reprimanded in any way because Afzal is like a god in the family.

I was shocked by this story, but then I started noticing how everyone was treating Tariq. Tariq could do no wrong. If he deserved to be reprimanded or punished, I had to do it. When I tried to discipline him, the family laughed and ridiculed me, which undermined my authority with my own son.

Tariq spent most of his time with his father and the other men of the house. I felt I had already lost my first son, so I concentrated on Afraz.

I thought, "Afraz will be my son!"

Afzal did not pay much attention to Afraz, as he was just a little baby. However, when Afraz turned six months old, Afzal told me to stop breastfeeding him, which devastated me again, but I had to obey. It did not make any sense at all this time—breastfeeding was safer and easier, and it was a wonderfully comforting and peaceful experience for me and my baby. The thought entered my mind that maybe Afzal was jealous; this was an experience he was not part of. But I could not shame my husband in front of his family by standing up to him. Afzal had always jokingly reminded me when we lived in Denmark that he had 90 percent of the power, and I had only 10 percent. I'd thought back then that he was teasing me. Now, the reality hit me—he was indeed serious.

Chapter 15

The tragedy of life is what dies
inside a man while he lives.
—Albert Schweitzer

Afzal changed in many ways, when we set foot on African soil and started living with his family. The responsibility of taking care of his family—his father, mother, brothers, and sisters—weighed heavily on him. He was stressed, and we barely made love anymore. Afzal was usually a passionate man and lover, and we still loved each other despite our differences. As a very sexual person, I needed sex regularly to feel whole, but in Uganda, weeks would go by without us making love.

Our lovemaking had been conventional and straightforward until we moved to Uganda. One night, Afzal requested that I put his penis in my mouth. At first, I was put off, but of course, I indulged him. I discovered that I really didn't mind, but I wondered why he wouldn't return the favor. From my experience in Sweden with the young Danish man, who dove for my genitals, I knew that men did that. I later learned that some Muslims consider oral sex immodest and reprehensible because the mouth and tongue come in contact with "impure" secretions. It was apparently okay for me to come in contact with impure secretions, but not for Afzal to do the same. Otherwise, Afzal was a very good lover. I felt I was missing something, though, but I didn't dare ask for it. I was too inexperienced and still a little shy about sex.

One day, Afzal told me that his mother had come to him and asked him to give me a message. Amma's message was that after Afzal and I had sex, I was supposed to wash my hair, as a cleansing ritual, according to Muslim traditions.

I was flabbergasted and blurted out to Afzal, "Your mother is just curious about how often we have sex!"

Afzal just smiled. He didn't demand that I comply with Amma's ridiculous request, so I ignored it. Amma never knew.

Afzal was working very hard trying to get his medical practice started. We remodeled one of the vegetable stores below our bedroom into a doctor's office with an examining room and a waiting room. We waited for months for the electricity and water to be connected, but nothing happened. Afzal received vague excuses and no real answers from the people in power on the town council. The real reason was politics. Afzal was facing opposition from the other doctors in town, who were all Hindu. They were not happy about the arrival of a new English-educated medical doctor who was also a Muslim—and an adversary in their eyes.

The Hindu doctors had a strong influence on the politics in town; many were members of the town council. Afzal realized after a few months that these doctors were actively trying to prevent him from opening his practice, as we still could not get electricity or water. He became increasingly frustrated and stressed over the situation.

To make a little money for us to live on, he took a job as a doctor at the dilapidated local hospital. Several English doctors worked there, and some of them befriended him professionally, but we never saw them socially. The English families lived on the periphery of town, and the Indians and Pakistanis, who were mostly businesspeople, lived in town. Most of the Africans lived in huts out in the countryside. I was the only white person living in town, and I was a great curiosity to everyone whenever I ventured outside.

Since the Hindu doctors had cornered the market on patients in town, Afzal decided to go on "safaris," which meant traveling by car to visit patients in their houses and huts. I was expected to assist my husband on these adventures as well. I was now stretched very thin, so we had to hire some domestic help. We hired an African man to help me with the heavy chores, such as washing clothes, cleaning the house, and doing the dishes. He also killed and plucked the chickens for me.

We hired an African woman to help babysit our children while we were out on our safaris. One early morning, I saw our babysitter come strolling across the street, clutching a little red handbag. Her hips were swaying back and forth in her high heels, and she was wearing a very tight, short red skirt. It was confirmed a few days later that she was a prostitute at night. She confided in me about a female problem, and it turned out that she had contracted gonorrhea, like so many other Africans. Afzal felt sorry for her and treated her for free. Frequently, I found her sleeping on the job while she was babysitting, so we finally had to fire her. Amma then helped with the boys when we went on our safaris, but eventually we found another woman for the babysitting job.

The news traveled very fast that this new English doctor was curing patients. Soon there was a long line of people waiting outside the medical office to see my husband. Afzal didn't have the heart to turn them away, so we started treating patients, even though we still didn't have any electricity or running water. I became busier than ever since I had to assist as a nurse. We saw patients at the medical office in the morning and went on safaris in the afternoon. I still cooked three meals a day, and ironed clothes in the evening.

Afzal discovered why so many patients never got well. Most of the complaints were sexually transmitted diseases, and the Hindu doctors never gave the patients the full course of antibiotics that they needed. This was all about economics and making money. If the patients didn't have enough money for the antibiotics, they would only get as much as they could afford. They would then be told to come back when they had more money. More often than not, the patients didn't return, and the disease became resistant to the common antibiotics.

When Afzal realized what he was dealing with, we drove to Kampala and bought broad-spectrum antibiotics in large quantities. We started treating the patients with a full course, whether they had all the money or not. We didn't really make any money on that venture, but the patients got well, and the line outside our building grew bigger by the day.

However, the political troubles with the other doctors hadn't disappeared, and we were still refused electricity and water. Afzal was trying so hard to do the right thing and support his whole family, but everywhere he turned, there was opposition. He became depressed and started having trouble sleeping, dwelling on his problems. Things were not turning out the way he had envisioned. It was a shock for him to return home and face all these challenges and difficulties that he was not prepared for.

One evening, a large group of women dressed head-to-toe in black robes sat down in front of our house and started an eerie chanting. It made my skin crawl. I asked some of the family members what was going on. I was told that the women were using voodoo to put a spell on someone. The women arrived every night at sundown and chanted throughout the night. It was very hard to sleep, and no pleading made them go away. They were clearly there on a mission. The whole family was very disturbed by the haunting noise and the malevolent intentions behind it.

Afzal became depressed and moody. One morning he came into the kitchen while buttoning his white shirt. He wore two shirts every day, one in the morning and one in the afternoon. So, did Tariq, and it was my responsibility to iron all those shirts. Afzal suddenly noticed that a button was missing. He reprimanded me, screaming loudly that I had left him a shirt without a button. With intense fury, he ripped the shirt off and all the buttons flew off, scattering across the dirt floor. I didn't say a word but picked up the shirt and threw it in the trash. I was calm and without emotion, while Afzal stormed out of the kitchen in a rage to get another shirt. We never discussed the incident, but I think my silence made my point.

Mahmoud confided in Afzal that his marriage was a failure and that he was considering suicide, but Afzal talked him out of it. He was so shocked about his brother's mental state that he confided in me. Mahmoud's wife, Nadira, was equally unhappy—she told me that her husband had not touched her since the wedding night. She cried hysterically as I tried to comfort her. Afzal would later tell me the real reason for Mahmoud's displeasure with his wife. Nadira had looked so beautiful in the picture before the marriage was arranged. But on the wedding night, Mahmoud had discovered that his wife was partially bald and had a deformed leg due to a car accident. Mahmoud felt cheated as this was not what he had signed up for. Nadira had gotten pregnant on their wedding night and gave birth to a lovely little girl, but Mahmoud completely ignored his wife and daughter, giving all his attention to our boys.

I was so busy with all my household duties, the children, and helping my husband in his practice that I really didn't notice the subtle changes in Afzal's behavior. I just worked, slept, and struggled to keep up.

One night, there was a big event at a fancy hotel outside Mbale. It was a fundraiser, and many items were going to be auctioned off. We had no money to buy anything, but Afzal wanted to show his face, as he knew all the important people in town would be there.

Before we left the house, I noticed Afzal swallowing some pills, and I asked him what he was taking. He ignored my question, but I was very persistent. He finally admitted that he had been taking amphetamines because he felt so exhausted.

I worriedly asked, "How long have you been doing this?"

He told me that he had been taking amphetamines during the day and Seconal (sleeping pills) at night for a few weeks. I was shocked, but there wasn't time to discuss the problem at that late hour. We had to leave for the auction.

At the hotel, Afzal ordered some cocktails for us to sip on during the auction. To my dismay, Afzal started bidding on things we couldn't possibly pay for. We barely had money for the drinks. He was playing a disturbing game in his euphoric state, and he told me not to worry. Thankfully, none of his bids won, but I was so upset by Afzal's risky behavior that I wanted to leave.

I said, "Since we don't have any money left anyway, even for a drink, I think we should just go home."

Afzal's face turned red with anger. He grabbed me hard by the arm and dragged me out of the hotel. Once outside, he yelled that it was not my place to tell him what to do; I was a Muslim's wife, and I needed to learn how to keep my mouth shut and be obedient.

Once inside the car, Afzal continued to berate me about my inappropriate behavior, saying how ashamed he was of me. He told me he had made a big mistake marrying a Westerner.

He said, "At least a Pakistani wife would have known her place and kept quiet and do as she was told."

These words tore into my very core. I had left my family and my country to go with this man, and he told me in the middle of Africa that it was all a mistake. I was devastated and started crying. My heart was crushed. My husband didn't love me like I thought he did. I wanted to flee this horrible scene. I opened the door to the car while it was still moving. I was going to jump out; I felt my life was over. When Afzal saw what I was trying to do, he slowed down the car enough so that I could get out without killing myself, but then he took off, leaving me on a desolate dirt road on the outskirts of Mbale. I thought he would come back for me, but he never did.

I was petrified. Alone in a dark, wooded area, I knew I could be a target for anyone who came along. I could be raped and killed, just like that. I removed my white sweater to be less conspicuous and started walking toward the town. I wasn't sure where I was exactly, but I knew the road would bring me to Mbale eventually.

After walking for half an hour, I spied the flicker of the town's lights in the distance. I sighed with relief, and as I walked on, I saw a fork in the road ways ahead. Three African men were standing on the opposite side of the road at the fork. I froze when I saw them and then dove into the ditch to hide and to decide about my next move. The men hadn't seen me yet. I knew I needed a plan in case they meant to harm me. I decided to continue walking toward the fork, as far away as possible from where the men were standing, but I would keep an eye on them and be ready to run for my life if they made the slightest move in my direction. The men were watching me intently as I approached. A chill ran up my spine. I instinctively felt that I was in danger and slipped my shoes off. Just as I was passing the men, they started running toward me, yelling and laughing. That's when I started sprinting—in my bare feet on the gravel road. The adrenaline and endorphins kicked in, so I didn't feel the stones cutting into the soles of my feet. I knew that I was running for my life. My heart was pounding so hard I could hear it. The men gave chase. I couldn't even look over my shoulder to see how close they were, for fear of losing time. I knew I had to prevent them from catching me, or I would, at the very least, be raped.

My aptitude for running was my saving grace because soon I couldn't hear them anymore. I finally turned around and saw them far behind. They had given up—their defeated postures showed that clearly. I ran until I found the street we lived on. I was shaking and out of breath, but I was safe for now.

It was now the middle of the night, and all the doors to our house were locked. I didn't have a key. I couldn't knock for fear of further shaming my husband. Afzal had clearly expressed his displeasure with me, and I couldn't let on to anyone that we had had a fight.

My brain was still high on adrenaline, so I decided to try to jump over the seven-foot-tall concrete wall to get into our backyard. I made several running leaps up the wall, attempting to try to catch the edge and pull myself over. I finally succeeded after many tries, and I tumbled onto the hard dirt with a thump but without any injury. I was finally safe and I sighed deeply with relief. Then I realized that I had another problem. I couldn't get into the house from the backyard because those doors were locked as well. I went into the backyard kitchen and lay down on the dirt floor to sleep, but roaches and other bugs kept crawling on me. I realized that I had to get into the house somehow. There had to be a way.

The so-called bathroom had a door facing the backyard about four feet up the wall and another door leading into the house. I looked at the lock on that door and noticed a loose nail. I got a knife from the kitchen and pried the nail out. After that, the lock was easily opened, and I quietly tippy-toed past all the sleeping family members in the first bedroom and on through the house to our bedroom. Nobody had heard me! When I entered our bedroom, I was surprised to find the babysitter still there, sleeping on the floor.

I asked her, "Why are you sleeping on the floor when there is a bed in the room?"

She looked surprised by my question and said she was not allowed to sleep in our bed. I shook my head in disbelief. Then I asked her if she had seen my husband, and she said she hadn't.

I was confused because I had seen our car parked in front of the building when I came running home. I sent the babysitter home and tried to go to sleep, but my mind was racing. I kept imagining where Afzal could be. Maybe he had gone across the street to see the sick boy he had seen earlier that day—I knew the little boy was very ill.

Hours had passed by this time. An ominous feeling was growing inside me. It suddenly occurred to me that maybe Afzal was in the medical office below. That would be the only way he could come home without me and not have to explain the circumstances to his father.

Amma and Mahmoud's family were not home that night, and they had taken Tariq with them to visit some relatives. Afraz was sleeping in his crib and Babba, Sadia, and Ashraf were in their bedroom. Nothing seemed out of the ordinary inside the house.

Filled with foreboding, I rummaged through the nightstands for the key to Afzal's medical office. I knew there was a spare key somewhere, but in my troubled state of mind, it took a while to find it. Finally, I found the key and ran downstairs with it and out the front door, and in seconds I was inside the office. As I entered, my gut told me that something horrible had happened.

Then I saw him. The sight that greeted me was indescribable. Cold dread coursed through me. My husband was lying face down on his desk—his face was grayish blue. I let out an agonized scream, and I didn't care whether I woke up the whole neighborhood or not. After my tormented cry, I became aware of the silence. The black-robed women were not out there that night, chanting their eerie tunes. The street was empty and quiet except for my blood-curdling scream.

I needed help. I yelled out louder for Babba while I gently rolled Afzal off the desk and onto the floor to get him into a better position. He was barely breathing, but there was still a pulse. I noticed an empty bottle of Seconal on the desk, and I knew what Afzal had done. It was unthinkable that my husband had tried to take his own life, especially after he had been so upset over Mahmoud's suicide wish.

When Babba arrived downstairs, he was stunned. He cried out in a voice full of pain, "No, no, no, Allah—Allah, not my son!"

There was a letter on the desk from Afzal, addressed to his parents. Babba picked up the letter and read it and then started crying with a deep moan, but I couldn't console him at that moment—I had to get some real help. I called for an ambulance, but none was available. Everybody was at the auction. Then I remembered that one of the English doctors had a station wagon, so I called him. He came over immediately, and we lifted Afzal into his car.

When we reached the hospital, the doctor immediately ordered a stomach pump, but by the time the nurses found it, there was nothing left in Afzal's stomach—the pills had already been absorbed. The doctor tried to find the hospital pharmacist to get the antidote for the Seconal, but the pharmacist was also at the auction. By the time the antidote was finally obtained, the sleeping pills had already gone into Afzal's system and were now affecting his breathing and other organs, including his kidneys and liver. It looked hopeless. The doctors were at a loss as to what more to do with their limited resources. The English doctor put an IV in, with my help, to get some fluids into Afzal. Then we waited. Afzal was now in a deep coma.

I stayed at the hospital for three days and nights, watching over him. On the second day, Afzal stopped breathing, and then his heart stopped. I was alone in the room with him at the time, and I was frantic with fear. I straddled his chest on the bed and resuscitated him myself. I was still hoping that he would make it, even though I knew intuitively that he would not. But hope was all I had. It was too painful to accept that my husband was dying. I guess you cling even harder to hope when there is no hope left.

Babba and Mahmoud talked to the doctors about other options because Afzal's kidneys had now stopped working. On the third day, it was decided that we would charter a plane to fly Afzal to the dialysis center in Nairobi to try to clean out the Seconal that was slowly killing him. The doctor was worried that Afzal's brain had been damaged by now, but we all wanted to do whatever we could to try to save him.

I had had no sleep for three nights and was living in a nightmarish limbo between life and death. The doctor depended on my assistance whenever he had to perform procedures, especially when placing an intravenous catheter. Most of Afzal's veins had collapsed, but before we had to transport Afzal to Nairobi we tried to put in one last IV. The doctor was pushing the needle deep into Afzal's arm to find a vein while I was assisting. I was overcome by a wave of nausea and dizziness, and I almost fainted. I collected myself, and concentrated on the task at hand, dissociating myself from the fact that we were working on my husband. The ambulance arrived just as we got the IV in. I was holding the bag of fluids while we rolled Afzal out on a gurney to the waiting ambulance.

A crowd of curious onlookers had gathered outside, surrounding the ambulance. I became enraged at these people's insensitivity and their display of unbridled excitement at the drama that was unfolding. My anger toward them was so intense, if I had had a gun, I might have shot them all.

After we rolled Afzal into the ambulance and I climbed in beside him with the bag of fluid in my hand, I went into a catatonic shock. The enormous psychological trauma of the last few days had taken its toll on me, which was probably the reason I went into a physical coma. I could sense everything that was happening around me, but I could not move my body.

I started repeating to myself, "Maud, you have to accept that Afzal is going to die! Maud, you have to accept that Afzal is going to die!"

After a few minutes of this, the words triggered an emotional release, and the catatonic shock suddenly went away, just as quickly as it had manifested.

I felt numb but calm as we drove on to Tororo Airfield, which was about an hour away. Afzal's mother and Mahmoud were sitting up front with the ambulance driver. The doctor and I were in the back with Afzal. At the very moment we arrived at the airport, Afzal stopped breathing. I knew it was the end. He had succeeded in taking his own life, in defiance of our heroic efforts to save him. I dropped the IV bag and looked at the doctor. He looked at me somberly, confirming what I already knew. Afzal was dead! It was February 6, 1967, three days before his thirty-fourth birthday.

I jumped out of the ambulance with a hollow feeling in my heart. I was gripped by crushing grief and indescribable fear.

I thought, "I don't have a husband anymore. What is going to happen to my poor boys, and how do I explain this to a two-year-old? Tariq will wonder where his Pappa went."

I didn't know what to do now that the battle was over. I stood there in a daze on the dry, dusty grass at Tororo Airfield, looking at the plane, which was still waiting to take my husband to Nairobi. I was frozen in place, but I did not cry.

Amma came running to the back door of the ambulance and screamed and threw herself on her son and shouted, "No, no, he is not dead! See, he is still breathing!"

I wanted to tell her to shut up because he really was dead, and her shrieking was intolerable. I felt so incredibly alone in the world, and I needed to feel a warm body. I walked over to the doctor and hugged him hard as if my life depended on it. He held me for a long time, feeling my pain. The doctor cried, and then I finally started crying, in heaves. Mahmoud came over and put his arms around me as well, and we both sobbed uncontrollably.

Mahmoud held me close, and I felt such comfort from his arms and body that I didn't want to let go. I needed to feel somebody who was alive and breathing and not dead. In a flash, all my warm feelings toward my husband were transferred to Mahmoud, and I clung to him desperately. The warm feelings were then suddenly mixed with sexual feelings. Why was I feeling like this? I was horrified. My husband had just died moments ago, and I was getting aroused by his weeping brother. I was overtaken by shame, and I quickly pulled away from Mahmoud.

I have since read that this is something that can happen when a traumatic death touches us closely—we grab on to life, and Mahmoud was a living, breathing person who reminded me of my husband. I have now accepted my response with a clean conscience, but I felt such shame about that incident for years.

Chapter 16

The most painful good-byes are the ones that are never said and never explained.
—Unknown

The following days were traumatic. I had no friends, and I was alone with my grief and shock. I felt a tremendous guilt since Afzal had killed himself after we had had a fight. I felt I should have recognized the signs, and if I had only done things differently, I could have prevented this tragedy from happening. I should have kept my mouth shut and been a good, obedient wife.

Another blow to my fragile heart and soul was the letter Afzal had written to his parents. Apparently, I wasn't even important during the last hours of his life. In the letter, he apologized to his parents for what he was going to do. Afzal had also written:

> *Send Tahira back to Denmark and bring my boys up to be good Muslims.*

My heart broke when Mahmoud read the letter to me, and I felt cold all over. Afzal had dismissed me so easily, even though we had been married for three years and had two children together. How could he be so heartless, to want my children taken from me and raised by his parents?

According to Muslim tradition, children belong to the husband's family, and I could stay with my in-laws as a servant for the rest of my life, or I could leave without my children. This is what I was told by the Khans. There was no one I could turn to for help. My mind was in a daze, and I didn't know what to do. Everything had happened so fast, and the emotional turmoil continued unabated.

Afzal's body was put in our bed for three days and nights, with his lifeless face uncovered. Routinely, ghoulish visitors would drag me to my dead husband's bedside and say, "Tahira, you better appreciate him while he is still here!" Then they watched my profound grief with sordid pleasure. This was very painful, and I frequently had uncontrollable crying spells.

The household became a surreal nightmare, full of strange and alien happenings. A mass invasion of strangers from all over Uganda and Kenya crowded into every corner of the house. Almost every piece of useful furniture was removed, and white cotton sheets were placed over every inch of the open, empty floor. Professional mourning women in black saris, with their heads covered, sat with prayer beads and books from morning till night and cried and prayed and prayed and cried, only to be relieved by the darkness, when sleep would overcome them on the cold, hard cement floor.

I couldn't sleep in my own bedroom because my dead husband occupied it. Another bedroom was saved for my boys and me, and Afzal's family had left one bed for us to sleep on. However, I could not lock the three doors opening into the bedroom, so we had no privacy. Strangers would come barging into the bedroom even when the boys were asleep, pick them up, and shake them until they cried hysterically in fear.

These strangers would cry out, "Look at these poor little orphan boys without a father!"

I grabbed my children away from them, telling them to get out and stop frightening my boys. I was mostly ignored, and they kept doing it over and over, traumatizing my little boys even further.

I had no place to go to get any peace and quiet, so one day I decided to hide in the medical office below to try to get some sleep. After an hour or so, I was discovered to be missing, and Mahmoud finally found me hiding in the office. Everybody thought I was trying to kill myself and then started to suspect that I had killed my husband. The police were summoned, and I was interrogated for hours on suspicion of murder. But, there was no evidence that I could have done such a terrible thing, and I was set free.

It would have been very convenient if the police could have made the charges stick, as I automatically would have lost my little boys. Moreover, suicide is a sin according to Islam, and finding someone else responsible would have solved two problems for the Khan family. Nobody cared about me; they only cared about my boys, Afzal's reputation, and the fate of his soul in the hereafter. But I was determined not to give up on my boys, and since Afzal and I had been married according to Danish law, the boys belonged with me, I reasoned.

Afzal had to be buried on the third day after his death according to Muslim traditions. He was picked up by the men and brought into the dining room and then placed on a large table for a ritual cleansing of his body. The men wrapped him in beautifully embroidered sheets provided by the women. One of the women asked me for some perfume for the body, as it did not smell very good after three days in the hot African weather. I gave her whatever I had. Soon after, two other thrill-seeking women grabbed me by the arms and pulled me into the dining room, where my husband was lying, covered in those gorgeous sheets like a mummy, with only his handsome face showing.

As I looked at his lifeless, serene face that I had known so well, kissed so often, and loved with all my heart, a woman blurted out, "This is the last time you are going to see your husband, so you better take a good look!"

I was overcome with emotion, and just then the perfume vapor hit me, and I fainted. Due to the density of the crowd, I was caught before I hit the floor. As I came to, I saw the men carrying Afzal's wrapped body high over their heads and down the steps. They were singing, and the women were wailing loudly. I sprang up and ran after the procession of men, but I was quickly stopped by the women.

I cried out, "Where are they taking him?"

I was told curtly, "They are taking him to the burial ground, and women are not allowed. You have to stay here!"

This was my husband, and I was not allowed to see him get buried and get some closure? I asked how Afzal would be buried, as I didn't see any coffin. I was told that he would be put in a hole in the ground just as he was. I was shocked and horrified. I couldn't accept that they would just throw him in the ground in such a primitive way. It seemed disrespectful. How little I knew, and how little I understood them—everything they had done was to show my husband respect, which I understand now, years later.

I stood at the top of the stairs, friendless in the large crowd of mourning women, watching the men carry Afzal away forever with tears silently running down my face. Feeling totally lost and empty, I ran to fetch my boys. I wanted to hold them and protect them from all this craziness.

When the English doctors came to pay their respects and saw the conditions I was living under, they suggested I come to stay with them. I had to decline, as I was afraid of what the Khan family would do. I had noticed that Mahmoud had checked through all the kids' and my personal belongings and had removed our passports so that we couldn't travel anywhere. I was trapped. I knew that everybody blamed me for what had happened, but I was carrying so much guilt, and I didn't need more piled on. I could barely handle this difficult situation.

The English family, however, didn't give up so easily. They could see that I was in deep trouble, and they approached Mahmoud. They asked him directly to give the passports back to me, so we could go to Nairobi to stay with my sister-in-law and her husband. To my astonishment, Mahmoud gave in, probably to save face.

So, it was decided that the boys and I would go to Nairobi and stay with Amira, Afzal's oldest sister. She was married to an international businessman, and they had two children. The English doctors felt secure that I would be better off in Nairobi until I could get a plane back to Denmark. I was relieved to get out of the madhouse in Mbale, with the mourning women and their crying.

Two of Afzal's sisters, Sahar and Mahira, accompanied me and the boys to Nairobi, along with Mahmoud. When we arrived at Amira's house, I was in for another shock—instead of finding a normal household, we walked into a duplicate of the one in Mbale. Most of the furniture had been removed, all the floors were covered with snow-white sheets, and mourning women in black saris lined the empty white walls of the house. One bedroom was set up for me and my boys, just as in Mbale, but the bed was bigger and more comfortable, and the room was larger, with only one door that I could lock behind me at night.

Once in Nairobi, I tried to settle into a routine with Tariq and Afraz and ignore the crying, mourning women as best I could. We went for walks, and I read stories and sang my boys to sleep every night. It was very hot in Nairobi, so when I went for walks, I refused to wear black, for which the family harshly criticized me. I was trying to stay sane and have days that were as normal as possible with my boys. I would have uncontrollable crying spells at times; sometimes I was afraid that I wouldn't be able to stop.

Amira's spouse, Khalid, noticed and advised that we go to a doctor to get me a sedative, and I agreed. I was given

Valium, which calmed me down, and I was finally able to get some sleep. Without Khalid's help, I would have been lost; I could not think clearly about what to do next. He suggested that I call my parents to let them know what had happened. At least a week had gone by since Afzal had died, and I hadn't even thought about calling my parents. I didn't know how. I couldn't think straight, and I was still in a state of shock. I was living moment to moment.

When I finally called, my mother was shaken by the news and wanted me to come home immediately. And she said very explicitly, "Make sure that both boys are with you!"

"Why wouldn't I have both my boys with me?" I responded.

Khalid took me to the Danish Embassy to help me get plane tickets for us to go back to Denmark. I did not have any money, so the Danish government had to lend me the money for the fare.

Mahmoud had gone back to Mbale, so I called him to tell him of my plans to go back to Denmark with Tariq and Afraz. He was furious. He said that the boys belonged to their grandparents.

Mahmoud reminded me of Afzal's farewell letter and said, "You can go back to Denmark, but the boys will stay here with us. That was Afzal's wish!"

Still astounded that I was expected to give up my kids, I said, "Your parents still have nine children. Why would they take the only children I have away from me? They are my children, and they belong with me!"

Then I asked Mahmoud to kindly find the suitcase with the children's clothes and some clothes for me, as this was February, and Denmark was in the middle of winter. Mahmoud promised to look for the clothes and come to Nairobi within the next few days.

When Mahmoud arrived, the only things he brought were old baby clothes, which the boys had already outgrown, and nothing for me. I had asked for my personal papers as well, but he brought none of that. I was empty-handed, except for Afzal's beautiful leather suitcase and camera.

As soon as Mahmoud came back from Mbale, the harassment and brainwashing ramped up. The women dragged me into the bathroom for hours at a time after the boys were asleep. I was repeatedly told that I was a terrible mother and that the boys belonged to their grandparents. I was bombarded with insults, verbally abused, and humiliated. I was told that I was a horrible person and that I had killed my husband. I was free to leave but without my kids. The torment continued day and night, whenever the kids were taking a nap or asleep in the evening. Khalid knew nothing about this insanity, as he was working long hours and was rarely home.

I was so mentally exhausted that I started to believe what they were saying. I hung in there, though, knowing deep down that this was all wrong and that nobody had the right to take my children away from me. The fear of losing my boys was palpable, and I started locking the door to our bedroom at night.

One day, after an especially traumatic episode with my persecutors, I ran out into the street, crying, and stopped a Volkswagen Beetle with a white man in it. I banged on his car window and pleaded in a shaky voice, "Please help me! They are trying to take my children away from me!"

The man looked perplexed and didn't have time to respond before Mahmoud and his sisters grabbed my arms, shook their heads, and said to the man, "Don't pay any attention to her. She is crazy!"

The man drove off, relieved, I am sure, that he didn't have to get involved, and the clan dragged me back into the house.

I knew now what I was up against, and I kept my kids close to me at all times. I just needed to make sure that nothing happened to my boys before we left for Denmark. I lived in constant fear, but Khalid assured me that I would be fine, and that the Khan family was just distraught over Afzal's passing.

When the day arrived to leave for Denmark, Mahmoud was the one who accompanied me to the airport. I had taken Valium to stay calm and collected, and I was carrying Afraz in my arms. Mahmoud was carrying Tariq. Both boys had fallen asleep on the way to the airport. I had only one suitcase and my two boys.

I was a bit dazed by the Valium when I boarded the plane. Mahmoud was following behind me with Tariq in his arms. I sat down in my assigned seat and looked around, expecting Mahmoud to be close behind. But I couldn't see him anywhere. Alarmed, I asked the flight attendant what had happened. She didn't know what I was talking about and sternly instructed me to take my seat, as the plane was taking off soon. I became agitated and said that my son did not make it aboard and that he was missing. I was ignored and treated like a crazy woman and again told to take my seat. The Valium had made me groggy, and I couldn't think clearly, but the realization hit me that Mahmoud had taken Tariq during the last few minutes before boarding the plane, and he was now gone. At what point Mahmoud had turned around, I didn't know.

The plane started taxiing down the runway. All I could think about was that all my careful watching had failed. My son was gone. I tried to assure myself that the Khans had been overcome by grief and probably just needed to keep Tariq for a little while until they came to their senses, and then they would send him back to me. I was still so naive and trusting, and I had so much compassion for Afzal's family losing their son and brother. People do strange things under traumatic circumstances, so I believed in my heart that the family would eventually return my son.

The eighteen-hour plane trip to Copenhagen was grueling, and without my ten-month-old baby, I would have had a complete meltdown. I had him to take care of, which kept me busy. But my heart was heavy, and at times I broke into uncontrollable crying while tending to my baby.

The cold, wet chill of Copenhagen hit me like a bucket of ice to my face, and Afraz and I had no warm clothes to protect us from the unforgiving Scandinavian weather. Pappa came to pick us up, but his face froze with fear and fury when he saw only me and Afraz coming down the escalator. When we arrived at the apartment and I walked past the window of my parent's kitchen, Mamma's shrill scream cut through the glass like a knife.

She cried out in intense agony, "I knew it! I knew it! They took Tariq, didn't they?"

I nodded in between my sobs. How could I have been so stupid to trust Mahmoud, when he had shown nothing but anger and contempt toward me when I had insisted that the boys belonged with me? I had lost my husband and now my son in just two weeks. I was despondent, but my mother was resolute.

She said, "You have to go down to the Ministry of Foreign Affairs this minute to report this. There is no time for you to eat! It has to be done now!"

I followed orders. At least somebody knew what I needed to do. The whole affair was so harrowing that I cannot remember much from that meeting, but the Ministry of Foreign Affairs took the kidnapping very seriously and closed all the borders around Uganda and Kenya. One thing I do remember was that I was told that if Mahmoud managed to make it out of Uganda to Pakistan with Tariq, I would never see my son again, as Denmark had no foreign relations with Pakistan.

So, started the waiting game by the phone. Day after day went by without any news of where my son was. Mahmoud had gone into hiding with Tariq, and nobody knew his whereabouts.

Apparently, Mahmoud had acted alone. Babba had no knowledge of his son's actions, and he was appalled to learn what his son had done. Babba was a fair and honorable man and wanted to set things straight.

Stuck in this limbo, I was wasting away. I could not eat from all the stress, and my stomach had become so acidic that I developed an ulcer—I weighed no more than 105 pounds, and I cried every day. The grief was unbearable. I felt like a hollow shell. I didn't know who I was anymore. There was no spark left in me—only emptiness, despair, and a tremendous, boundless grief.

Mahmoud finally heeded his father's command and came out of hiding after four weeks. The Danish ambassador in Nairobi traveled to Mbale to retrieve Tariq, who by then was a very confused and distressed little two-and-half-year-old. Tariq had lost his whole family within the span of two weeks.

When Tariq descended the escalator at Kastrup Airport in Copenhagen with the flight attendant holding his tiny hand, I almost didn't recognize my usually vibrant, energetic boy, except for his smile. Tariq was thin and undernourished, with dark circles under his eyes.

He came running toward me and threw his frail arms around my neck and cried out, "Mamma, Mamma, I was looking everywhere for you, but I couldn't find you!"

Then he turned to his brother and cupped his face in his small, skinny hands and said, "Chazi, Chazi, I missed you so much!"

Tariq couldn't say Afraz, so he had made up another name for his brother. He kissed his brother on the cheek, while we were all crying with happiness.

Chapter 17

Youth offers the promise of happiness,
but life offers realities of grief.
—Nicholas Sparks

It was wonderful to be home in Denmark again, safe from all the craziness. Afzal's death still haunted me night and day, and the guilt festered. I was like a walking zombie, just living in my head. The only thing I could feel was my enormous grief and sadness. Every day I thought the same thing over and over—I should have done something to prevent this tragedy from happening. I felt responsible.

The Khan family had told me that I had killed my husband, and I had started to believe them. My mind was now playing this guilt record over and over; I didn't know how to stop it. Nobody understood what I had been through, and I had nobody to talk to. Not even my parents fully grasped how traumatized I was. I had trouble sleeping, frequently waking up screaming and crying out in fear from the horrible nightmares. I was alone in my grief and sadness and so depressed that I wished I would die. But my sons kept me alive, as I was responsible for them. I couldn't do the same thing that their father had done.

Despite feeling an incredible pain in my heart, which manifested itself physically and emotionally, I persevered and tried to hold it together, even though I wished I were dead.

During the first few months at home, my parents took care of all of us, including my brother, who was sixteen and still in high school. Fortunately, my parents were young, in their forties, and they loved their grandchildren. They had to take care of all the practical things, as I was in a daze. I couldn't concentrate on much. I couldn't read a book or even concentrate on a movie. I watched the Flintstones cartoons with the boys. That's all I could muster. I was living but felt like a dead person inside without any good thoughts or feelings. I had lost so much weight and was again skinny like Twiggy, with a stomach ulcer to boot. Anything I ate made me sick, and I was constantly throwing up.

My parents moved out of their bedroom so that the boys and I would have a place to sleep. They bought bunk beds for the kids and a bed for me. We were six people sharing an apartment with two bedrooms, a den, and one very small bathroom.

Mamma and Pappa didn't understand why I grieved Afzal since he had treated me so bad. But I still loved him—we'd had children together—so how could I not grieve and miss him? I knew I could not talk to them about it, which made things more difficult.

Every night, I cried myself to sleep. I missed Afzal even though our marriage had been so tumultuous. I missed making love to him, but those moments had been rare during those last stressful months in Uganda.

After Tariq came back from Africa, he was different—a very scared little boy. At first, I couldn't leave the room without him panicking. He had anxiety about losing me again. I understood that and tried my best to keep him secure. There were other signs of dysfunction as well. One day when we went to the shoe store to buy him some boots, Tariq became angry with the salesperson and kicked her in the shin. He would also go around spitting on the floor and at people. At first, we were shocked, but then I remembered how the Khan family had approved of these behaviors and even encouraged them, as he was the oldest son of the oldest son. Afzal's family had been grooming Tariq to be the "god" who could do nothing wrong and the one with all the power, like his father. Over the next few months, I had to retrain him and explain proper behavior around people.

Now that we were all together again, we had to visit Momma and Morfar in Jämtland. We took the sixteen-hour journey by train at the end of March. Snow was still covering the ground, and it was very cold.

While we were in Sweden, Tariq would become hysterical the minute I was out of his sight, so I had to be mindful at all times about where he was.

Momma was so happy to see me and my boys. She said that God had answered her prayers.

I asked her what she meant, and she replied, "I have prayed to God every day since you went to Africa. I have prayed that you and your boys would come back. I am glad that Afzal is dead because that's what had to happen."

I was taken aback by her answer, but I understood that this was her love speaking. Momma had not intended that any harm come to Afzal, but she saw it as God's solution for our return.

The necessity of making a living haunted me daily after I got back from our visit to Sweden. I couldn't live off my parents' generosity forever. I needed a job, but before that could happen, I needed to find daycare for my boys. My parents both worked, so that was not an option. The daycare center in our area had a long waiting list. I signed up, hoping for the best. After a few months, two spots were available in a daycare center not far from where we lived. Afraz was placed in the nursery section and Tariq with the children over two.

By the time Tariq entered the daycare center, he was doing much better and had become quite a little gentleman, compared to his previous outrageous behavior. I was very proud of him.

The next step was finding a job, which wasn't difficult in the field of nursing. I accepted a position at the biggest hospital in Copenhagen, Rigshospitalet, but I wasn't prepared for the pressures and the demands of such a job. This was my first official position as a registered nurse since I had graduated. My immaturity, inexperience, and emotional state made it doubly hard, and I had no clue what I was getting myself into. All I was thinking about was making a living for myself and my boys. The rest would fall into place, I thought, being young and naive.

Since nobody in Denmark could pronounce the name Afraz, my mother and I decided to call Afraz by his middle name, Tore. Tore was a little over a year old and had never been separated from me. When I left him at the daycare each morning, he would scream hysterically. I would hear that scream all day at work. It probably hurt me more than him. I would cry out all my sadness and grief while riding my bike to work, and somehow manage to pull myself together before starting my day. On the inside, I was an insecure, scared mess. How I managed from day to day was a miracle. During that time, I didn't see any other way but to continue my uncomfortable job and just bear it.

Nurses usually start work early in the day. I was not a morning person and never have been, so it was very difficult for me. My day started at 4:30 a.m., and I had to be at work by 7:00 a.m. Before leaving for work, I had to get the boys ready and then take them to the daycare. Having no car, I had to use the buses—one to take us to the daycare and then another two to get to the middle of Copenhagen, where the hospital was. When the weather got warmer, I bought a bike and bicycled back and forth. I would load the kids on the bike and pedal them to the daycare—Tore in front of the bike and Tariq in the back. It was a little easier that way, as I didn't have to depend on the busses and their schedules.

The winter mornings were dark, cold, and wet. I would get off at 3:00 p.m., and by the time we arrived home at 4:30 p.m., it was dark again. In the winter, I rarely saw any daylight, but in the summer the sun was high in the sky, and each day grew longer until there was barely any night at all.

I didn't fully comprehend that what I had been through was the cause of my severe depression and anxiety. I was still in a state of shock.

I finally made a doctor's appointment to get some help, but all the doctor said was, "Time heals all wounds!"

It felt like a slap in the face. I wondered how much time that would be. It was probably good that I didn't know that it would take many, many years before the pain would subside to a manageable level. I did not know that it was possible to feel such pain and still be alive.

After the doctor's appointment, I realized that I was on my own with my grief and sadness. In a moment of desperation and total hopelessness, I went home to the empty apartment, took some sleeping pills, and locked the door. I wanted some peace and to sleep for a long time, as I was so tired of all the daily struggles. I didn't do it to kill myself; I just wanted a little momentary respite from my life and pain.

My mother had gone to Copenhagen that day with my aunt Britt, who was visiting from Sweden. When they came back in the afternoon, Mamma found my bedroom door locked and became alarmed. She managed to get into my room with another key. According to her, I was lying lifeless in my bed. She called an ambulance, but she was so angry with me that she didn't go with me. I was rushed to the hospital in my lifeless state without any family support. Mamma excused her action by saying that somebody had to pick up the kids from daycare, but Aunt Britt or Pappa could have done that. Mamma was furious with me—for good reason—but she had no comprehension of what was happening. There was no compassion for me, and I had no compassion for myself, only hopelessness.

When I woke up in the hospital and opened my eyes, I found a very angry young emergency room doctor glaring back at me.

He told me in a loud, furious voice, "I have better things to do than to take care of stupid girls like you!"

I felt cold all over. While staring into the doctor's hard blue eyes, I was gripped by unsurpassable shame for not being strong enough, or good enough, and for being such an idiot. I didn't know how to deal with my problems—all I wanted was somebody to talk to about my pain.

My stomach had been pumped. Once I could walk and my head was clear, I was sent home. This was the second slap in the face that day. I felt like a total failure as a human being. In addition, I had been abandoned, again, during my darkest hour. The only person I could count on was myself, and I was an emotional wreck.

The nursing job was very difficult with enormous responsibility and incredible demands. Just a few weeks after I started, I was required to take a night shift for two weeks. I was petrified; I would be responsible for seventy patients because at night two units were combined. It took all night to familiarize myself with each individual patient so that I could give a thorough report to the day nurses in the morning. Expectations were high, and the unit nurses were critical of any mistakes or lack of information. I was expected to know all the lab results for every patient if they were abnormal. When the day nurses arrived each morning, I was a nervous wreck.

My depression worsened after I started working. I felt I was not dealing adequately with the pressures from the job due to my imbalanced state of mind. There was also an intense anger brewing in me toward Afzal. How could he betray me like that after I had given up everything for him? I had been betrayed, abandoned, and disqualified as a spouse. In all aspects of my life, I was a failure.

After a few months of work, I felt restless and needed to get out among people my own age. I went to a dance party for young professionals, but I couldn't relate to these pampered, spoiled kids who knew nothing of the world or any hardships. We were worlds apart. I had already lived a lifetime, and now I was widowed, with much responsibility and little money at age twenty-four. All my money went to raise my boys—buying them clothes, food, and paying for daycare. There was nothing left at the end of the month. Pappa would sometimes put a hundred kroner (about fifteen dollars) in my pocket to soften the situation.

One Saturday night, I was restless again. I needed to go dancing and have some fun. Dancing had always helped me in the past, as it would always make me feel happy for a while. I was insecure about going alone; I still had no friends. So, I talked my brother into coming with me. Peter obliged and borrowed my father's sport coat. I had heard about the dances at the student club at the University of Copenhagen, and with a sponsor, we might be able to get in. We approached a student and persuaded him to get us into the club. It was a fabulous place, with three dance floors at different levels playing rock music, jazz, and rhythm and blues. The place was packed with young men and women, and I felt an exhilaration and excitement that I hadn't known in a long, long time. In my mind, I wasn't looking for anybody, but subconsciously, I guess, I needed sex. I was young and full of hormones, and I was used to having sex on a regular basis while married, and at this point, I was starved for attention, affection, and sex.

Peter disappeared somewhere, probably to have a beer. It was legal to drink at any age in Denmark back then. It didn't take long before I hooked up with a younger medical student, Kurt. We danced to one song after another, trying out all the different dance floors. We ended up in the rhythm-and-blues section, where people just did the cling-on thing. Feeling a man's body against mine again sent chills up my spine, and I was turned on so fast that it was embarrassing. My whole body sizzled, and my juices flowed.

After the dance, Kurt and I decided to go home to his place. He still lived at home, but his parents were gone for the weekend. There was one problem—Peter. We decided to take him along because I couldn't send him home alone in the middle of the night. We lived on the outskirts of Copenhagen and the university was in the middle of Copenhagen, about forty-five minutes away, and the buses had stopped running after midnight. Kurt's house was on the way to my parents' house, so Peter tagged along. What happened next is something I felt guilty about for a long time.

Kurt and I went into his bedroom while Peter waited in the living room. We had wonderful, wild sex. I was quite noisy and couldn't contain myself, as it was so amazing to feel alive again. I wasn't dead inside anymore; I was alive with incredible, sensuous feelings all over my body. I couldn't get enough. I have no clue how long this passionate encounter lasted, but it must have been at least two hours.

Afterward, I felt that I had been selfish and put my sixteen-year-old brother in an uncomfortable position. When I finally showed up in the living room, Peter looked like he had been asleep. When I asked him about this incident, years later, Peter said that he didn't even remember if he had heard anything.

He said, "It was not a problem, Maud, I know you needed that, and I know you needed my company, and that's why I came with you."

Despite his young age, Peter had understood that sex was something I needed more than food and water that night.

Scandinavians are freer about sex than most other people. We know and accept that sex is part of living. I was very grateful for my brother's answer; it set my mind at ease.

After that wonderful night, Kurt and I started dating. Our frequent sexual encounters caused us both to get quite red and sore. I went to the doctor for a checkup.

The doctor smiled and said, "Why don't you give it a break for a week, and you will be fine!"

The relationship only lasted a few months, until Kurt's parents found out that he was dating a widow with two children. That was not exactly what they had planned for their one and only bright twenty-two-year-old boy. They ordered him to stop seeing me or all support for his medical school would cease. Kurt tearfully told me that he couldn't see me anymore, as he couldn't throw his education out the window. There was no great love there anyway! It was just carnal sex, and I knew that, so I was fine.

Now, though, I needed to find someone else to fulfill my needs for sex and pleasure. Being able to dance the night away and have sex revived my zest for life. The deadness I felt inside disappeared during those moments, and I could forget my troubled, sad life for a while.

Chapter 18

Life may not be the party that we hoped for,
but while we are here, we should dance.
—Unknown

At work, the demands grew, and I felt very insecure. I was scared to death that I might not be able to handle a problem such as a patient dying. The patients were very ill, and several had died since I had started working there. The fear grew in me that I would have to deal with such a situation soon.

We rotated shifts every two weeks between the day, evening, and night shifts. I found the two-week-long night rotation immensely arduous. I already had difficulty sleeping due to my regular nightmares and sleeping during the day was even harder.

There was a patient on my night shift who was close to death, and every time I went into his room I held my breath, dreading what I might find. During those two weeks, I prayed hard to God to let this man live, at least until my night shift was over. I felt relieved every time that was the case.

When I returned to the day shift after two weeks, I found to my horror that the man was still alive and was again my patient. After receiving the morning report, I went to check on all my patients. When I entered that man's room, I found him dead in the bed. Panicked, I ran out of the room and hid in the bathroom, shaking all over. I stayed in the bathroom for a long time, to make sure that someone else would find him and deal with it. This incident made me question my own capability. I decided that I could not work as a nurse in the hospital if I had these problems with death and dying. Afzal's death had changed me in many ways, and I knew I needed to find myself a less stressful job.

After some soul-searching, I decided that I wanted to work in preventive medicine, or at least outside of the hospital. I entered a program that would prepare me for a university education to become a health-visiting nurse who visited mothers after their babies were born. Before starting the university studies, I had to complete a two-year rotation program at various institutions, including a geriatric care center, a couple of children's hospitals, and home health.

Eight months after Afzal's death, I finally had a complete nervous breakdown, and my family doctor put me in a mental hospital. I was given insulin shots in the morning as shock therapy. Since the shots were given before breakfast, I almost passed out every time. The doctors had me drugged so heavily that I slept for three days and three nights.

Every few days the doctors would ask me how I was getting along. I just answered, "Okay," and that was the end of the conversation.

There was no talk therapy about my grief and depression, only drugs.

When the other patients found out that I was a nurse, many came to talk to me about their problems, and I discovered that many of them were repeat visitors at this mental facility. The patients would go home on drugs and feel calmer, but they always ended up coming back. I didn't see anyone get better, only worse, and I knew that I wanted to avoid the same fate. I did not want to become a helpless mental patient like them.

I intuitively knew that I had to get out of there and away from the drugs, so I called Pappa and asked him to pick me up. Pappa was more than willing to do so, as he could also see that this treatment was all wrong. The doctors were furious, but they let me go after I signed a form stating that I left against medical advice. It was a relief to be back home, and it took several weeks to get off those awful drugs, but I was able to pull myself together and get back to work.

For recreation and stress relief, I continued to go out dancing and meeting men at the university student club. My parents offered to babysit whenever I needed it. Life was getting a little better, and I had several short-term relationships with various young men, mainly for sex, but I would quickly get bored. Still numb and grieving, I had no feelings for anyone.

On June 1, 1968, which was a Saturday, I met a wonderful man from America at the student dance. He was so cute and handsome that he took my breath away. His name was Bill. He was short and stocky with dark-brown, slightly curly, overgrown chin-long hair, and kind hazel eyes. He looked goofy, as his ankles and socks were showing below his too-short pants, but he was a relaxed and interesting man with keen intellectual qualities and a sharp wit. When we danced, I felt an instant connection, and when his arms were holding me, I felt as if I belonged there. We talked and danced all night. We were so immersed in each other that we didn't see anyone else. For the first time since Afzal, I had stars in my eyes. I knew that this man was special.

Bill was traveling through Copenhagen to Paris, en route from Bergen, Norway, where he had attended a scientific conference. He was a microbiologist. I wasn't quite sure what a microbiologist did. It took me a while to understand that he had a PhD and that he was doing his postdoctoral fellowship in Paris. In Denmark, a PhD is called something else, so there was some language confusion.

While in Copenhagen, Bill had been given a place to stay at the Carlsberg Laboratories in return for giving a lecture, which he was more than happy to do. He was still a poor student and was relieved to have free lodging until he could get a flight back to Paris. In the meantime, he wanted to explore Copenhagen and savor the different cuisines at local restaurants, as he loved good food.

Bill explained that he was stuck in Copenhagen for a while, maybe for days, as the social revolution in France had cut off all air transport. The unrest and protest had started in May, with demonstrations by millions of workers and students that paralyzed the country. The uprising was against an archaic and rigid society by a paternalistic government under Charles de Gaulle. In just four weeks, France experienced a fundamental political and cultural revolution, and nobody died, which was amazing.

When the evening was over, Bill asked to see me again. He wanted to take me out to dinner on the following Tuesday. He was hoping that I could direct him to an authentic Danish restaurant. Tuesday evening was three days away, and all I could think about was Bill for those three days. It baffled me. Why had he made such an impression on me? I wasn't sure. It was mostly a feeling, but he was also the cutest and most interesting man I had ever met. He was so genuine and kind that he went straight into my heart.

We had a wonderful time that evening, and Bill was such a gentleman in every way. This bright, handsome man mesmerized me completely. And when he kissed me, I felt an electrical current go through my body. I was instantly turned on, but I thought I had better hold out a little. Bill was different from the other men I had been seeing, and I was a little perplexed by my feelings. For the next couple of days, I was daydreaming all day about him. We went out for dinner again that Thursday.

When I found out that night that Bill was Jewish, I knew this could be complicated. I had promised myself when I came back from Africa that I would never again fall in love with a foreigner or even leave Denmark, for that matter. Bill was from America, which was also far away, and I reasoned that this romance was totally doomed. But I was unable to resist this fascinating, happy man. There had been very little joy in my life since Afzal's death, and now someone had lit my fire. I knew it was crazy, but I was willing to take a chance, go with my feelings, and risk getting hurt.

The very next day, Friday, when I was off, I invited Bill home for lunch at my parents' place. I made a perfect filet mignon with vegetables and potatoes. The dessert was a classic Danish version of an apple cobbler—cooked apples, cinnamon, and fried breadcrumbs with whipped cream on top.

Bill fell in love that day. The love traveled through his stomach to his heart—that's what he told me later. We met again on Saturday and went dancing at the student club. When we left the dance, he asked me to come to his room, and I knew what that meant. I could not decline the invitation. There was no defense left in me when he kissed and caressed me, as my whole body was already on fire. He was so tender and loving, yet so magnetic. The chemistry worked in wondrous ways when we made love on his hard pull-up bed. It was so incredibly beautiful and more satisfying than with anybody else I had been with so far. I was amazed by the fireworks erupting in my body, and my heart ached with longing for more. I had feelings again—feelings that I'd thought were all dead and gone. I had fallen head over heels in love with a stranger from another faraway country. I was worried enough to confide in my mother.

I said, "What am I going to do? I have fallen in love with a Jewish man from America."

"Just enjoy, and forget that he is Jewish and from America," she replied, and that is what I did for the remainder of the short time Bill stayed in Copenhagen.

Bill and I had enjoyed pure bliss for just a week, and then he was gone. He wrote me immediately when he got back to Paris. His first letter started like this:

> *Paris is beautiful, but violent again! The night I returned, there were more riots. Last night police*

and students were in the streets, and tear gas was streaming past my windows.

Then he wrote at the end:

I can't believe that I am writing this letter as soon as I am. I thought I could hold out for at least a week. It just goes to show how weak of mind I am. Love, Bill.

A long-distance romance had started, and it wouldn't be easy. We lived separate lives far apart, but we kept writing to each other several times a week, and a strong bond developed.

Bill dated and went to bed with other women, and I still danced and dated others. Before Bill left on that last Sunday of the single week we were together, he had invited me to come to Paris for my summer vacation. I was excited about the prospect of seeing him again so soon and to have the opportunity to see Paris. Bill said that I could stay with him, but he was worried that he had been too forward in suggesting such an arrangement. I felt, however, that staying with him was the most natural thing in the world, and I accepted excitedly.

Bill reminded me again in his letters that the invitation to come to Paris was still there, and he hoped that I would take him up on it. It didn't take me long to make up my mind and start arranging my trip, which would be in August for ten days.

Shortly after meeting Bill, I became very busy, as I was finally lucky enough to get an apartment in the same high-rise as my parents. I had to prepare and clean the apartment before moving in. I varnished the floors, stripped some old furniture my mother had given me, and made curtains. My parents also helped. Mamma upholstered a beautiful antique chair she had given me as a gift. I spent my precious money on some new furniture for the living room and a new carpet. It was exciting, and I worked feverishly to make it as comfortable and tasteful as possible, within my means. The children and I had a home of our own, and it felt very good.

My parents lived on the sixteenth floor and had a great view—you could see all the way to Sweden on a clear day. My apartment was on the bottom floor, which was perfect for the boys, who could then run in and out as they pleased. There was a large playground right outside and a park nearby with an open field for playing ball games, especially soccer. The kids loved their new freedom of being able to go out and play on their own. Tariq always looked out for his brother, who was still so young. All the neighbors looked out for the children, so there was no danger in letting the children roam and play. I had a small patio in the back where I could see the playground, and during the summer I would sometimes sit there topless, enjoying the sun and reading on my days off.

My life was finally falling into place, and I was happier than I had been in a long time, but the depression and grief still lingered. I couldn't get Afzal out of my mind. My responsibility and love for my boys kept me going, but dancing and sex were what truly made me feel alive.

I saw my parents every day. Whenever I needed a babysitter, they were always willing, and whenever I worked a night shift, they would take the kids to nursery school in the morning. I wouldn't be back until 8:00 a.m., and then I had to sleep until the boys came back in the afternoon. Without my parents' help, it would have been impossible to manage such a schedule and still be able to have a life of my own. I was very grateful for all their help. They loved the boys so much that they were willing to do almost anything just to be with them. Pappa loved to spend time with my boys, telling them stories and teaching them how to play soccer, even though they were only two and three and a half years old. That was the Scandinavian way. All boys played soccer.

Chapter 19

Good times become good memories
and bad times become good lessons.
—Nicholas Sparks

Thanks to my parents, I had time for dancing and dating. One night, I met a black man from Ghana at the student club. He was a medical student studying at the University of Copenhagen. My friends saw me dancing with him and warned me, but I thought they were prejudiced. There was something about this man that reminded me of Afzal, so I let him pursue me all night at the club. Since the Ghanaian man was a medical student, I thought he was safe. He was, after all, an educated man in the healing profession. I was so naive!

My friends and I usually danced until the wee hours of the morning, and then we would go to a bakery for breakfast when it opened at 5:00 a.m. The Ghanaian student suggested he come home with me for breakfast, but that didn't feel right at first instinct, so I said, "No!" However, he didn't take no for an answer, which should have been another red flag and an indication that my first instinct was right.

I didn't drink alcohol or smoke, as so many other young people my age did, so I was perfectly sober. After much persuasion, though, I finally gave in. He was persistent, and I was tired. I reasoned that it was daylight outside, so I told him we could have breakfast together, but absolutely no sex, and he agreed. I didn't want to have sex with him, as that just didn't feel right.

We had a Danish breakfast at my apartment with baked goodies from the bakery across the street. I made coffee, and we had cheese, soft-boiled eggs, and jam. While we were eating, we had a pleasant, intelligent conversation, and I was oblivious to any imminent danger. When breakfast was done, this big man suddenly grabbed me, picked me up like a feather in his arms, and locked me in tightly. Then, he carried me into the bedroom and pinned me down on the bed. I could not move. He was six feet tall and weighed at least two hundred pounds. I weighed only 110 pounds and was five feet six inches tall. Everything happened so fast and unexpectedly that I didn't even have time to cry out. Moreover, the fear was paralyzing because I knew what was going to happen. I told myself not to fight it, as I thought that would be safer. He raped me vigorously and hard, but I never moved or said a word. Afterward, I just lay there on my new bed, stupefied with fear, staring at the ceiling. Then I heard the sliding glass doors to the patio open and close, and he was gone.

I blamed myself for my stupidity, and I felt filthy, used, and betrayed. I went into the shower to wash the dirt, humiliation, and shame off. I sat down under the running water for what seemed like an eternity, sobbing like a baby. Later in the day, I noticed that he had robbed me as well. There was no use in reporting it, I reasoned, because I had invited him into my home, so the police would blame me like I blamed myself. I didn't tell anybody about the rape, and that made me more depressed. I dealt with it by telling myself that I had not been beaten or physically hurt, and I should be grateful for that. I tried my hardest not to think about it. It was a traumatic, scary experience, and it took a long while before I went back to the university-student dance club.

The rape became my shameful secret for decades. How foolish I was—not talking about it with anyone made it even harder. I brushed away the rape the best I could and pretended it had never happened. It was just a bad dream, and that was how I managed to live with it.

August was getting closer, and I was counting the days until I would see Bill again, but I couldn't tell him about the rape. I had butterflies in my stomach, just thinking about him. I was leaving by train on August 8 and arriving in Paris on the morning of the ninth.

I had reserved a bunk, as it was an all-night trip. The sleeping compartment was for both males and females, as was normally done in Europe. Nobody else had arrived to claim his or her respective bunk, so I was all alone. However, a non-European man saw me enter the sleeping compartment, and after I had settled down to sleep, he quietly slipped through the door. I had had to leave the door unlocked, as other people would arrive at the next train stations to claim their bunks. I thought that he was one of my fellow travelers and therefore didn't pay much attention, until I felt him climb into my top bunk.

The man tried to climb on top of me, and I yelled out, "If you don't get out of here, I will pull the alarm!"

"Oh, baby, let's have some fun," he said and laughed.

I reached for the bell string, and once I had that in my hand, he scrambled back down and out the door, as quietly as he had come. I waited to go to sleep until the rest of the passengers had arrived.

When I stepped off the train in Paris, I saw Bill running toward me in his too-short ankle-length pants. He grabbed me hard into a wonderfully tight hug. One hand gently held my head, while the other was around my waist. Then, he kissed me with his soft, delicious lips for a long time, and all those warm, fluttery feelings flooded over me. I was ecstatic. We smiled and looked lovingly into each other's eyes. I never knew one could feel so good just seeing and being with another person. It was pure magic.

Bill's apartment was in a very central part of Paris, close to shops and various attractions on Rue de St. Jacques. His apartment was messy according to my standards, with papers everywhere. It was a one-bedroom apartment with a tiny kitchenette, a small sink, an electric burner, and a fair-size bathroom with a shower. The queen-size bed was up against the wall to the left, and his cluttered desk was near the window on the other side of the room. The room was dark and gloomy, but Bill lit up the room with his presence, his warm, kind eyes, and glorious smile.

As I stood there in the middle of the room taking all this in, I felt my body tingle all over, and I was longing to hold him again. The tension was building, but I felt unsure all of a sudden and didn't know what to say or do. I had only seen this man for a few days in Copenhagen and had made love to him once. We had corresponded for about two months, and I had gotten to know him a little. The more I had found out about him, the more in love I had become, but suddenly I felt shy and awkward.

Bill turned toward me and embraced me gently. I hugged him back and snuggled my face close to his neck, breathing in his scent. His smell made me giddy, and I was aching for him to touch me. Bill guided me toward the bed while he kissed me and caressed my body with his warm, soft hands. I responded eagerly and lovingly to his every move. Our clothes were quickly removed, piece by piece, and there we were in a passionate embrace, and everything was all right with the world. I found heaven in his arms.

The next day, Bill had to go to the laboratory for a while, and I started cleaning his apartment. When the mail arrived through a slot in the door and fell to the floor, I picked it up and put it on his desk. I noticed that it was addressed to someone named Dr. William Steinberg. I was shocked, as Bill had told me his name was "Bill." I started wondering who this person was that I was visiting and whether he was lying to me.

Being very direct as usual, I confronted him as soon as he walked through the door. Bill laughed out loud when I questioned his identity. He explained that in America people often have nicknames and that he was sometimes called

Willy, but mostly Bill or Billy, instead of William. I was so relieved to find out that I hadn't misjudged him after all and that he was the Bill I knew.

Paris was truly magical. During August, most Parisians leave the city to go for holidays in the country, which made the city less crowded. Bill was a fantastic planner and tour guide. Even though he had to work some of the days I was there, he managed to thoroughly entertain me and keep me busy.

The grandest adventure was visiting the Louvre (the largest museum in the world), and then we walked across the bridge over the Seine River to the Musée d'Orsay, where we enjoyed the impressionists' and postimpressionists' greatest and most famous art pieces. We visited the Eiffel Tower and walked along the Avenue des Champs-Élysées with the impressive Arc de Triomphe towering over the traffic below. We toured through the Latin Quarter and Sorbonne University, one of the oldest universities in Europe.

Bill took me to dinner every night at small, intimate side-street restaurants, and after dinner, we often walked along the romantic paths on the Seine River, which runs through Paris. The food was incredible in all the places he picked, and of course we had wine with every meal. I wasn't used to drinking wine, and one night I drank too much red wine. When we arrived back at Bill's apartment, I became violently ill. I vomited explosively at first and then had bouts of dry heaving. Bill lovingly held my forehead while I spilled my guts into the commode. I was thoroughly embarrassed, as I had never been drunk before. I realized then that Bill was a very compassionate and loving man, and an unusual human being. After that night, I stuck with white wine or maybe a rosé in moderate amounts. Bill didn't seem to have any problems with wine and had learned to love a good wine with dinner while living in France.

We made fabulous love every day, and in ways I hadn't experienced before such as oral sex, which I had wondered about for such a long time. Bill was a master at it, and he expressed such enthusiasm that my pleasure was magnified. Bill was so enthusiastic about everything he did, and he had more zest for life and its pleasures than anyone I had ever met. His face was so bright, full of sunshine, and happiness, and he was so loving and sweet that he truly made me feel alive.

While staying in Paris, I realized that I was seriously in love with this man, and I wondered how it would end. Our chances were slim, at best. A relationship like ours was almost impossible and certainly unrealistic, but what did any of that have to do with love? We promised to write to each other until we could meet again.

Our lives continued as before, but we wrote to each other several times a week. Bill's letters were what I lived for from then on. Sometimes Bill would call me on my parents' phone, and I would tremble listening to his sweet voice telling me how much he missed me. I had neither a phone nor a TV because those things were luxuries I couldn't afford. Bill and I had made no promises except to continue writing to each other.

Shortly after returning to Copenhagen, I went dancing again. On my first night out, at the student club, I met a physics student named Frank. Frank was quiet but sweet and attentive. He was also quite handsome, with a mop of black hair, dark-brown eyes, and a very strong, slender physique. He turned me on sexually, and he was an excellent lover. I needed sex all the time or as much as I could get, and Frank met my needs better than any other Danish man had so far. But I was not in love with him. I was in love with Bill. I told Frank about Bill, and he accepted my long-distance romance.

Frank became increasingly more involved in my life, however, and I even introduced him to my boys, which was an exception. I usually kept my personal life separate from my home life with the kids.

Frank's big passion was photography, and he was always taking pictures of me and the kids. We spent many pleasant afternoons on the weekends together with the boys, but he never spent the night. I would usually go to Frank's apartment after we had been out on a date.

Chapter 20

Feelings are something you have;
not something you are.
—Shannon L. Adler

During the fall, I started working in home health as part of the rotation of the different disciplines I had to finish before entering the university to study maternity, childbirth, and the role of the health-visiting nurse for newborns. Most women give birth at home in Denmark, and then they enter a national program in which a nurse visits to ensure the proper nutrition and health of the baby for the first few months.

Home health care was a challenging job in many ways. For transportation, I used a heavy black bicycle provided by the home health care agency. The bicycle had a rack on the back for my big, black medicine bag which contained supplies, including narcotics. I rode my bike in all kinds of weather, and in two shifts every day. I visited patients in the morning, and then again in the evening. It felt as if I was working nonstop, even though, I had a few hours off in the middle of the day. Riding a bicycle during the wintertime was especially hard as it was dark, cold, windy, and wet. It was also hazardous navigating the traffic during the busiest hours of the day.

The job made me feel free, autonomous, and in charge, and I loved helping people who were sick at home. I was the angel who came in the dark to help them and make them feel better. I felt great satisfaction in doing my job well, and I received much appreciation from my patients, which made everything worthwhile.

The days were busy with many chores. Bill's letters were always the highlight of my day. Every day when I came home for lunch, I hoped for a letter, and on the days, I received one, I was smiling. We wrote about our daily lives, our experiences, our feelings, and our dreams about the future. We both realized too well the obstacles to our fragile relationship. We openly discussed our feelings, and we questioned everything. We were drawn to each other by an invisible force beyond reason. Neither of us could stop writing.

We had promised each other not to tell if we went out with anyone, so Bill didn't know about Frank. But he knew that I was going out dancing and dating. When Bill broke our unwritten rule and told me in a letter that he was going out with girls and had relations with them while he was thinking of me, I became quite upset and jealous. I reasoned that I was doing the same, so who was I to complain? I was jealous for the first time in my life, and I couldn't help but openly express my discontent in my next letter. Bill answered that he didn't write those things to make me jealous but to make me understand that I was someone special and that he had a deep, warm need for me, despite having had all those experiences with other women in Paris. He wrote:

> *I choose you, and now my only problem is where do we go from here?*

On October 10, 1968, Bill wrote:

> *What is the weather like in Copenhagen around Christmastime? This is my roundabout way of saying that I would like to come to visit you.*

I was thrilled, and of course Bill was welcome. I had my own place now, and he could stay with us. I didn't think twice about breaking my own rule of keeping my family life apart from my social life. I wanted to have him with me day and night. It sent chills of sheer delight up my spine, knowing I would see him again.

Bill's original plan had been to go home to New York in December to see his family and to look into a teaching position at various universities for the fall semester of 1969 and then make a quick stopover in Copenhagen on the way back. But then he was advised to go while the schools were in session, and therefore February would be a better time for him to make the trip. Now he could visit me instead, and the timing was perfect.

It was not easy to tell Frank that Bill was coming to see me during the Christmas holidays and that he had to stay away during that time. Frank looked crushed but accepted the situation. After all, he knew about Bill and that we were corresponding. One day he even took a picture of me reading Bill's letter. I have always wondered whether he knew that I was reading Bill's letter while he was there with me. If a letter came through the door slot while Frank was there, I couldn't wait to read it.

I also think that Frank hoped that Bill would go back to the States, as I knew how much he cared about me. I knew I could trust him, and I liked him very much. The only problem was that I was in love with someone else. If I had not met Bill, things would have been different with Frank.

I counted the days until Bill would arrive, and I planned the best I could to be off as many days as possible while he was visiting. Bill was going to stay with me in my apartment, and he would finally meet my boys. He arrived at the Copenhagen train station in the early afternoon on December 22, 1968, and I was waiting with a yearning, throbbing heart. When I spotted his sweet face, I ran to him, almost toppling him over with my exuberance. This time, I was not so shy, and I kissed him over and over.

Bill's visit was truly magical. He brought heaven with him, and all my sorrows and grief disappeared. He was here with me, where he belonged. I felt that so strongly that it was frightening.

How could we possibly have a future together? He was another foreigner from a distant land, with a different religion and culture. It was too overwhelming to think about, so I pushed it aside and decided to live in the moment and enjoy all that I could for as long as it lasted.

When we arrived at my apartment, we embraced again with a passion that ignited every cell in my body. We had waited so long for this moment. It was as natural as the ocean waves moving in rhythm on the shore or the birds singing in the morning. We made love fluently, lovingly, and yet with a consuming desire, savoring every touch and kiss. This man ignited my fire like no one else had. He had the magic touch and a magic tongue in more ways than one. I could listen to him for hours without ever being bored.

We had the rest of 1968, about ten days, to learn more about each other. Now it was time to introduce Bill to my boys, who were staying with my parents on the sixteenth floor. With their exotic looks, my boys always made the Danes turn their heads in surprise and admiration. There were few non-Europeans living in Scandinavia in the sixties, and Tariq and Tore were good-looking, with dark-brown complexions, blue-black hair, and deep dark-brown eyes. I was frequently stopped on the street and asked if the boys were mine. When I answered, "Yes," people always looked surprised, but they smiled and remarked how gorgeous my boys were.

I was proud of my boys and loved them more than my own life. But now, I had another love that I wanted to share with them, and I hoped it would work out somehow. Crazy daydreams! How could this possibly work? My boys' father had been Muslim, and Bill was Jewish.

To me, however, everyone was the same. I had not learned that other people looked at religion and race differently. I also believed in love above everything else. I could not understand Afzal's hatred of the Jews, and I did not know how Bill would react to my boys, even though I had told him my story. Would he see little Muslims, or would he see my adorable sons?

How could I have doubted Bill? He saw two sweet little boys with curious, excited eyes looking up at him. This was the man whose letters made Mamma happy, and that is all they needed to know. Tariq had told me one day that he wanted a daddy and that I should find one for him and Tore.

"Who do you suggest I marry?" I asked.

Tariq quickly responded, "I think you should marry the mailman who brings you all those letters that make you so happy!"

That was the day I had to explain about the mail and that the letters were from Bill.

Later at the apartment, as I was preparing dinner, for four this time, Tariq came up to me and said, "Why don't you ask Bill to marry you?"

I blushed a crimson red but realized to my relief that Bill didn't understand Danish.

Bill had seen my reaction, though, and asked, "What did Tariq say?"

I blushed again but smiled and said, "Nothing!"

The kids were enamored with Bill immediately, and it seemed that Bill liked them too, even though they were rambunctious and sometimes naughty little boys.

The Christmas holiday was pure bliss, and it was easy to be together. One dark afternoon, we went to see the Christmas decorations in Søborg (a suburb of Copenhagen), where I lived. I remember standing in front of the town's big, brightly shining Christmas tree, holding Bill's hand, with the boys in front of us. Some people were singing Christmas carols, and the falling snow was slowly covering us in a light blanket of white. I looked up at Bill while the snow was melting on my face, and I felt complete in that moment. My heart overflowed with love. I thought of how right it felt being together like this, just the four of us. It had the makings of a far-fetched dream from a romance novel, and I couldn't shake the feeling. I reveled in every minute of the love and closeness I felt in that precious moment.

We celebrated Christmas Eve with my parents, and Bill had his first education in how Christmas was celebrated in Denmark. My mother made roasted duck with sweet-and-sour red cabbage, caramelized potatoes, and some other typical Danish side dishes. For dessert, we had a special rice pudding called *risalamande* (rice with almonds). Risalamande has whipped cream blended in to make it light and fluffy, and it is served with a cherry sauce. A single blanched almond is hidden in the pudding, and whoever finds it gets the marzipan pig. It was a game we played, and sometimes the person who found the almond would conceal that fact so that everybody would eat more dessert than they really wanted on top of the big Christmas dinner. The kids would eat themselves silly to get that marzipan pig. (Marzipan is an almond paste made from almond meal and sugar, and it is frequently eaten as a candy or used in baked goods as a filling.)

We spent New Year's Eve with my parents and watched fireworks from their balcony. The explosions painted the sky over Copenhagen in an array of rainbow colors. We toasted in the New Year with champagne then kissed for a long time, knowing that Bill's departure was near.

I had managed to be off from work for eight out of the ten days that Bill stayed with us. The only thing that mattered was being with him, talking to him, and making love to him during those days. It felt like an unreal, magical dream.

When it ended, it was a brutal shock to have to face my daily life with all its mundane chores. I felt abandoned and lost. My harsh reality returned along with my deep, unrelenting depression and grief.

My grief over Afzal was like a black hole, a void that Bill had filled for a while. After Bill was gone, my nightmares and sleeplessness continued. During our beautiful holiday together, Bill and I had reached another level in our relationship, and the parting was harder than ever.

The day after Bill left, I sat down to write him a letter telling him how much I missed him and that everything felt so empty without him. Bill wrote to me the minute he got back to Paris on the same day:

> *I feel lousy with a capital L. I am really a hard shell until I am on my own thinking. So now I am back in my apartment and you are not here, and I feel lousy. Do you hear? I know that I have never been more honest and forthright with any girl before, and that's why I know that what we've got is so special.*

Bill finished the letter with this line:

> *'I love you so very much and now you finally got it on paper.*

I had told Bill about my past, so he knew about my pain and grief, and he had honestly expressed that he couldn't predict how that would affect our relationship but that he hoped it would work out somehow. Bill thought we ought to look beyond the past and think of the future for us, even if it meant only a few days together between January and August. During the Christmas holidays, we had started planning a summer vacation together in August, but that was so far away. However, it was something to look forward to.

At the beginning of January 1969, I began another rotation, at a hospital for children. Children's hospitals were the worst—I was again confronted with my fear of death and dying. This rotation involved children with cancer, which made it even harder. When I came home each night and looked at my healthy, vibrant boys, I reminded myself of how lucky I was. Fortunately, each rotation only lasted a few months.

The correspondence continued feverishly between Bill and me. After Bill had openly declared his love for me, I was scared to lose him. The fear of him leaving Europe and going back to America for good was real.

In February, Bill traveled to the United States to look for an assistant professorship in microbiology for the fall. He was also going to New York to see his family. To me, it seemed impossible that this bright, accomplished young man would be interested in an emotionally unstable girl from Denmark with two young children. Moreover, his family was also a problem, because he was Jewish. I knew enough to understand that much.

Bill had warned me about his family's potential negative reaction when they found out about me. He was planning to tell them when he saw them. All I could do was wait and see what would happen, but deep down I already felt hurt. It seemed eerily familiar to be in a position of not being accepted, as had happened so many other times in my life.

To be divided because of a religion or culture felt wrong. Bill's sister, Rachel, had married a Catholic, and that hadn't gone over too well with Bill's parents. Rachel had been alienated from her family for a long time, but eventually her parents accepted the marriage. Bill was another firstborn son, like Afzal, and the family had major expectations for him. He was the first to go to college and to get a PhD. He was Dr. William Steinberg, which garnered prestige and pride for his family. He was expected to marry a Jewish girl. Bill wrote in his third letter:

> *You are right. It is almost impossible and "almost" is a pretty big word. There is so much that tells me "no," especially after all you told me about yourself, but you see, I can only see the goodness in you. They*

say love is blind, but I suppose it has to be that way or else no one would ever love anyone. I want to see you, be with you, and I'll let time take care of the rest. Marriage is not out, you know.

He continued:

As far as I am concerned, I don't give a damn how this will end. I just think how happy I am to know you and to have your love. Whatever comes later is okay with me, but I know I've got to reach out and grab that bit of happiness now because no matter how bad it may be later, it can never overshadow the happiness of the present. I should probably feel much worse if someday I should suddenly realize what a terrible mistake I had made by not taking that chance. I know we have a problem. Believe me, I know, and it certainly is more difficult for you than for me, which is why I made no demands on you. 'I don't want you to commit yourself. You just give me your love and your thoughts and don't worry about anything else. You can be damned well sure that I'm not giving you up that easily. I'm bound to you too strongly to be able to do that. I just hope that I don't do anything to really hurt you. That's something that only time can take care of and usually does. Love, Bill.

Bill wrote four letters in succession during his first week back in Paris, telling me about his plans and his trip to the United States. He had written to his parents and told them about me but had only said that I wasn't Jewish. He figured that was enough for now.

While Bill was planning his trip home and planning for his life in the States, I was thinking of ways that we could be together after he left to go back for good in September. I came up with the crazy idea of going to the States on a student visa. I could postpone admission to Århus University for a few months without losing my spot. If it was only for a few months, I wouldn't lose my apartment either. That way, we could find out if it would work between us. Bill pointed out that we couldn't live together as an unmarried couple, as that wasn't done in the States. Moreover, since he'd be a university professor, his reputation would be at stake. I was dumbfounded that Bill was rejecting my plan. I had already talked it over with my parents, and they would take care of the boys. It would be very difficult to leave the kids. It would certainly be a hardship for all of us. After much discussion, Bill started to entertain the idea but was hesitant in his commitment.

The fact that he was leaving soon made me more emotional and insecure. I started feeling conflicted about making the drastic decision of going to the States. I had responsibilities—I was the mother of two boys who depended on me. This was too difficult a situation to even contemplate any further. I wrote an impassioned second letter saying that we should just end it if he couldn't make a commitment. The uncertainty and pain I felt were too much for me to bear. It was all or nothing for me at this point.

Chapter 21

Follow love and it will flee,
flee love and it will follow thee.
—John Gay

As I always had in the past, when I had an emotional problem, I went home to see Momma. I took sick leave and left for Sweden with the kids. I felt abandoned and scared after Bill left, even though he had declared his love for me in his very first letter. I had also read all those wonderful letters full of love, tenderness, and his concerns and hope for our future, but I reacted like a wounded animal when Bill wrote:

> *There is so much that tells me no, especially after you told me about yourself.*

I lashed out at his doubt. I wanted him to accept me fully with all my baggage of pain and grief and not have a second thought, because I childishly believed that love conquers all. I wanted his unconditional love, and I didn't hear that in the letters, or I didn't want to hear it. I heard only his concerns and brainy analyses of the situation, when in fact he was baffled by his own emotions and was trying to make sense of it all.

Bill had never been in love before or ever had any feelings of this magnitude, and he was expressing this to me openly. I heard his fear and doubt, and I could comprehend how improbable it was that he could love someone as scarred and broken as I was. I wanted to give him an out and release myself from the pain and anguish of loving someone so impossible to attain. So, I went hiding high in the mountains of Jämtland at Momma's house to try to forget this man who had turned my life upside down in a matter of months.

All in all, we had only been physically together for less than a month and corresponded for six months, and now we were already talking about the possibility of marriage. I was scared because of the implications of such a decision, and I was also scared of losing Bill, because of my feelings for him. My feelings were overpowering, but I did not want to complicate his wonderful, uncomplicated life. I was willing to sacrifice my love to protect him from a bad decision that would forever change his life. I didn't see any benefit for him if he married me. It was in this state of mind that I wrote Bill a final farewell letter.

When Bill received my third letter full of sadness and hurt, telling him I wanted to end it, he immediately called my parents, hoping to talk to me. My mother told him that I was with my grandmother and that I would be back the following weekend. Bill called again once I had returned.

When I heard Bill's wonderful, loving voice full of care and concern, I melted. He reassured me that I was no burden at all and that he loved me very much. He said he wanted to marry me and that he hoped the future would somehow provide an answer for the decisions we had to make.

"It must be love," he said, "or I wouldn't feel so miserable and wait so impatiently for your letters! Oh, Maud, you are so wonderful! Do you realize what a beautiful person you are? I love everything about you—I really do. I know you consider yourself imperfect, but you must remember that beauty lies in the eyes of the beholder, and that person is me."

I not only heard his words of love, but I felt them more strongly than ever. I had to accept his love, as he had accepted mine. All the problems we faced were still looming, but maybe love would conquer all in the end. Only time would tell.

When Bill made his flight reservations to New York, he found out that he could make a quick stopover in Copenhagen on his way back, for three days in March, and asked if I could get off work on those days. I couldn't believe I would see him again so soon. He also requested that I send him some Swedish cookies called *drömmar* (dreams) before he left for the States. I had made drömmar for him before, from my grandmother's recipe, and had sent him care packages with various goodies. Bill would send me small presents too, including Grand Marnier bottles and French Camembert cheese. He loved my cooking, and I was more than willing to please him, even though my days were filled with work, children, cooking, and cleaning.

Meeting Bill and getting into this intense long-distance romantic relationship caused me to be more fearful of the future. The past came roaring back with nightmares, sleepless nights, grief, and anger. I tried to explain to Bill in a letter that I was mixed up and needed to fix myself, or he wouldn't be able to live with me for long. To love someone again was scary because I knew too well that lives can change in an instant. I was also afraid of being abandoned again. Bill represented everything that was good for me. When I was with him, life was once more beautiful and full of light. It was when we were apart that fear arose in my mind. Bill had never had a care in the world before he met me, and now I was putting all these burdens on him and complicating his peaceful life. I felt that Bill was better off without me. I was concerned about his parents' reaction and being rejected by them. Abandonment and rejection were part of my past, and I was setting myself up for another one. Maybe it would be easier to walk away.

This is how my thoughts churned every day, and I was making myself crazy. I managed to send one more letter to Bill before he left for New York, saying that I was letting him go for his own good. Of course, this resulted in another phone call from him, assuring me that everything would be fine. He wouldn't accept my decision because he loved me too much, he said. He also admitted that he was intimidated by the prospect of taking on two children and becoming an instant family. However, all he knew was that it felt right to be with me. In his next letter, he wrote:

> *It's like magic, a very special magic and we make love to each other with more than our bodies, which makes me feel so good and whole.*

Then he included a poem that he had written:

Your kiss how sweet and full it is;
tightening around my body
—embracing loving all.
Your body next to mine—absolute heaven
divine ecstasy.
Your love for me—the essence of life itself
That we should feel this way;
so deeply do we love—afraid of what will be, yet
sure of what we feel for each other
In a new world at last—hold me
all this goodness—in you I live.

After all this emotional turmoil, I finally collapsed out of pure exhaustion. I went to see my family doctor, who ordered me to take some time off and gave me some pills so that I could sleep. I took the kids for a second time to see Momma, for a week of relaxation in the mountains of Sweden. The serenity and beauty of my childhood home as well as

Momma's love were the elixirs I needed. It was easier to talk to her than my own mother, who was still somewhat distant. My mother and I had not completely bonded, even though my parents were my rock of support when I came back from Africa, broken and traumatized.

Chapter 22

Your intellect may be confused,
but your emotions will never lie to you.
—Roger Ebert

During all the emotional turmoil after the Christmas holidays, Frank came back into my life. Frank was a good friend and lover who cared, and I was not strong enough to be all alone and waiting. I felt Bill and I had no real commitment. All we had was a very strong bond of love. Bill had to approach his family, whom we both knew would not be approving of our union. There was too much uncertainty, so I had to go on living my life the way I had before I met Bill. I could not put all my eggs in that one basket of unknowns.

While Bill was in the States, we wrote to each other, and he described his family's reaction when he told them about me. It didn't go over very well. He was bombarded with responses that were meant to create severe guilt and doubt.

His mother's first outburst was this: "Do you want me to be ashamed to walk in the streets? What will the neighbors say?"

His aunts said, "How could you do that to your mother after what Rachel did?"

His mother added, "Is this what I raised my children for?"

The family also wanted Bill to take a job in New York City to be close to them, but Bill was tired of New York. He wanted to live in a smaller town with more greenery around. Moreover, he had to go where the jobs were, and the family didn't seem to understand that either.

Bill was very upset with his family's narrow-mindedness and selfishness. There was no concern for his happiness. They wanted to live their lives through him, which he found disturbing. He realized how much his views had changed during the last two years abroad. He was finally growing up.

When Bill told his family about our plans for the summer and that we couldn't get married for a while for economic reasons, everybody was relieved.

"Many things can happen between now and then," was the reply.

They knew Bill would leave Europe for good in September and come back to the United States to work, and they figured that would be the end of our relationship. In other words, Bill didn't get very far with his story about our plans. He was treated as a wayward child for not following the family traditions. He wrote that he was ashamed of how they acted, but he still loved them because they were his family. Bill wrote these last words as he closed his final letter from the States:

> *I can't wait to be with you again, to kiss you, to smell you, to feel you with me, so close, it hurts, and to know that what I feel toward you is something that few people even get to realize. These are the things that make me happy and grateful to be alive. My darling, I love you.*

He interviewed at several universities, which resulted in two serious considerations. One was in Chicago and the other one in Virginia. He thought the University of Virginia (UVA) in the town of Charlottesville would be the best choice for a small family. He was already thinking as a family man. This gave me some hope and comfort.

On his way back to Paris in the middle of March, Bill stopped off in Copenhagen as planned for three wonderful days. Bill was fatigued and slept a lot during those days. When he got back to Paris, he came down with a terrible cold and had to get penicillin shots from a visiting nurse. A few days later, I became a victim of the same affliction. We were both sick for weeks.

Bill and I missed each other so much. We were trying to figure out a way to see each other again before August. Bill came up with the idea that I could come to Paris for a while. We wanted to learn more about each other and find out by living together whether we could stand each other on a daily basis. With much planning, I was able to quit my current job and leave for Paris without anybody knowing where I went. My parents, who were taking care of the kids, were the only people who knew my whereabouts. My absence, if known, would have compromised my apartment and the daycare for my kids.

I was deeply concerned about leaving the kids, as I didn't know how much hurt my absence might cause them, especially Tore, who was too young to understand. Tariq seemed to understand that I was visiting Bill and would be home soon.

Tariq and Tore loved Bill. They often asked about him and why he couldn't join us when we went to the zoo, Tivoli Gardens or other excursions. Tivoli Gardens in Copenhagen is the second oldest amusement park in the world, after Dyrehavsbakken, north of Copenhagen. Both places were favored by us all.

I was supposed to stay with Bill for three months, but I was only gone for six weeks. I couldn't do it. I missed my boys too much, even though I was with the man I loved. It was wonderful being in Paris again, and this time it was spring, my favorite time of the year. I arrived after the first week of May and left before the end of June. I worked as a private nurse during the day for the very rich, which was a unique experience.

Being together with Bill was wonderful, as always, but it also made me appreciate what I had back in Denmark. I missed my home, my parents, my friends, and most of all my darling boys, so I left in haste, leaving Bill disappointed and lonely. Moreover, despite my great, undying love for him, I saw a weak, indecisive man. I was filled with foreboding that he would not be able to stand up to his family, leaving me hurting in the end. At least Afzal had stood up to his family, breaking off his arranged engagement and marrying me in the face of all obstacles.

Pappa met me at the train station, just to help me with the suitcases and to get me a taxi. He was always so thoughtful and caring, which warmed my heart. Pappa was always there for me, no matter what. How could I leave such unconditional love and support for an uncertain future in a foreign country again, where nobody except Bill seemed to want us? It wasn't good enough, and I was terrified of being let down again.

Tariq and Tore didn't know which foot to stand on when I met them at the nursery school. For a few weeks afterward, I had to make up for the time I had been gone by being extra attentive and loving. Tore had been very upset while I was gone and had cried for his mamma many times. This gave me crushing guilt when my mother told me about it. How could I be so selfish? The boys needed me more than anyone. I could not play with their future. How could I uproot them and move to the States and take them away from such secure and loving surroundings? In Denmark, we had people who loved and cared for us, but in the States, even Bill's family didn't accept us. It was an impractical, romantic fantasy, and I was trying to be realistic, even though it hurt like hell.

Once back at home, I wrote some long letters explaining to Bill why I couldn't marry him, but he wouldn't hear of it. Whenever he got a letter that upset him, he would call to set things straight.

Bill always renewed my hope with his love declarations that it would all work out somehow. We were still planning to be together in August and to take a month-long vacation together with the kids to visit my grandparents in Undersåker. After that, I figured, the relationship would be over after Bill went back to the States to work.

Bill accepted a generous offer from the University of Virginia and was planning to start the job on October 1, 1969. He wanted me to wait for him, hoping that his family would come around. I rebelled the only way an Aries does, by backing out and claiming my freedom. Bill continued to refuse to accept my decision. He made me promise to wait until after the August vacation we had planned before I made up my mind.

It was a good thing to be a nurse and in high demand, because I had no difficulty getting another job for just a month and then taking off again. I had quit jobs and started new ones just to be with Bill. It was crazy. My life was a continual flood of unknowns. My plans for the university were on hold too. I doubt that Bill was fully aware of how much I accommodated him and put up with just to see him for a short while.

When Bill arrived on August 5, we were together again, and all was right with the world. I had the uncanny ability to live in the now and not worry about tomorrow while we were together. The more time we spent together, the deeper the love grew between us. It was effortless loving Bill. Since Tariq and Tore were with us, my happiness was complete.

We borrowed my father's new Saab for the trip, but I had to drive since Bill did not have a driver's license. I found it strange that a guy from America did not know how to drive, but he explained that he had grown up in New York City, where people really didn't need cars.

We drove from Copenhagen to Stockholm and then to Nynäshamn to see my aunt Ruth and uncle Herbert for a few days. Then we headed west toward the mountains of Jämtland.

Momma and Morfar greeted us with such warmth, and Bill was captivated with Undersåker and Jämtland. Momma never batted an eye that this time my love was a Jewish man, but she requested that I tell Bill about Jesus. I nodded, but I knew it was of no use, as Jews don't believe in Jesus the way Christians do.

I knew we were all God's children, regardless of color or creed. I did not believe in the notion that one religion was above another, or that you had to be saved to get into heaven. I looked upon religion as something people had made up to control the masses. Religion had caused too many conflicts in the world, and too many wars had been fought in God's name. I believed in God in my own way, and I didn't think I needed to go through Jesus or anybody else to talk to God. I respected others' views, and I had a right to have my own.

I understood that Bill was born Jewish and that he honored his roots. He was very secure in his own beliefs, and we had had long discussions in our letters regarding this topic. I had gone to the library to learn more about the Jewish religion because I had been so ignorant about Islam before I had married Afzal. I believed that understanding and tolerance could overcome most differences, and I was very tolerant and idealistic, believing in love above all.

On the trip back to Denmark, we drove from Undersåker over the mountain to Trondheim in Norway. In Trondheim, we picked up a highway (E 6) which runs through Gudbrandsdalen (Gudbrand Valley in English) all the way to Oslo. What a spectacular sight it was, every time I made that trip! The road was built on the side of the mountain with several hundred feet drop to Gudbrandslågen, or *Lågen* (the river) which runs through the valley. In some places, the cliffs were so steep and the road so close to the edge that guardrails had been erected for safety. The kids screamed with fear and excitement when they looked out the window. I had wanted to share this beauty with Bill, and his excitement and awe delighted me. Bill had such a scientific mind, and he explained how the mountains and valleys had been formed by glaciers during the last Ice age. He had the wonder of a child when he took in nature's beauty.

Everything we did together was so magnificent because of his brilliant intellect and enthusiasm. I was a better person with him than without him. During our whole trip together, I was on a cloud and felt anything was possible.

The emotion that can break your heart is
sometimes the very one that heals it.
—Nicholas Sparks

After our month-long summer vacation to Sweden, Bill and I were more in love than ever. It was perfect and easy to be together, even with the kids. We lived and traveled as a family, and we both felt like we belonged together.

Before Bill left for Paris, he sang the song "Leaving on a Jet Plane" by John Denver as he was packing up his things:

All my bags are packed, I'm ready to go
I'm standing here outside your door
I hate to wake you up to say good-bye

So, kiss me and smile for me
Tell me that you'll wait for me
Hold me like you'll never let me go

Within a few days of returning to Paris, Bill sailed for New York City by ship. His family was waiting at the dock with a limousine.

After Bill's departure, I was haunted by the fear that Bill's family would never approve of our union, no matter how hard he tried to persuade them. Bill had never been up against adversity before, and I worried that he wasn't strong enough to go against his family's wishes. All I could do was wait. My life had been on hold for over a year, and all my educational plans were up in the air as well because of Bill. I was in limbo, and I didn't like that feeling.

Bill had assured me during our vacation that he loved me and wanted to marry me. We had planned that I would come to the States to see him for a couple of weeks over the Christmas holidays. We would then marry in April 1970, after he had settled into his new job in Charlottesville. Bill felt that he needed to give his family time to adjust to the idea of us marrying. He said that he wanted to do it gradually with caution to prevent everyone from getting too upset. He was planning to talk to his family again when he returned home.

Bill's first letter from home carried awful news. My fears had been accurate. His parents refused to listen to reason, and Bill felt trapped. Bill wrote that he was sorry that he had gone back to the States or even accepted the position at UVA as an assistant professor. He wished he had stayed with me in Denmark and pursued opportunities abroad instead.

Over the next few months, we both lived for our letters and monthly phone calls. I started a challenging new job as an EEG technician, which required extensive on-the-job training. I loved the job, and I only worked six hours a day with no night shifts or weekends. It was perfect for now, and by December I would find out if I had passed the initial trial period, and then the job could be permanent. The pay was less, but my taxes were lower as well, so, in the end, my income was about the same as before. Now I had more time at home with my boys. Bill had been kind enough to occasionally help me out with money because I had quit several jobs just to be with him. What I had done was crazy, but I was in love, and Bill meant everything to me.

Even though we had plans to marry, I felt very insecure because Bill's parents had not given their consent. This was very important to Bill, though I didn't understand why he needed their approval. So, regardless of Bill's assurances, I felt that everything could unravel at any moment.

Bill acquired a driver's license and bought a fancy new Ford Mustang. He drove to Washington, DC, for the Vietnam antiwar demonstration, and then in November he drove to New York City to talk to his family again about us marrying.

At the end of November, I received the letter that I had feared for so long. I had known for a while, somehow, that this would happen, but the pain was worse than I could have imagined. I felt I was going to die that day. Bill wrote the following:

My dearest Maud,

I just spent the longest weekend of my life, perhaps the saddest also. My parents absolutely refuse to listen to reason or even to meet you. They will not let you enter their house and not me either if I am with you. I am sick of this whole situation, for me as well as for you. I have come to the edge of my rope and I am hanging myself on it.

This weekend all seems like a nightmare, one I hope I shall never have to relive again. Maybe God is punishing me and indirectly you also. I have let myself down, and more importantly, I have messed up your life too. I thought I was strong enough, but I am not.

In spite of the handicaps, I thought I could work things out and that my parents would understand. I now realize what a fool I have been to trust in humanity and superstitious, bigoted people. It's all the more difficult and all so unbelievable now that we are this close.

My parents refuse to allow us to get married. They do not have the legal right to do so, as I am over 21. They are hysterical people. They will never permit us to enter their house. That plus the deteriorating health of my mother has placed a burden on my shoulders the likes of which I have never held before. What makes this all so frightful is that I love you so much and it's come to the point where I had to decide between my love for you and the family I cherish, which seems to be falling apart before my eyes. I never thought it would be this way. I have been spoiled to think that people are reasonable and understanding.

It was my honest intention that we should get married, but what do you do when your mother is crying and begging and claiming that you are taking her life away, and you see it slipping away right before your eyes. My God, what do you do? It's a horrible mess.

"Your sister put the knife in my back and now you want to destroy me and our family?"

I don't see how I can do it, but it is impossible for them to understand. Impossible for them and horrifying for me to see our chance for happiness destroyed.

I am sorry for you; I am sorry for myself. I am ashamed of my parents. I am so profoundly miserable because of all the things that I have forced you to put up with. I hope one day you will find it in your heart to forgive me. Believe me, I was not leading you on. I love you too much for that. I never intended for our relationship to come to this. So, I have had to make my decision and now I must live with it for the rest of my life. I hope to God that I can.

I realize that you have made plans to come here, but they can be of no good now, not the way things are. I cannot ask you to wait, that would be the cruelest thing of all. I shall continue to help you out if you still have money problems because I love you.

I am not myself anymore. This constant fight between my love for you and my family's health was too much for me and I can't take it any longer.

It is now your turn to tell me to go to hell and God knows, I deserve it. Why couldn't I see it coming? Why am I so trusting, such an optimist? I am ashamed of myself, I am ashamed of what has happened and for the way this will affect you.

I give you your freedom and I put myself in chains. Please, please, please, my darling, forgive me and I know that I shall continue to love you, as I can never love another woman again. Bill

The day the letter arrived, I knew it was coming. I usually picked up my kids on my way home from work, but on this day, I went home first because I knew that letter was waiting for me. I collapsed after reading those heart-wrenching words. I felt my whole world fall apart in an instant.

I tried to walk to the daycare center, but I was so shaky that I had to call a taxi on the way. Once inside the taxi, I started crying uncontrollably, and I don't remember how I managed to get the kids home. I cried for hours, and the kids looked helplessly at me and asked what was wrong.

I told them the truth, and Tariq blurted out, "Bill can't take his words back if he has made a promise to marry you."

He was angry and disappointed because his dreams fell apart that day, too. We all cried together.

I needed to tell my parents, and I needed their emotional support. They were more shocked than I was. Peter was furious on my behalf and couldn't understand why Bill had even asked his parents for permission to marry.

After I'd spent three days of crying and thinking about the situation, my spirit resurfaced, and I decided that I could not give up on Bill. I loved him too much, and I knew that I had to be strong for him. My father had already bought me a ticket to New York City for December 13, and I decided to go to see Bill no matter what. How could I fight for him while in Denmark anyway?

I had to see him and talk to him, so I sat down to write him a letter. I felt his pain and misery, and I knew he needed my understanding and strength, not my anger.

If Bill had written that he didn't love me, it would have been different. I assured him that I was not going to tell him to go to hell but that I loved him and that I understood the difficult situation he was in. I told him that he did not have to choose between me and his family and that I hoped he would be there when I arrived.

When Bill received my letter, he called immediately, and he sounded relieved. He had realized that he couldn't live without me. He wanted to marry me despite his parents. We made plans to marry while I was in the States, and Bill arranged for us to stay with his sister in New York City when I arrived.

Since Bill was also a practical man, he gave me pointers about what to bring as far as papers were concerned, so that getting married would go smoothly. I had my personal papers translated into English and made sure my vaccination certificate was in order. Before I left Denmark, I received a short letter from Bill:

> *My darling Maud,*
>
> *I cannot wait till I see you again. I need you more than ever. I pray that life will be kind to us. We care too much for each other for things to turn out otherwise.*

Chapter 24

Life is like a steering wheel,
it only takes one small move
to change your entire direction.
— Kellie Elmore

I arrived at John F. Kennedy Airport on December 13, 1969, and Bill drove up from Charlottesville to meet me. What a sweet sight he was, standing there waiting for me in his too-short khaki pants and a dark-blue winter jacket. His hair was curling down below his ears, and he was wearing dark-rimmed glasses. His right shoulder drooped slightly, due to always carrying his heavy briefcase on that side.

Our greeting was tender and slow this time, but his kiss still sent electric shock waves through my body. Pure bliss swept over me—I was home again in Bill's arms, where I belonged.

Bill's sister, Rachel, was the cutest and friendliest person I had ever met. She walked right into my heart, just as Bill had. Rachel was short with bleached-blond hair and hazel eyes. She looked like a cute Barbie Doll, with a sweetness all her own, and she spoke with a very heavy Brooklyn accent, which I had not heard before. "How could these adorable people have such an unpleasant mother I wondered."

Rachel and her husband lived in Brooklyn in a small apartment. Despite the cramped conditions, Bill and I were given a room to ourselves. How sweet it was to be together again after so many months with so much confusion.

The next day, Bill and I drove down to Virginia in his beautiful aquamarine Mustang. Bill must have disregarded the worry about his reputation because I stayed with him in his apartment on campus. He had work to do at UVA until the Christmas vacation, but we enjoyed all the time we had together when he was off.

The day before Christmas, we drove back to New York City to see Bill's parents and to get married. I was very nervous about meeting them after all the things I had been told.

When we arrived, Bill's mother, Etta, gave me a cold, hard look, but reluctantly let us in. She didn't greet me, but instead, she started ranting loudly. She worked herself into hysterics, punctuated by fierce, shrill screaming. I guess the nurse in me surfaced, as I had only seen mentally unstable patients behave in this manner.

As I slowly walked over to Bill's mother and touched her lightly on the shoulder in a comforting way, I said, "Mrs. Steinberg, why don't you calm down a little and sit down here on the couch."

Etta totally lost it and yelled at me, "Don't you dare come here and tell me what to do in my own house!"

She never regained her composure, so we left.

I had bought a beautiful hand-carved Danish teak bowl for Bill's parents, but I never gave it to them. I didn't feel like it after that rude reception. I could also see that the bowl's quality and modern design would not have been appreciated in that home.

Their apartment was dark and messy, and all the chairs and couches were covered in plastic. It was surprising that this tacky, dirty apartment had been Bill's childhood home. How could this wonderful human being come from such a background? It didn't change anything, though. I adored Bill and loved him with all my heart. It didn't matter where he came from. Bill was genuine and beautiful in my eyes.

After that visit, Bill finally realized that his parents, and especially his mother, would never change, and they would never give their consent.

So, we married on December 29, 1969, in New York City in a civil ceremony, with Rachel as the only witness. Bill's parents knew nothing about it.

Since there was no reason to stay in New York, we drove back to Virginia as husband and wife, and I stayed there until I had to go back to Copenhagen on January 4.

Being back in Copenhagen was a mixed blessing. I was so happy to see my boys again. Tariq and Tore were eagerly awaiting me with flowers, presents, and a decorated apartment with a sign that said, "Welcome home, Mamma." My father had helped them engineer all this, and they were so proud. Tariq and Tore were more interested in seeing me open their presents than receiving their own. I was so proud of them.

But after a few days, I began missing Bill. We were married, but we were still apart, and it would be that way for a few more months. It took three weeks to receive the first letter from Bill. I was devastated that I didn't hear from him for so long, but he was overloaded with work and all his new responsibilities as an assistant professor at UVA.

My EEG training was complete, and I was accepted as a full-time employee, even though the administration knew I was leaving soon. They wanted me for however long I could stay, which was gratifying.

My mother informed me, after I returned to Copenhagen, that Frank had written me a letter. She had returned the letter to Frank instead of giving it to me, writing on the envelope, "Maud is married now!" This angered me. I have always wondered what Frank had written. He could have told me to go to hell, or he could have pleaded with me to not go to the States. Frank had been a very good friend and a great comfort to me during a very difficult time, and for that, I was very grateful.

Tariq was concerned about his last name. He wanted to have Bill's name, and I agreed that it would be practical for us all to have the same surname. So, I changed my kids' last name to Steinberg and applied for a visa for all of us to enter the United States. After selling everything and giving up the apartment, we moved back in with my parents.

The immigration visas finally arrived at the beginning of March, and I left on March 18, 1970, to join my husband in Virginia. The plan was that the boys would come at the beginning of July, accompanied by Peter. Bill and I needed some time to ourselves for a few months, and we needed to prepare a home for the kids. I was planning to work at UVA to make a little money before the kids arrived so that we could buy some furniture.

Our plans were practical and sound, but we didn't realize how much this upheaval would affect the kids.

It took a lot of courage to pack up and leave Denmark and my family, even if it was for love. I left with only a couple of suitcases. The boys would bring one suitcase each containing all their earthly belongings when they followed in July. Bill was taking on a lot of responsibility with this instant family, but he would not be facing it alone. I was the strong one, I thought, and Bill needed me. My heart had led the way, and now I hoped that my life would be good with this wonderful man, the love of my life.

When I arrived at JFK International Airport, I had to go through US Customs and Immigration Enforcement before transferring to LaGuardia Airport, and that took some time. To my horror, I could not get a taxi to drive me to LaGuardia. The taxi drivers' excuse was that it was too far to drive. I was dumbfounded at their indifference. I had limited time to catch my next plane. I pleaded with several taxi drivers, and then one said that if I found another passenger who needed a ride to LaGuardia, he would take me. How in the world could I do that? For a moment, I lost all hope. I stood there near the taxis, frustrated, letting my tears flow.

Several minutes later, the taxi driver suddenly called out to me. "Come on, lady. Get in. I have another passenger who needs to go to LaGuardia."

The driver collected two fares for one trip, leaving me to wonder what kind of cold, harsh country I had moved to. It didn't feel good.

At LaGuardia Airport, I had to run to make my flight. I was struggling with my heavy suitcases when two men suddenly appeared on either side of me.

They grabbed my suitcases from me, and for a moment I panicked, but they were smiling, and one said, "Don't worry, young lady! You look like you need some help! Where are you going?"

I sighed with relief and gave him a grateful smile, and said, "I am going to Dulles International Airport."

He replied, "That's perfect! That's where we are going too. Come with us."

We managed to get to the plane on time. We talked during the flight, and they told me that they were from Charlottesville.

These Southern gentlemen had restored my faith in the American people, and I realized that New York City was different from the rest of the country.

When we arrived at Dulles International Airport, the men helped me again with the suitcases, escorted me through the airport, and made sure that I found Bill. I never got their names, which was a great shame, as I wanted so much to thank them.

Bill's face lit up when he saw me. He thanked the men for their help and then gave me that forever-love hug I so desperately needed. I was worn out from the stress, but now I could relax and let Bill take over for the rest of the journey. We had much to talk about on the way. I enjoyed the scenery and was amazed at the wide and multiple lanes on the highway. Everything was bigger than in Denmark, even the cars.

When we arrived in Charlottesville, Bill wanted to show me the town, so he drove through the downtown area on the way to the university. I was horrified at how ugly everything looked—bland, commercial cinder-block buildings and dilapidated old houses lining Main Street. I was disappointed by the aesthetics of the place and wondered if I could tolerate living in this town. I also noticed that there was quite a bit of litter everywhere, which offended my senses. However, when we drove through the university area, I noticed a marked improvement in the architecture—grand classical-style brick buildings all through the university village. Grassy quads were shaded with huge old trees, and the nineteenth-century structures were in better shape than those on Main Street.

Later, I found other areas of Charlottesville to have a certain appeal. We often visited Shenandoah National Park west of town, which lies astride the spectacular Blue Ridge Mountains. Skyline Drive, a one-hundred-mile-long parkway through the Shenandoah National Park, was a favorite outing whenever we had guests.

When the boys grew older, they frequently attended nature camps in Shenandoah National Park for a couple of weeks during the summer.

The Blue Ridge Mountains, which are part of the Appalachian Mountains, made me feel at home because they reminded me of the mountains of Sweden. Geologically, the Scandinavian Mountains and the Appalachian Mountains are connected, and the heights of their peaks are very similar. However, due to the colder temperatures in Sweden, the tree line is much lower, whereas in the Blue Ridge, the trees grow all the way to the top. This makes the mountains in Sweden look taller, and the barren tops are covered with snow all year long.

Virginia eventually grew on me, mostly because of the warm climate, with so many sunnier days than in Scandinavia. I never liked the harsh, dark winters of Sweden and Denmark.

The Charlottesville downtown area had been neglected through the sixties, but in the seventies, a revival plan created a pedestrian mall on East Main Street. The first phase was completed in 1976. The restoration of the Downtown Mall continued, and it is now one of the most attractive and successful pedestrian malls in the nation.

There was only one movie theater when I arrived, and only one place to go dancing. The university had a theater for the performing arts, and that helped.

Charlottesville is a small southern town, with a population of around forty thousand people, but Albemarle County, which surrounds the town, adds another sixty thousand. The University of Virginia added an international dimension to the place, and without that it would have been even more difficult for me to adjust coming from a diverse city like Copenhagen.

Charlottesville is a historical attraction as well, having been the home of two US presidents, Thomas Jefferson and James Monroe. Thomas Jefferson founded the University of Virginia in 1819.

A great marriage is not when the perfect couple comes together. It is when an imperfect couple learns to enjoy their differences.
—Dave Meurer

We arrived at our split-level brick house on Mimosa Drive in the early evening. Bill had picked this house for practical reasons. The house had three bedrooms and one bath, and its location was secluded, close to a creek with woods in the back. It was a faculty rental through the university, and the rent was cheap. We had to buy a washer and a dryer, and there was no air-conditioning. The house was old and not modern as in Scandinavia, but I managed to make it a tasteful, comfortable home for us.

During the first few months, we rented the furniture we needed. Later, we drove to Washington, DC, to buy some Danish furniture at the Scan store, as I couldn't stomach the Early American design. I bought cheap unfinished-pine bunk beds and dressers for the kids at Woolco.

One day, I decided to paint the kids' furniture red, white, and blue. Since paint is not my friend, I started getting paint all over my clothes. I figured it would be easier to clean the paint off my body instead of my clothes, so I undressed and painted in the nude. When Bill came home, he found me in my birthday suit covered in all the colors of the American flag. He was quite amused.

A week after I arrived, I started working at the University of Virginia Hospital on a cancer ward as a foreign exchange student. I didn't have the registered nurse credentials from the States, so I was given a temporary job as an exchange student. It was a depressing job, and I had never seen such sick patients before. Most patients had stage-three or stage-four cancers, and I realized that patients in the United States didn't go to the doctor until it was too late, due to lack of insurance or money. One man had only half a face left with big, rotten cavities that needed to be flushed out every day. I was given the worst jobs to do and became quite depressed. On most days after I came home from work, I just sat in front of the TV watching soap operas, which were the simplest shows for me to understand, but they probably depressed me even more. I couldn't wait for the kids to arrive.

Fortunately, this situation had an end. Bill and I made a decision that I would not work after the kids joined us. We were also planning to have a baby soon. The urgency was for practical reasons because we didn't want the kids to be too far apart in age.

Bill had certainly picked a unique place to live, but in the beginning, I felt a little out of place. One day while I was shopping at A&P, an old man started talking to me in a very strange dialect. I couldn't understand most of what he said. I looked at him totally confused and wondered what kind of language it was. I tried to explain to him that I didn't understand. The old man gave me an awkward, toothless smile, but he had a bewildered look on his face. I realized later that the man had simply been speaking with a very extreme southern American accent. I had a lot to learn.

Life was different in the States in other ways. For example, in Denmark, I would usually wear short shorts with a tank top and no bra during the summer months. One day, when I went to downtown Charlottesville wearing this, the construction workers whistled and hollered at me. I felt violated, as it was too much attention. I realized that it had happened because of the way I was dressed. I never wore short shorts again in public. It felt like a restriction, though, and I was annoyed that people were so archaic.

On another occasion, after coming home from work on a beautiful, sunny day, I decided to sit topless behind the house facing the woods. I wanted to soak up some sun, and I figured that if anyone came walking down the trail across the creek, I could quickly cover my breasts with the newspaper I was reading. Unfortunately, Bill decided to come home early that day. He had taken the bus instead of calling me to pick him up. Bill walked down the trail, and before I could see him, he appeared behind the house, surprising me in my glory.

He was upset and scolded me for my behavior saying, "Maud, this is not Denmark. You cannot do things like this here in the States."

I thought he was being square and stuffy, and I felt my freedom was being taken away. I knew I had to adjust if I wanted to live in this country. I had always been good at adjusting, and I could do this as well. But, I thought it was silly to be so old-fashioned.

My boys arrived in July, accompanied by Peter. My heart had ached for them for three whole months. Tariq seemed fine, but Tore had changed. Tore seemed nervous, and he had started stuttering. At night, Tore would come crawling into my bed, like he used to do in Denmark. I thought he needed to learn to sleep by himself, so I carried him back to his bed every night. Then, to prevent me from noticing that he was in my bed, Tore started crawling in at the foot of the bed, sleeping at my feet. When I discovered him, I would carry him back to his bed again. This went on for months. After I was finally onto his foot-of-the-bed-approach, Tore started sleeping on the rug next to my bed, like a little puppy. I agonized over it, but I wasn't sure what to do. When Tore finally accepted that he needed to sleep on his own, he started wetting the bed, and I felt that I had to handle this very carefully. I was afraid to punish him in any way, as I realized that this might have happened because I had left him behind. The bedwetting went on for about a year until I finally lost it one morning when I found the entire bed soaked with urine.

I yelled at him, "This is it! I have had enough, Tore! This is your mess, so you can take care of it yourself."

I told him to take the sheets off the bed himself and put clean ones on. I remember the shocked look on Tore's face, and I worried that I had caused more damage. The surprising thing was that he never wet the bed again, but I felt guilty.

Later, when I talked to Tariq and Tore about why I had to leave them behind, Tore said, "Mom, we just wanted to be with you. We didn't need beds. We could have slept on the floor, as long as we could be with you."

It broke my heart to hear this. But Bill had also wanted me to himself for a while. I had been very torn.

The kids had to learn English, and for Tariq, this was the second time he'd had to do that. I continued speaking Danish with them, but eventually, that fell by the wayside because Bill did not know Danish. I had to speak English when Bill came home, to not exclude him from the conversation. The boys learned English very quickly and started answering me in English whenever I spoke Danish to them. They wanted desperately to be Americans. I knew that speaking Danish with them was a losing battle, so I gave up after a couple of years.

Our first summer in Virginia was incredibly hot and humid, which was almost too much for me. I bought a wading pool for the boys, so they could play in the yard. Tariq and Tore did not have bathing suits because we didn't need them in Denmark. In Charlottesville, we lived in a subdivision with other faculty families who had children.

One day as my kids were playing in the wading pool, my next-door neighbor came over, looked at my naked boys, and then angrily said, "You better get some clothes on those boys, or somebody is going to call the police."

I was shocked. I had swum nude until I was nine years old, and now it was a crime that my boys were nude at the age of four and five? More restrictions to abide by. After I had bought swimming trunks for the boys, we would go swimming at a local pool and sometimes in a small creek north of town.

After a week of relentless hot sun, I started wishing for a rainy day, as I was mentally exhausted. I wanted rain, so I could relax and have the weather complement my underlying mood. I was still quite depressed. We were finally a family, and everything seemed fine for a while. I had naively thought that marrying Bill would solve all my problems. On the contrary, my fluctuating moods resurfaced as we settled into our daily routine, and so did the nightmares and sleepless nights. Again, I was waking up screaming in the middle of the night. I didn't understand why. My life was good, and I was loved, but I was miserable and depressed. I didn't understand that my past was following me and that I was still quite traumatized by what had happened in Africa.

Bill was a very busy man with his new job as assistant professor at the university. He was teaching at the medical school and trying to do research as well. Research was his love, and the teaching sometimes felt like a hindrance preventing him from doing what he loved.

He said one day, "I am a very lucky man because my research is my hobby."

There were many times when I felt neglected. Bill found it difficult to take time off for his family. He would get up early to go to work, come home for dinner late, and then leave again in the evening to go back to the lab until midnight so he could finish his endless research projects. On most evenings, I was alone after the kids had gone to bed.

Tariq was barely six years old by the time school started in the fall, so I decided to hold him back for a year before beginning first grade. I wanted him to start with a more solid foundation in English and be settled a little more before starting school. I also didn't want him to be the youngest in his class. I saw that as a disadvantage. Therefore, that fall Tariq started kindergarten, and Tore started preschool at a Montessori school. They seemed happy with that.

During the winter of 1970, I became pregnant, and our child was expected to be born the following year in August. My pregnancy was difficult due to severe nausea throughout most of the nine months. Bill was very excited, and we decided to go to Lamaze classes for natural childbirth since Tariq and Tore's deliveries had been so difficult for me.

I started having different nightmares about Afzal, and one night, I dreamt that my child was born without a head as punishment for marrying again. Afzal had told me more than once that if he died, I was not allowed to marry again. I was petrified after that dream that my child would be born deformed.

When the time came to give birth, Bill was of little help. He forgot everything we had learned in Lamaze class because he was so excited about what was happening during the delivery. I was in terrible pain. The doctor gave me an epidural, but it only worked on one side, which wasn't of much use. I was very happy, though, to have my husband by my side this time.

Our baby boy was born at the beginning of August in 1971. Bill grabbed his son the minute he appeared, forgetting to show him to me in his exuberance and joy.

He ran around the delivery room saying, "This is amazing! He is beautiful. He is perfect."

I cried out of happiness and relief that my child was normal. When Bill finally calmed down, and after the doctor had stitched up the tear in my vagina, I reminded Bill that I would also like to see our son.

I told Bill that he would have to name our son because I hadn't even looked at boys' names. I had hoped, for the second time, that it would be a girl. Our baby boy was indeed perfect, with his chubby cheeks, white skin, and an almost bald head. He weighed eight pounds and looked very healthy, which was amazing since I had felt so sick during most of the pregnancy.

After the delivery, I was put in a room with five other women. Of course, I was going to breastfeed again and informed the nurses of that. When the time came for the babies to be fed, everyone was given their little bundle of joy, except me.

When I asked the nurses why they didn't bring me my baby, I was told, "There is no point in bringing you the baby, since you don't have any milk yet. We gave him some sugar water instead."

I was livid. I was the only mother who was breastfeeding, and apparently the nurses did not know that I had colostrum in my breasts, which is often referred to as "the first golden milk of life." Colostrum is a thick yellow fluid, packed with antibodies and three times as much protein as mature milk. The colostrum is also full of immunoglobulins to protect the baby against bacteria and viruses. The breast milk usually comes in within seventy-two hours after birth, and until then, the colostrum is very important for the baby's immune system. I was so upset about the nurses' ignorance that I demanded a private room for myself and my baby. I didn't trust that the nurses would properly care for my baby boy while he was out of my sight. After all, they had given him sugar water.

Once in my own room with my baby, the doctor came in and questioned my decision. I was told that I was a hysterical woman, blowing things out of proportion. Due to all this animosity from the nursing staff and the doctor, I left the hospital against medical advice the next day. I didn't see any reason to stay in the hospital any longer, as neither my baby nor I were sick. At home, I could relax, but the following day, I was already out shopping for food. I had two other children to care for, and they needed me, too.

I did most of my grocery shopping at A&P, where the cashiers were very friendly. My two older boys would frequently receive much attention because they were so cute and handsome.

One day, while I was greatly pregnant, a friendly female cashier asked, "So, is your next child going to be dark and beautiful like these two gorgeous boys?"

I blurted out, "No, they all have different fathers!"

I realized that I had misspoken, but the woman gave me a judgmental look. She never spoke to me again.

Bill's parents did not know that we were married until Tariq and Tore arrived in July 1970. Bill's mother was quite upset by the news, but surprisingly enough, it didn't kill her, as she had predicted. A year later, when our son was born, Bill informed them immediately, and our baby boy was their first grandchild.

A week after the birth, my parents, Bill's parents, and Bill's brother and sister arrived, and they were all accommodated with a place to sleep in our small house. Bill's family wanted to be part of our baby's circumcision ceremony, called *Bris Milah*, and the naming of our child, which would happen at the same time. I knew nothing about this almost four-thousand-year-old Jewish tradition and trusted Bill to arrange what he thought needed to be done. Tariq's and Tore's circumcisions had been done very humanely, and I'd had no problems with their procedures, as my boys had seemed okay during and after the circumcision. Their circumcisions had been done in a hospital setting under anesthesia.

On the eighth day after birth, our baby boy's circumcision was planned to be done by my obstetrician at the hospital, with a rabbi present for the ceremony. I walked into this ceremony totally ignorant and trusting and handed my baby over to the rabbi. Our baby was placed on a table with a white cloth, then unwrapped and given a small amount of an alcoholic drink. The obstetrician proceeded very quickly with the circumcision, without any analgesic for the pain. He cut my son's foreskin with a surgical knife, upon which my baby screamed in agony, with his arms and legs flailing in the air. When I cried out in protest, I was grabbed and escorted out of the room. I was again called a hysterical woman—by my obstetrician—because of my maternal instincts to protect my baby.

I was furious and felt that Bill had betrayed my trust. I told Bill off for letting his Jewish faith dictate this barbaric tradition and force it upon our son. I was inconsolable, and then Bill cried as well, as he had had no clue that the circumcision would be done without pain medication. Our son was named Daniel on that traumatic day. His penis healed well due to my careful attention and care.

The reason that the circumcision was done on the eighth day is that the newborn's blood-clotting agents—prothrombin and vitamin K—have reached normal levels on that day, thus preventing excessive blood loss.

There is some scientific evidence that circumcision can have a few health benefits, but I question the religious rationale behind cutting a piece of flesh off a helpless baby without any pain reliever. This was very traumatic for everyone, and most of all for my little baby, who had had no say in the matter. My parents were equally disturbed by the whole barbaric procedure. Scandinavians do not circumcise babies unless it is medically necessary.

It didn't take long for Bill's mother to start causing trouble. She was criticizing everything I did, including how I cleaned my pots and pans.

One afternoon when I was in the bedroom breastfeeding Daniel, Bill came in, dragging his mother behind him, and said, "Mom, I want you to repeat in front of Maud everything you said about her behind her back."

Etta looked embarrassed but refused to speak. Instead, she kept pinching Bill on his upper arm to make him shut up.

This made Bill even more annoyed and angry, and he said, "If you have come here to cause trouble between us, then you are not welcome. I want you to apologize to Maud or you can leave to go back to Brooklyn in the morning."

Bill's parents left the next day.

Bill did not speak to his mother for six months, until finally one day, I said to him, "Bill, she is your mother, and I know you love her. You don't have to stay angry with her for my sake. Please call her."

Bill gave in and called his mother, and things were tolerable after that. We would occasionally travel to Brooklyn to see Bill's parents, but it was never a pleasant experience for me or the kids.

My parents stayed with us for a month. They were so helpful and pleasant to have around. My father played with the boys (they could still remember Danish), and they all had a grand time.

Before my parents left to go home, Bill drove them up to Washington, DC, to see the White House, the Washington Monument, the Lincoln Memorial, and the Smithsonian museums. I stayed at home, as the trip was too much for me and Daniel.

Chapter 26

But grief makes a monster out of us sometimes,
and sometimes you say and do things to the people
you love that you can't forgive yourself for.
—Melina Marchetta

After Daniel was born, postpartum depression set in on top of my other depression, and then slowly an intense anger surfaced. I would blow up over insignificant things that didn't make any sense. The boys became afraid of me. When they saw my fury rise, Tariq and Tore would run and hide under their beds. One evening during dinner, I totally lost it, and the whole dinner with meatballs and spaghetti ended up on the dining room wall. I was disgusted by my behavior. I realized that I needed help. I didn't care about myself, though, because I hated myself as a person. I felt I was the worst possible scum living on this earth. I needed to improve because I felt that my family deserved better than what they had right now.

During the terrible dinner incident, Bill looked horrified, but he told me in a very calm tone, "Maud, just go and lie down. I will take care of this."

My heart overflowed with love for this patient man, and I was more ashamed of myself than ever.

Bill would sometimes say, "When you are bad, you are so bad, but when you are good, you are so incredibly good that it makes up for all the bad."

I didn't think that was good enough for my husband or my boys because I wanted to be good all the time. I felt I had a demon inside that I had little control over, and it scared me.

I found a psychiatrist who I hoped could help me understand what was happening to me. I started seeing Dr. A once a week. During my sessions, I learned that my depression was due to the tragedy and trauma that had happened in Africa. Afzal had killed himself and discarded me as if I did not matter at all. I had sacrificed much, left my country, and given up my whole family for him. In return, Afzal had written a letter to his parents, telling them to keep Tariq and Afraz, bring them up as good Muslims, and send me back to Denmark. Afzal's traumatic death, the abuse by the Khan family, and Tariq's kidnapping had taken a heavy toll on me. Mahmoud was never charged or imprisoned for what he had done, and I had lived in fear for the last three years that either he or other family members would show up in Denmark and kidnap my boys.

Psychoanalysis helped me understand why I was so angry, and that the intense anger toward Afzal as well as the grief had caused my depression. I never told the psychiatrist about the rape and I am sure that was a factor as well. There was a lot to be angry about, and now I was taking it out on those I loved. I had a long road of intense therapy ahead of me, but I wasn't doing it for myself, but for my family. I hated myself, and not even the beautiful Virginia sun could elevate my precarious mood.

Breastfeeding Daniel was a respite from my inner turmoil because it made me sit down and relax several times a day. It was like a wonderful meditation, and my son's dependence on me for his daily nourishment made me feel needed and important. I read many books in English during this time and listened to music that filled my heart. Since Afzal wasn't there to stop me from breastfeeding, I nursed Daniel for a whole year. I loved every minute of it.

Bill was very concerned during the first two years of our marriage. He admitted later that he had been very worried about who he had married. My angry outbursts declined after I started therapy, and my depression was at times better, yet it never went away completely. I struggled with depression for years, and the nightmares continued. My doctor would not give me any medication, even though there were antidepressants on the market then. Psychoanalysis continued, but it didn't really help my depression, only my understanding of what was happening.

Bill's lack of attentiveness did not help. He had a difficult time understanding my depressive moods and anger, but after I explained why I had all this anger, he would sometimes invite me to hit his upper arm when I became angry. He was such a good, loving person despite his absent-mindedness and obsession with work. But, I had to beg him to spend time with me and our boys. I knew his work was his first love and I was his second. I missed spending quality time with him, as I loved him so much. Bill did not have my insatiable sex drive either, so I was sexually frustrated most of the time.

As many women do, I dove into my roles as a mother, wife, and housekeeper, as well as hostess, when we had parties for the faculty. I became known as the great cook and baker in the neighborhood and at social functions. Bill was very proud of me for that. Despite my variable moods, I was always able to rise to the occasion for special events.

On a good day, I had the energy of ten people, and if I stayed busy, there were moments of great joy in my daily life. I was, after all, married to the love of my life, and I adored him.

When the kids came home from school, I would always have cake or cookies with milk waiting for them, and we would often have neighborhood kids join the fun. We played games in the afternoon, especially on rainy days, and watched Walt Disney movies in the evening. I either read a story or sang some songs to the boys before bed. I spent much of my time with the kids, and Bill was mostly absent.

Occasionally, Bill would give me a whole weekend of togetherness, and those were my most precious moments.

We went dancing a few times, but not enough, and Bill was a great dancer. We were still very much in love, and when he held me in his arms, all my dark moods would vanish.

When my parents visited in 1971 after Daniel was born, my father had serendipitously run into a woman who was speaking Danish with her kids, right there in our neighborhood. Since my father didn't speak English, he heard the Danish language from far away and immediately approached this tall woman, with his winning smile and gift of the gab. After a short conversation, he invited her to meet me and my family. We lived at the end of a cul-de-sac street, and Helle lived only a block away. Helle was six feet tall and lanky with straight sandy hair and sagacious blue eyes. She dressed in an unpretentious but European way and always wore flat shoes, because of her height. She was intelligent and insightful, and we quickly became good friends and confidantes. She had two tall boys who were about the same ages as Tariq and Tore. Helle's outlook was somewhat conservative, with a slightly religious overtone, which is unusual for a Dane. She had married an American, like me, and had been born in Scandinavia, and that's where the similarities ended. Helle was a good sounding board for my unpredictable mood swings and emotional ways. She brought me down to earth many times with her sound advice. I admired her very much and appreciated her friendship. We were close friends for many years until she divorced and moved away.

During the summer of 1972, we made a trip to Denmark to see my parents and, of course, to Undersåker to see Momma and Morfar. Momma was getting old. She was so delighted to see our new baby as well as Tariq and Tore. She was amazed at how loving my boys were, showering her with hugs and kisses, in comparison to her other grandchildren, who rarely displayed any affection toward her. Maybe I was doing something positive after all.

We were gone for a month. Bill and I had a whole week to ourselves, touring the beautiful island of Bornholm. I gave up breastfeeding during that trip so that Bill and I could devote that time to each other, as the togetherness was sorely needed. My parents stepped in as babysitters whenever we needed them. Tariq and Tore reunited with their old friends in Høje Gladsaxe, where we used to live. At this point, they could still understand and speak Danish. It was shortly after this trip that the Danish language was forgotten in our home back in the States.

Chapter 27

I cannot erase or change the past,
but I can try to learn from it and accept it.
—Maud Steinberg

The boys were growing up, and Daniel started nursery school at the Montessori school when he was three. On his first day, he seemed confident enough until I was ready to leave. Daniel started crying and asked me to stay. I stayed with him for two hours until the teacher finally enticed him with a story.

Suddenly, Daniel turned around, smiled, and said, "You can leave now, Mom."

I was relieved that I didn't have to suffer the agony I had had with Tore when I had to leave him behind at the nursery school in Denmark. Of course, I didn't have two hours to spare back then, and Tore was much younger.

Daniel was a different child—exhausting at times because he was so bright. He was reading street signs by the time he was two years old, and he walked on the street as if he owned it.

At night when Bill came home for dinner, I would hand Daniel over to him and say, "I have had him all day, so now he is all yours."

Bill didn't seem to mind at all, and he enjoyed this little bundle of energy and brightness. They had a great relationship.

From early on, Daniel wasn't interested in fairy tales or children's stories, as Tariq and Tore had been.

He would say, "I want real stories," which meant that he wanted factual information, so I handed over the "storytelling" to Bill. I like fairy tales and other fun stuff and find scientific information boring as a basis for a story. Bill was happy to oblige and was quite amused by it. On that level, they were very much alike.

My parents visited us again in 1974. It was always wonderful to have them, as they were easy guests. They pitched in with the household chores while I did all the cooking. The boys loved having them around. We would play different games in the evening before bed, and there was much laughter and fun in the house.

During my parents' visit that year, I wanted desperately to talk to my mother about my problems, but she was always so distant and unapproachable. I was curious about how she had felt when she was pregnant with me, knowing full well that I had been an unwanted child. I tried to get the courage many times to talk to my mother, and when I finally did confront her, she clammed up, became angry, and refused to talk to me about it.

Thanks to Dr. A, I understood that this was her problem, not mine, and I realized with a certain clarity that I was only responsible for my own problems. I had to accept the fact that my mom would not talk to me about her feelings or the pregnancy. My mother never showed much affection toward me, but she adored her grandchildren and my husband.

At night, the demons and troubled thoughts were ever present. I frequently stayed up late after everyone had gone to sleep to ponder why I was feeling so bad and why my depression would not leave. I was a grown woman, but inside, I was just a vulnerable, wounded little girl. When would I grow up and become wise and feel secure within myself, I wondered.

I continued having strange nightmares about Afzal. One frightful night, I dreamt that Daniel died, and Afzal was still alive and had come back to see me. It was a very confusing and scary dream. My past would not leave me alone.

One evening as we were watching the news after Idi Amin's takeover of Uganda, I recognized Mahmoud on the TV screen. He was being interviewed by a journalist on a street in Kampala, but he was very careful about what he said. I later found out that Mahmoud had fled Uganda while wearing only his slippers. The Ugandan government seized all property belonging to the Khan family, and everyone was thrown out except Mahmoud. Mahmoud was an engineer and therefore needed by the government. I realized how small the world was, and seeing Mahmoud again brought back all the traumatic memories from the last few weeks in Uganda.

To my father's consternation, I had kept the lines of communication open with some members of the Khan family. I felt that Tariq and Tore might want to know their father's family later in life. A few years after marrying Bill and moving to the States, I felt more secure, so therefore, I sent photos to their paternal grandparents, who now lived in England. My father did not understand how I could still communicate with this family, who had hurt me so much. I knew I would never forget what happened, but I could forgive, I reasoned. My father was furious with me, but I knew even then that not forgiving a wrong would only hurt me in the long run.

Several members of the Khan family had fled to Canada, and among them was Afzal's brother, Atif, whom I had always liked. Atif was mild mannered and very easy to talk to. He came for a visit during the summer of 1974, after my parents had left. Atif had settled down in Toronto, where he worked as a pharmacist in his own pharmacy.

Atif and I had long conversations into the night when he visited, and the boys were quite taken by him. I was very frank with him and told him about everything that had happened when Afzal died. It was so good for me to talk about my troubled past and my heartache over losing Afzal in such a traumatic way.

Helle and Dr. A warned me not to trust Atif or get emotionally involved with him, but I loved him like a brother and felt very comfortable with him. Bill seemed to like him, too. I was amazed how welcoming and open Bill was of my previous husband's brother.

Atif told me that nobody in his family talked about Afzal's death, as they felt much shame and anger over it. He also said that Afzal had created many problems for the family with his suicide. It was a deplorable and grievous event affecting everyone. The Khan family had taken their anger out on me, and now I was taking my anger out on Bill and our kids. When would all this anger and hurt stop?

Atif's visit was very good for both me and the boys, and I felt he had put a Band-Aid on the bleeding wound in my heart. We promised to keep in touch.

Chapter 28

Breakdown

The gloom of being, the desperation
Is sometimes hard to take
How do I find some joy in life?
How do I correct each mistake?

I feel a congestion, a suffocation
The walls are closing in on me
But I still continue my existence
Urging stubbornly to be free

And then things are done, and things are said
With the regrets for every day
While emotions stir a storm inside
And I wish to fade away

—Maud Steinberg

During the summer of 1975, Bill and I had a terrible fight. I felt neglected and starved for attention, and my heart was like a bottomless pit that could never be filled. After the fight, I left the house in anger and went for a drive to cool down. I don't even remember what the fight was about.

I parked the car near the university and went for a walk. While I was walking on Main Street, I decided to go dancing.

Dancing had always made me feel happy, and I missed having fun. We didn't have much money to spend on going out, and Bill was always working, so dancing rarely happened. If we went out, it was usually to some university function, which was boring, and there was never any dancing. I was still so young, only thirty-two years old, and it seemed that all we ever did was work.

As I was walking toward a dance club called 1776, a young man came up to me and tried to start a conversation. I ignored him. But after I entered the club, the same young man approached and offered me a drink, which I reluctantly accepted. We had a couple of drinks, and then we danced.

At midnight, I thought of calling Bill, but I didn't. An hour later I thought of calling him again but still refrained. I wanted a respite from my life for a few hours.

The young man I was with was the artistic type—very different from Bill. After we left the club, he picked up his guitar from his truck, and then we sat in an alley, talking for hours while he played the guitar for me. I was getting some attention for a change, and it felt good. I stayed out all night and didn't come home until 7:00 a.m. Bill was furious and with good reason. It was very irresponsible and childish of me to do such a thing, and I had no excuses for my behavior, except that I felt very unhappy, neglected, and unloved.

Bill had been riding around in a taxi for part of the night looking for me, since I had our only car.

When I saw Dr. A that same day, I told him about the incident. Dr. A remarked that I wasn't acting in a rational way, and he suggested that I go to Arlington House (a local mental hospital) for a few days.

We were supposed to move in a week because we had bought our first house, north of Charlottesville. I felt anxious and overwhelmed about the upcoming move, so I agreed because I thought I would have some peace for a few days before moving.

Arlington House, I soon found out, was a prison of sorts. The doors were locked. I had willingly walked into this prison, and now I couldn't get out. Every day there were group meetings with other patients, and the patients decided what each of our privileges would be. I had no privileges, as I had to earn them. The other patients would vote as to whether I was fit to have visitors or go home to see my kids.

After a couple of days, I realized that I had made a colossal mistake, so I called Dr. A and Bill and asked them to come to the hospital. Bill had forgiven me for my transgression because Dr. A had explained to him that I was not myself.

I had started packing my things and had already removed all the linens from the bed. When Dr. A arrived, he told me that he wouldn't let me leave because he thought I was better off where I was. I felt that I was being punished like a wayward child for my one-night infraction. Bill was stone-faced, showing no emotion when he arrived. I explained that I didn't belong there, and since I had voluntarily admitted myself, I reasoned, I should be able to leave (just like in Denmark). That was a wrong assumption on my part, and my pleading got me nowhere. Bill didn't say a word. I became angry and threw my pillow on the bed, which probably convinced Dr. A that I was unstable, and he pointed this out to Bill. Dr. A told Bill not to listen to me, and then they both walked out of the room and down the hallway. I called out to Bill, but he did not respond.

I wanted to talk to Bill in private, but I heard Dr. A say, "Don't pay any attention to her!"

Bill never turned around, and he walked out of the hospital completely ignoring me. I was crushed.

I saw Dr. A motion to two six-foot-tall orderlies. Immediately, the two men seized me by my elbows and forced me back into the room. While they were still holding on to me, a nurse came into the room with a syringe in her hand.

She said, "You can either do this the easy way or the hard way. It's up to you."

She jabbed the needle into my hip. I didn't put up a fight, as I was outnumbered anyway. I had been so sure that I had rights as a patient and that I could go home if I wanted to, but I had been so wrong. It didn't make any sense to me. The injection worked incredibly fast, but before I fell onto the bed, I asked the nurse to put some new sheets on for me. When the nurse came in with the sheets, I was lying on the bed in a daze. I couldn't move.

The nurse threw the linens on the bed and said, "Put the sheets on yourself!" and walked out the door.

I never saw her again. Since I could not stand, I tried crawling on the floor to put the sheets on. I didn't succeed because the injection finally knocked me completely out. I don't know exactly how many hours I was lying there on the bare mattress. I was hallucinating, seeing strange things on the ceiling, and bugs crawling on the wall. It was a hellish nightmare of the worst kind. I remember becoming very thirsty, but I couldn't reach the bell to call the nurse, and I couldn't get up to get myself some water. I was in this nightmare all afternoon, and nobody checked in on me.

Finally, in the late afternoon, my roommate came in, noticed my predicament, and gave me some water to drink. Around eight o'clock, Bill came to see me, and by then I was able to walk a little again, but I was too fogged up to talk much.

The next day it was clear to me what I had to do. I had to play their little game to get out of there, and I made a careful plan in my head. It took me ten days to earn the votes to get out of that insane asylum. I had hoped I would get out before we had to move into our new house. Unfortunately, Bill had to take care of everything himself. I felt very bad about that.

During our group meetings, I never revealed my feelings to anyone, even though some of the doctors seemed to be all right. I was very cautious and tense the whole time I was locked up.

When I got home, the dam of my troubled soul broke, and I sobbed for a long time before I was able to tell Bill what had happened with the injection and how the whole system had worked.

I was angry with Bill for leaving me there and said, "Don't you ever do that to me again!"

I was not a crazy person, and nobody should be treated the way I had been at Arlington House. My rights as a patient had been violated. I had the right to be treated with dignity and respect, the right to be fully informed regarding treatment, the right to refuse any treatment, and the right not to be denied my personal liberty by reason of mental illness without a fair jury trial. I was neither a danger to myself nor to others. Yes, I was a depressed person, and with good reason, but I was not suicidal. I should have had the right to leave if I had voluntarily admitted myself. I did not know my rights, but my doctor should have known, and he overstepped his power. I had a hard time forgiving Dr. A for what he had done to me. I never saw him again as he moved away. I was angry with him for years, and I felt betrayed.

Bill was shocked when he heard my story and apologized. Then he cried, too. He had trusted Dr. A. After all, Dr. A was the doctor. The injection was unjustified and a gross violation of my rights, as I was not out of control or hysterical in any way. The whole scene was outrageous, and I wonder how many other unfortunate patients have been treated this way by overzealous doctors.

It was wonderful to be in our new house. We lived in a great neighborhood with plenty of other children for our boys to play with. I made new female friends and tried to forget the terrible experience at Arlington House. I became very busy with decorating and gardening. I sewed curtains and covers for our *dyner* (Danish for "down comforters"). I increased my indoor plant collection and even made macramé hangers for the pots. There was little I could not do. I started taking classes at the community college because I wanted to learn something new. I felt unfulfilled just being a homemaker. I had great yearnings for more, but I wasn't sure for what. I didn't think that I could ever go back to nursing because of my fear of death and dying.

Our boys seemed happy with school, Boy Scouts, and sports. I served as a den mother for the Boy Scout group one year. Like most American mothers, I was an around-the-clock chauffeur, taking the boys to their various after school activities.

We were a regular family with a busy schedule. Bill continued to work very hard, always going back to the lab in the evening after dinner and tucking Daniel in, rarely coming back before midnight.

I put a lot of effort into making family dinners every night, and I always thought about what Bill would like to eat. He was complimentary of my cooking, which made me try even harder to please him. We shared great communion as a family during dinnertime and had wonderful, interesting conversations at the table mostly because of Bill. There was still deep love between us, and that hadn't changed, regardless of what had happened.

Chapter 29

Glorious Day

In the bittersweet darkness
every thought and pain
seem more difficult to bear,
but when the sun comes up
the thoughts disappear
like vapor from the morning mist
You glorious day
which gives me hope to live

—Maud Steinberg

My parents discovered during their first visit to Virginia that the summers were too hot and humid for them. Therefore, they changed the timing of their visits to spring or fall.

When my parents visited in the spring of 1976, my aunt Britt accompanied them. I remember that visit rather fondly. My father was very sentimental and would be as excited as a child, for months before each visit. He would make me just as excited waiting for them to arrive. It felt like Christmas every time my parents came with their many delightful surprises for all of us. We received many small, interesting trinkets, presents, and games that would keep us occupied during their stay. In 1976, Tariq was twelve, Tore was ten, and Daniel was now five years old.

In the evening, we often played games with the kids, and I would frequently break into laughing fits. One night, we played the game Clue with Britt. Since Britt was so religious, she had a hard time voicing her accusations of who was guilty.

She could barely squeak out, "Mr. Mustard did it in the dining room with the candlestick."

She felt guilty about verbalizing the accusations because murder was a sin, so even playing this game was a sin in her mind. Since she was having so much fun, she continued playing anyway.

After Britt had gone to bed, my father said, "I bet you that Britt is now on her hands and knees in her room asking God for forgiveness because she played Clue with us."

That's when I started laughing so hard and long that I ended up peeing in my pants. Laughter is healing, and it was very healing to have my family with us, even though I still could not speak to my mother about my problems.

One night my father dragged me out of the house and made me stand in the street, looking toward our beautifully lit house in the darkness.

He said in a dramatic, but sentimental tone, "This is the most beautiful house I have ever seen."

He continued. "Look at the bright lights shining out into the street. Can't you see how warm and welcoming it looks? You are so lucky to be living in such a beautiful house with a wonderful husband and great kids."

I knew my house was not the most beautiful house—far from it—but he made me see the beauty in it, and he also made me realize how lucky I was. I almost cried.

My father spent more time with Daniel on this visit because Tariq and Tore were bigger now and had many activities to attend to, with school still in session. There was a problem with communication between my father and Daniel, though.

Daniel did not know Danish, and my father's English was limited. This caused some friction in the relationship. I wrote a piece about this delicate union for my community college English class:

> Daniel's cute, sleepy face looked up into the sky where the lights from the plane appeared, and he smiled in anticipation. Mormor and Morfar (the Danish words for grandmother and grandfather) were arriving. He knew that they lived far away across the Atlantic Ocean and that they loved him. All the postcards, little trinkets, and lovely presents were signs he understood, and now he was curious to see the persons who had bestowed all this upon him. He felt instinctively that the next few weeks would be important to him.
>
> Daniel looked curiously at the smiling couple who approached him. Somehow Morfar did not look like the person in the photograph. Morfar's face was partially covered with a beard, and what a stomach—good grief! Everybody was laughing and greeting each other, while Daniel quietly watched the long-awaited newcomers. Unable to resist the temptation after a while, he touched Morfar's stomach ever so lightly, but his hand was quickly caught. Morfar squeezed it gently and lovingly and smiled at him. Daniel felt embarrassed!
>
> Mormor inquired about him in accented English, but when Morfar talked, Daniel realized that the old man could not speak English very well. The initial disappointment was so great that Daniel withdrew into complete silence.
>
> For the first few days, Daniel paid more attention to Mormor, with whom he could at least talk. They chatted and played games while Morfar, slightly disillusioned, watched them in their fun.
>
> Well, Morfar could not be ignored that easily, not even by a five-year-old, and eventually Morfar's natural charm and winning manner completely captured Daniel.

Once the friendship was established, they became inseparable. In spite of their substantial spoken-communication problem, they got the meaning across by using fingers, hands, and facial expressions. Morfar knew a few important, simple words that he used often, such as "good boy," "big boy," and "nice boy," to which Daniel would immediately respond.

Everything seemed perfect and peaceful for a while until suddenly one day the frustrations that had slowly gathered in both parties became too much. The confrontation was inevitable, as the relationship was a unique one. Daniel became impatient with his friend of such few words, and Morfar's feeling of inadequacy finally got to him. The fight was unpleasant, and everyone suffered.

Morfar took a long ride on the bike to cool off and to think things over. Daniel sat in his room and looked glum and sad. He was not about to listen to an old man who could not even speak English properly.

Somehow Morfar managed to mend the broken friendship, but how this was accomplished is still a mystery. Regardless of Morfar's shortcomings, Daniel learned to love and respect the old man, and their friendship became stronger than ever.

Over the past year, they have kept in touch by mail, and at the prospect of seeing Morfar again, Daniel made this lovely comment: "That will be nice because I haven't talked to him in a long time." When I pointed out that Morfar does not know English very well, Daniel softly replied, "But Mama, we still talk you know!"

My boys were all so different and so unique. Tariq was quite an athlete, always on the move, and playing all the sports. In high school, he was the captain of the football team and the quarterback. Tariq got into trouble often, but then he would write cute little notes to me, apologizing for what he had done. Tore, on the other hand, was the quiet type, and he rarely got in trouble. He became a video game champion at the local arcade in the mall and achieved fame for a while because of an article about his achievement in the Daily Progress. Tariq and Tore were A students in school, and I was very proud of them.

Daniel started kindergarten and remained a handful. He was a challenge, but fortunately he was quite capable of entertaining himself for hours. His hobby was collecting rocks, and I helped him organize his growing collection into labeled plastic containers. He would often be out in the yard or in the driveway collecting or watching bugs for hours. He even created an ant farm.

Daniel had now advanced from watching Sesame Street to Nova. This unusual five-year-old could sit for an entire hour watching a very advanced science program on PBS and seem to take it all in. I was amazed.

After my parents left, Tariq, Tore, and I traveled to Toronto, Canada, for Atif's wedding. Of course, my father was opposed to this, as I would be seeing many members of the Khan family, including Mahmoud, who had kidnapped Tariq. Atif was marrying a medical doctor named Mahnoor. Mahnoor was a Muslim of Pakistani descent, but it was not an arranged marriage, as Mahnoor was a modern and independent woman. I immediately liked her; she was easy to talk to and very wise.

The most memorable conversation I had during my visit was a talk with Mahmoud's new wife, Laila. Mahmoud had divorced his first wife, the one he had married in Uganda. Laila was only eighteen years old when she married Mahmoud—another arranged marriage. Laila confided in me about her sad life. She cried when she told me her story. She was now only twenty-one years old, and she had already given birth to three boys. Mahmoud was working in Saudi Arabia as an engineer and was making much money, and Laila was living in Toronto.

Laila said, "I am only a sex slave and a breeding machine for my husband when he comes home for visits. There is no love or affection, and Mahmoud is cold and distant."

Laila felt stuck, as she had no say about her life and no hope for further development outside the home. She was very unhappy. I realized how lucky I was to have such a good, loving husband who was not controlling in any way.

Mahmoud was much different from the jolly person I used to know while he lived in England. I had a brief, uncomfortable conversation with him one day, and he did indeed come across as a cold, bitter, and angry person. I felt a chill just being near him, so I avoided him for the rest of my stay. Mahmoud didn't scare me anymore, and I felt secure, even though I had my boys with me.

I had finally told Tariq and Tore about what had happened in Africa and about their father's suicide. Many years went by before I could tell them the truth. Initially, I didn't want to tell them about their father's tragic death. But as they grew older, I felt they deserved to know. I never said anything bad about Afzal; after all, he was their father.

Our visit to Toronto was eye-opening. I felt lucky to have come this far. I wanted my boys to know their father's family. It would be up to them, when they grew up, to decide whether they wanted to keep the connection. All I was doing was giving them options for later on.

Chapter 30

Traveling in the company of those we love
is home in motion.
—Leigh Hunt

Bill stayed home with Daniel when Tariq, Tore, and I attended Atif's wedding. He was busy finishing up his latest research and planning our trip to San Diego, California. Bill was taking a sabbatical year to do research at the University of California, San Diego, located in La Jolla.

The trip to California by car took six weeks. We had sold the Mustang when Daniel was born and bought a Ford Torino station wagon, a real family car. We had also adopted a female mutt dog named Toby. At first, we thought the dog was a male. Toby was a great learning experience for us all, and I had to educate myself on how to train her. She was the most stubborn dog I had ever come across. It took me several months just to teach her how to come when she was called. Toby would get carsick whenever she was in the car, and that created a big problem for us while driving across the country. She had to be medicated during the entire trip.

Bill had spent many hours planning this trip, down to the last detail. He was interested in visiting national parks on the way, and maybe a few sightseeing spots.

We camped in a tent every night during the trip, and I cooked our meals on a propane burner. We didn't have money to spend on hotels or restaurant food, but I loved every minute of it. I had Bill with me every day and night, and that was a treat. It felt like the honeymoon we had never had, even though lovemaking was difficult with the boys sleeping in the same tent.

We managed to crawl into each other's sleeping bag at night when the kids were asleep. It was heavenly having my husband so close all the time, and our love flourished.

We started out heading for Asheville, North Carolina, and then to the Cherokee Indian reservation. The next day we went toward the Great Smokey Mountains in Tennessee and from there to Hot Springs National Park in Arkansas. We traveled through the northern part of Texas, into New Mexico, where we visited Carlsbad Caverns National Park. The most incredible natural wonder was Grand Canyon National Park in Arizona. We stayed there for a few days. I wished we had had the money to go on a horseback ride through the canyon, but we enjoyed our own cheaper tour, walking on foot where it was safe for the kids.

Bill was relaxed and happy during the trip, and he was, as usual, an excellent tour guide. Everything was planned well, which made traveling easy.

We rented an old single-family house in the middle of San Diego, and Bill commuted to La Jolla every day. I started taking accounting classes at the local community college in the morning. To make some extra money, I babysat another little boy, Jason, who was the same age as Daniel, in the afternoon after nursery school. I stayed quite busy while Tariq and Tore were in school during the day.

My life was full and happy because of all the extra attention I received from Bill. On the weekends, we went camping and sightseeing. Life was a blast and full of adventure.

Daniel, Jason, and I would go to the natural history museum on Tuesdays because it was free on that day. Jason wasn't really that interested in going every Tuesday afternoon, so one day I thought we should do something different. When Daniel heard that we weren't going to the museum that day, he became very upset and cried because it was his favorite outing. I was shocked at how upset Daniel became, so I gave in and we went anyway.

When we were at the museum looking at rocks, Daniel asked me to read the information about a certain rock. As I started reading the metal plaque, Daniel exclaimed, "Mom, you are reading the wrong thing!"

I looked at him in surprise.

I heard a man behind us say, "How does it feel to have a child who is smarter than you?"

I just smiled, because I knew Daniel was smarter than me.

Bill loved the Pacific Ocean, even though it was ice-cold. During lunch, he would go swimming at Black's Beach in La Jolla, and since it was a nude beach, he went without his swimming trunks. Bill invited me several times to go with him, but I could not get into that cold water, so it never happened. It wasn't the nudity that bothered me—just the freezing water.

I asked Bill one day, "How will you feel if you meet one of your students on the beach?"

He smiled and said that he wasn't worried about it. That surprised me.

In Virginia, we had bought a small lot at Lake Monticello, where we would go swimming during the summer. Sometimes on a weekend evening, we would load the kids into the station wagon, and once they were asleep, we would go skinny-dipping by ourselves. This proved that Bill had a daring streak after all, which I appreciated.

We had a great time in California that year, but I found California crowded. You had to stand in line to get to the beach.

We made a trip to Tijuana, Mexico, which the kids enjoyed. For me, it was a horrible experience because of all the poor people and kids begging in the streets. It reminded me too much of Africa. We never went back.

During the summer of 1977, we returned to Virginia, but we made a trip up to Vancouver first to see some friends who lived there. On the way, we went to visit the active volcano Mount Saint Helens in the state of Washington. After leaving Vancouver, we camped in the Rocky Mountains in Montana. It rained so hard that night that the tent leaked, and we had a foot of water in it.

Most other people were sitting pretty in their campers, high off the ground. How I wished we had a camper that night. We had to pack up all our wet gear in the evening and head to a motel. The next day, we drove straight through the Midwest to New York City to visit Bill's family. Since I was the night owl, I drove the entire night.

Our year in California was relaxed and happy, and I received much love and attention from Bill. Every weekend we made special camping trips to national parks all over California and beyond, and life was one great adventure after another. I loved it, and I felt better than I had in a long time. When we returned home, all that changed, due to Bill's teaching responsibilities and research and college for me. Daniel started first grade, and Tariq and Tore were in middle school.

Chapter 31

Happiness is seeing your family
and friends after a long absence.
—Maud Steinberg

During the summer of 1978, the boys and I flew to Denmark for six weeks to see my folks, Momma, Britt, and Dagmar. My parents paid for our trip, which troubled Bill, but that was not the only reason he didn't go with us. He had a grant proposal to write and felt he couldn't take the time off to come with us. Even though I could understand the reason he stayed behind, I was quite disappointed and sad to not be sharing this adventure with him. Whenever I was experiencing something beautiful, I wanted to share it with him. If Bill was with me, the experience was magnified and became more beautiful and special. I was hurt that Bill didn't go with us, and Daniel was upset as well, as he missed his papa. It was a long, tough trip and a big responsibility taking care of three kids.

My oldest and dearest friend, Helena, whom I hadn't seen since before I married Afzal, had called my mother in 1967 to find out how I was doing in Africa. Helena was shocked to find out that I was widowed and back in Copenhagen. We could not meet then because she was moving to Norway with her Norwegian husband, who was a doctor. Helena had given birth to fraternal twin girls back in 1967. We lost contact because Helena moved so much during the first ten years of her marriage, due to her husband's job.

A few days after the boys and I arrived in Copenhagen in 1978, the telephone rang, and it was Helena. She told my mother that she wanted to talk to me. Helena didn't know that I had married again and moved to the States. It seemed coincidental that I should be at my parents' place when she called, but maybe there are no coincidences.

My parents and I had talked about Helena the night before, and I had expressed how much I wanted to find her and see her again. That same night, Helena talked to her husband about me, expressing the same wish of wanting to reconnect. So, Helena and I reconnected after twelve years, and it felt like we had never been apart.

I had planned to take the kids to Legoland in Jylland the following day, and Helena lived in Esbjerg, only half an hour away. After Legoland, we visited Helena for three hours before taking the train back to Copenhagen.

Helena's girls were beautiful, and Tariq and Tore had a great time playing with them. A few days later, Helena came to Copenhagen, and we spent another twelve hours together, reminiscing about the old days and sharing our life stories. My father had just as much fun as the kids, playing games with them and telling them wild stories.

For years I had wondered about my biological father, Sören, and I had a great desire to meet him. I found Sören by writing to a public registrar in Sweden, and then I wrote him a letter. Sören was very pleased to hear from me and wrote that he had wondered about me for many years. Sören was married and had three boys, and he lived with his wife in Karlskoga, Sweden. All his sons were now grown, and two were married.

Sören was delighted that I wanted to come to Karlskoga to see him and his family, so we planned to stop there on the way to Undersåker.

Since Pappa was coming with us, the visit to see Sören became a problem, as Pappa felt threatened by Sören. The night before leaving to go to Sweden, I had a heated argument with my father and my brother, Peter, who were against me looking up Sören. I felt that this was something I had to do, but nothing could change their minds. I stuck to my guns and embarked on the long trip without reconciling this problem with Pappa. I was quite anxious about meeting my biological father and having a distraught stepfather on my hands didn't make it any easier.

Pappa drove us to Karlskoga, but he didn't want to meet Sören, so he dropped us off at his house. Pappa was quite upset about our plan to spend the night, and I found out later that he was afraid of losing me to this long-absent father.

Pappa had adopted me when I was twelve, and all ties to Sören had then been dropped. I had only seen Sören once when I was around two years old, and I have no memory of that.

When we arrived at Sören's house, he hugged and kissed me and told me how happy he was to finally meet me. Sören was open and expressive of his feelings. I was surprised because Swedes do not normally express their feelings that easily. My impression of Sören's family was positive. Sören was a handsome man with thick, nearly black, slightly curly hair and deep-blue eyes. His physique was slender and wiry, and he was quite talkative and jovial. I noticed upon inspection that I had inherited his hands, jaw, and hair. Sören played the guitar beautifully and sang with a crisp, wonderful voice that sounded much like Willie Nelson's. He gave me a tape recording of him singing and playing the guitar. I was quite taken with him. I noticed, however, that Sören drank quite a bit, and his speech became increasingly more slurred as the evening progressed.

That same evening as I was coming down the stairs after visiting the bathroom, Sören met me halfway and cornered me in the staircase. He grabbed me by the waist as if he wanted to hug me, but then things suddenly changed. He started groping me and tried to kiss me on the mouth. I was horrified. How could he do this to me? I was his daughter. I felt violated, and I quickly slithered away from him.

This incident gave me a sudden insight into this man, who at first had dazzled me so. But I had already made plans to spend the night with the kids, and I couldn't get hold of Pappa, so we had to stay.

When Pappa came to pick us up in the morning, he looked distressed. He still refused to meet Sören. He was acting like a child, and I could tell he was relieved to whisk us away quickly. I felt violated by both men, but I couldn't tell Pappa about the unpleasant incident with Sören.

Later, when we got back to Copenhagen, I told my mother about what had happened and said, "Thank you for not marrying Sören."

She was shocked to hear my story.

Everyone else was so nice, including Sören's wife. Sören was the only problem. I was very disappointed and didn't really care to get to know Sören any further, but I stayed in contact with my oldest half-brother and his children.

Even though Pappa was jealous and insecure, I was very grateful to have such a wonderful, caring father. I had an emotional talk with him a few days later and told him that he had nothing to worry about.

"You have always been my real dad, and I love you very much," I said.

My mother had made a good choice by marrying Pappa.

We continued driving to Undersåker to see Momma, Britt, and Dagmar. Morfar had died of pneumonia at age eighty-nine in 1976, after being bedridden for months due to a broken hip. The doctors thought he was too old to have an operation, but I think that might have saved his life. He was in perfect health otherwise.

It had been six years since I had seen Momma, and she was now seventy-eight years old. The old childhood home had some improvements, such as modern bathrooms with showers, a new covered entryway, and a small balcony on the third floor. Otherwise, everything else looked and smelled the same, with aromas from food and baked goodies.

Britt had baked sweet bread and seven different kinds of cookies, and I warned her to hide those large cookie jars from my boys. Tariq and Tore raided the jars whenever they saw a chance, and Aunt Britt had to find new hiding places for them several times. There were coffee breaks with sweet bread and cookies twice a day, one in the morning and one in the afternoon.

Daniel said one day, "These cookie times are the worst!"

He was worried about gaining weight at age seven, so he started exercising vigorously, but he still couldn't stay away from the cookies.

My father kept us busy with excursions, and Momma's favorite pastime was a car ride. She would beam like a small child at Christmas whenever we went for a drive. We often went on picnics at a waterfall or a lake in the mountains, bringing coffee, sandwiches, sweet bread, cake, and cookies. On every outing, there was much *hygge*, as they say in Denmark, and we would sit and chat for a long time about everything and nothing while the kids explored their surroundings or played in the water.

Hygge is the feeling of sharing moments of togetherness with friends and family while having a cup of coffee or tea with a piece of cake, some cookies, or a special meal. I missed my hygge moments with my family when I moved to the States, but I continued the tradition of always offering a cup of tea or coffee with cake whenever I received visitors.

During every minute of my visit to Denmark and Sweden, I missed Bill and sharing this time with him. I enjoyed my family and seeing them, but I missed Bill every day. My life was not complete without him. Even Daniel called out for his papa several times during the night on our trip.

Momma was getting old, and her hair had turned snow-white. She had had a stroke at age seventy-one, and that worried me. She had been the one constant in my life, and the one person who loved me for me, and I was still her guld-klump (golden nugget). Her laughter was still infectious, and her eyes sparkled with love when she looked at me, and my boys.

Britt had moved back home to help out after Momma's stroke, and Dagmar was still living at home. Dagmar would grab the boys in big bear hugs and show her love by planting wet, sloppy kisses on their cheeks. There was teasing and playing going on between Dagmar and the boys, and the house was filled with laughter and fun while we were visiting. Daniel gave Momma much love and attention. He would give her kisses on her cheeks every day and picked flowers for her many times. Momma beamed and laughed out loud whenever the kids showed her love and affection.

Momma was surprised how often Bill wrote to me. Bill wrote thirteen letters during our six weeks in Denmark and Sweden, and I wrote six long letters. Bill would write a little every day, as he missed us all so much. I always write long letters, it seems, and that made up for the infrequency of mine.

Bill wrote:

> *It's amazing that I am writing to you this often after almost nine years of marriage, but I miss you so much, and I wish I was there with you. You mean everything to me.*

Bill kept us informed about his daily life, and about Toby, our dog. He had been working on a project to finish off an office for himself in the basement. I was worried that he was working too hard and straining himself too much, as he had complained about a swollen vein in his arm before we left. In his letters, Bill let me know that the vein was better, but that he was sleeping more than usual, and that he had lost some weight. I was a little concerned about him.

I must have said goodbye to Momma at least five times before we left. It was especially hard this time because I lived so far away and couldn't just take the train to visit her anymore. I didn't know when I would be able to come back.

Chapter 32

Perfect love cannot be sustained in an imperfect world.
—Maud Steinberg

After we came back to Copenhagen from Sweden, there was only a week left of our vacation, and I was tired and worn out from all my social responsibilities and busy schedule. I couldn't wait to go back home and be with Bill. I was deep down quite upset with him for not coming with us.

Helle was visiting her mother in Copenhagen that summer, and we met with the kids at Tivoli Gardens. Helle had divorced and moved to Chapel Hill, North Carolina, so I hadn't seen her in a while. I enjoyed seeing and talking to her again, but I sensed that our friendship had changed.

I also reunited with Tove, my friend from nursing school. She had married a dentist and moved to Germany. The last girlfriend I reunited with was Birgit, from the time I lived in Odense.

The day before Birgit arrived, I went shopping in Copenhagen for some presents to take home with me. I was feeling adventurous and silly that day, feeling free and on my own.

When a young man approached me at the Anva store in Copenhagen, I pretended to be an American, as it is difficult to figure out my accent. Alex was Italian, and he flirted with me, so I flirted back. He had lived in Denmark for five years and spoke Danish, as well as English. Alex suggested that he show me part of Copenhagen. I didn't tell him that I was already familiar with all the places we visited and that I knew Danish. It was a silly game that continued for a few hours.

When I told him that I was married and had three kids, it didn't seem to bother him. Later in the evening, I finally told him the truth, and he thought it was hilarious that I had fooled him for so long. We had a great time going out dancing in the evening. I felt young and carefree after five weeks of looking after kids, dealing with my two fathers, and saying goodbye to Momma.

I was caught up in the moment, and one thing led to another. Alex talked me into going to his place, where I spent the night. He was sweet and tender, but I realized immediately that this was a big mistake.

I didn't want to call my parents, as I didn't want to wake them up, so I waited until morning. Of course, my parents had noticed that I hadn't come home from my shopping. They had been worried about me and had called the police. When I called my parents at 7:00 a.m., they were quite angry with me, but were relieved that I was okay.

Birgit was supposed to come to Copenhagen that morning at ten o'clock, so I told my father that I would pick her up since I was already in town. It was a little uncomfortable seeing Birgit again, as we did not have much in common. Our lives were very different. Birgit still lived in Odense, she was not married, and she had never had any kids, so we were miles apart. We went out in the evening to the Tivoli Gardens, and we managed to have a good time chatting and sharing stories despite the big divide.

Alex, however, wasn't going to let me go that easily, and he insisted that we meet again before I had to leave to go back to the States. I told him that I loved my husband and that I was not interested in continuing anything. I met Alex for an hour at a restaurant to say goodbye a couple of days before we left Denmark. To my surprise, Alex told me that he loved me, and then he cried. I cried, too, because he was so sweet, like a vulnerable little boy, and I felt that I had hurt him. I had no idea a little fling was going to be that painful for so many people. I had yet to tell Bill.

It was finally time to go home, and I was feeling very guilty about my little affair. It didn't mean anything to me, and I loved Bill with all my heart. I was so angry with myself for doing such a foolish thing. How was I going to tell Bill? I knew I couldn't keep it a secret, and that Bill would be able to read me like a book.

When we got off the plane at John F. Kennedy Airport, and I saw Bill standing there waiting for us, my heart jumped, bursting with love and fear at the same time.

Before Bill hugged me, he looked curiously at my face and asked, "What is wrong?"

I blurted out, "I had an affair!"

A pained expression crossed Bill's face. He took a deep breath and said, "We will talk about it later."

I was sure it would be over between us and that I now had lost his love. I was in agony. I hated myself more than ever. I was a jackass of the worst kind, and I had no explanation for what I had done. Bill loved me, and I had betrayed him. It was unforgivable, and I deserved whatever would happen to me.

We were staying at Bill's parents' apartment the first night; then we stayed with Rachel for another night before going back to Virginia.

To my surprise, Bill reacted unexpectedly regarding my confession and he kept asking questions about my affair. In a way, he seemed excited that I had had sex with another man. He was hurt, but he wasn't threatened at all by Alex. Maybe it was because he knew that I loved only him. I was a wreck because I had a hard time forgiving myself, so I needed Bill's undivided attention for the next few days. I was more affected by the whole thing than Bill was, or so it seemed. I was relieved that Bill had responded the way he had, but it didn't ease my guilt.

Even though Bill had handled all this surprisingly well, I still felt terrible about what I had done. How could I do such a thing when I loved my husband with all my heart? Was it because I was always pining for him and he never gave me enough attention and love?

As time went by, I started to think that maybe Bill didn't care that much about me, because of his lack of anger about my affair. When I got home, I wrote in my journal:

> *If only Bill would love me a little more, spend more time with me, make love more often, talk to me, and notice me. I am just a shadow. I love being with Bill and doing things with him, but he is always busy and then too tired.*

Our daily lives continued, and things didn't seem to change despite what had happened. I became more withdrawn and depressed, and Bill was even harder to reach because of his schedule and research.

I was descending into a black hole of despair. I had developed a pelvic infection because of an IUD and I was quite sick with pain, anemia, and fatigue for a few months. I was becoming increasingly more despondent and hopeless and I didn't see a reason to live anymore. I had no therapist to talk to and I was stuck with myself and my own distorted thinking.

One night, a couple of months after I had returned from Denmark, and after having been rejected again by Bill because he wanted to sleep, I couldn't take it anymore and started thinking about how I could kill myself. My thoughts were overtaken by guilt and the fear that Bill didn't love me anymore. The affair with Alex had not rattled him that much, so that was the same as not caring about me. Bill had started going to bed earlier and sleeping later, and I thought that he was just tired because he worked so hard. He still had problems with the vein in his arm and he had lost quite a bit of weight, but he never complained about anything or talked to me about it. Bill was also clueless about my feelings, as I was not talking either. I didn't know then that he was very sick.

I had gradually hardened into a mass of anger, sadness, hurt, and despair. After a disastrous Saturday evening out, it all came to a head in my mind. I took six Valium, and a few hours later, another six, and then I wrote Bill a note. I kept taking more of whatever I could find. I tried to cut my wrist, but it hurt too much, and then I passed out on the bathroom floor. While lying on the floor, I heard crying and then sirens, and that is all I remember.

Bill had gone to work, even though it was a Sunday, without noticing anything or even reading my note, which said something about his absentmindedness and nonobservance.

In the late morning, Tariq had come into our bedroom with breakfast, which the boys had prepared for me. Tariq found me on the bathroom floor, bleeding from my arm and unconscious. My poor children had to see that terrible sight. I have had to live with that my whole life. I wrote in my journal:

> *I hope my children can forgive me for all my wrongdoings. They certainly can't have much respect left for me.*

Later, I wrote:

> *When I send my watch in for repair, I get it back ticking and sparkling with new life. Is there a repair shop for brains? I need a complete clean-out. I want the fear, insecurity, and anger replaced with joy, confidence, and peace of mind. Can you imagine how great I would be then?*

I was a tortured soul, dealing with a crippling depression that seemed to have no end. No matter how much I was loved, I couldn't see it or feel it.

The doctors in the hospital called me a "complicated woman," and it was suggested that Bill and I undergo couple's therapy, but that never happened

After I came back home from the hospital, I broke down and threatened to leave Bill. I needed to feel that Bill loved me and cared about me. On the other hand, I didn't feel that I deserved it because of the affair. Bill got down on his knees and begged me to stay. He told me repeatedly how much he loved me and needed me. Bill's declaration of love gave me an infusion of energy and hope. I had never wanted to leave, but I desperately wanted a reaction out of Bill and the reassurances of his love.

Bill had planned a trip to the Florida Keys for the Christmas holidays to make up for his absence during our trip to Denmark and Sweden. We camped again, to save money.

The family togetherness soothed my soul, and warm, loving feelings surfaced again between Bill and me. We fell in love all over, and I felt complete.

Chapter 33

Yours is the light by which my spirit is born:
you are my sun, my moon, and all my stars.
—E. E. Cummings

In February 1979, about a month after getting back to Charlottesville from our Florida vacation, Bill started having some new symptoms that deeply concerned me. His ankles had swelled up, he looked paler and was sleeping even more. Bill finally listened to me and went to see the doctor. I was worried about his kidneys. Our family doctor put Bill in the hospital for observation and tests. Bill did not seem too concerned, but I sensed that something serious was going on.

The doctor sent Bill home after a few days, saying, "It is probably just an inflamed kidney, and it will resolve itself soon."

This answer didn't feel right to me, and Bill continued to get worse. His legs kept getting increasingly more edematous, he lost more weight and had severe fatigue. I begged him to see a specialist in nephrology (kidney doctor) to get an expert opinion. Finally, a few weeks later in March, Bill gave in and made an appointment with a nephrologist, Dr. B, at the University of Virginia Medical Center. Dr. B seemed quite a bit more concerned than the previous doctor. He ordered more tests, and then, in April, a kidney biopsy.

My mother arrived at the end of March with my uncle Herbert. My parents had offered Herbert a trip to Charlottesville if he would help us finish the basement. Bill could not do much anymore—he was too weak and tired.

Herbert was an expert carpenter as well as an engineer. He put up studs and sheetrock for a family room, hallway, a bathroom, and an additional bedroom. Mamma and Herbert worked feverishly every day and only took off a few times to do some sightseeing. I helped out as much as I could while taking care of the house, cooking meals for everyone, taking Bill to his doctor appointments, and making sure the kids had clean clothes.

The results from the kidney biopsy came back a few days before Mamma and Herbert left to go back to Europe at the end of April.

Bill and I went to see Dr. B to get the results from the biopsy. Dr. B asked Bill to wait outside in the waiting room while he talked to me. I found that very strange, but Bill did not object, which I found even stranger.

Dr. B looked at me somberly and said, "The biopsy shows that Bill has amyloidosis, which is a fatal disease without any cure. He may have three to five years left to live."

A deep fear engulfed me; I felt ice-cold in the warm consultation office. It felt as if a hand had squeezed my heart until there was no blood left. My mind went blank, and I stared in disbelief at the doctor.

I wanted to scream, but instead, I blurted out with as much control as I could muster, "What is amyloidosis?"

Dr. B explained that amyloidosis is a condition in which a protein called amyloid builds up in your organs. The amyloid deposits make the organs rigid, eventually leading to organ failure.

After hearing this brief explanation of Bill's condition, I felt a tremendous rage toward the doctor, who had now left it up to me to tell Bill the bad news. What a coward!

When I walked into the waiting room where Bill was sitting, Bill didn't say anything or ask any questions. We drove home in silence, and my mind was churning with the heavy responsibility of telling Bill the truth. I was going over the information in my mind and also trying to figure out how I would tell Bill about the diagnosis and the terrible prognosis. I asked myself if I would want to know the truth, and I knew I would.

Once at home in our bedroom, I asked Bill if he wanted to know what the doctor had said, and he said yes.

Then I asked if he wanted the whole truth, and he said yes again.

It was difficult to tell Bill that he was going to die without breaking down crying first. I told him the most optimistic prognosis—that he had maybe five years left to live—but my intuition told me that he would die much sooner than that.

Then the tears came. I thought my whole being would dissolve into nothing, just a pool of tears, with all my pain and grief drowned in it. We embraced and cried together, and I wondered how Bill must feel about this nightmare.

Later, when I told Mamma and Herbert about the diagnosis and prognosis, Herbert looked at me as if he wanted to flee from the fear of it all. He looked horrified.

We celebrated everybody's birthday before Mamma and Herbert left to go back home. Bill was thirty-eight years old, and I was thirty-six. Tariq was fourteen, Tore had just turned thirteen, and Daniel was only seven.

After Mamma and Herbert left, we had to face the uncertainty of Bill's serious condition alone. I knew I had to be the strong one for Bill's sake.

The next day I wrote this in my journal:

> *Is this really happening to us? Is it all going to end soon? What about the love, the hopes, and the wish to grow old together? I cannot bear the thought of being alone again. Bill must live because we all need him so much. Oh, Lord, we are too young for this! We haven't even had our honeymoon yet. On a daily basis, I act normal, but there is a deep sadness inside*

me. Why Bill? Why not me? Oh, Bill, darling, I feel so helpless, as there is nothing I can do, and yet, I would give my own life, if it would secure yours.

I felt it would be a big mistake if Bill died, and I was very angry with God for making such a bad decision. It would have been a much better choice if I died since I found life to be difficult and painful most of the time. Bill had so much promise as a scientist and so much to give the world in comparison to me. He loved life. It didn't make any sense to me. But I knew too well that life goes on regardless of tragedy and sorrow.

I wrote in my journal:

The sun still shines, and the birds sing more beautifully than ever. The trees seem greener and happier this year, because of so much generous rain. All this beauty hurt my eyes and the birds' singing is a torment to my ears. I feel a rage toward life itself, a life I have no desire to live without Bill. Bill has made me see all the beauty through his eyes. How do I learn to appreciate the time that is left, instead of thinking of the dreaded end and the excruciating pain that will eventually follow? I know too well what is in store for me because I already know what that pain and grief will be like. I went through it once before. How will I be able to pick up the pieces? Will the children again be the ones who will force me to stay alive? Where is God? I know life is not fair, and I don't expect it to be. I don't even ask anymore, "Why Bill and me?" That is just the way things are; fate, being unlucky, that is what we are. What about my poor, poor children? God, at least have mercy on them and pour all the shit on me, as I don't really care anymore. The pain is complete, anyway.

Amazingly, Bill went to work every day despite his weakness and fatigue, but he slept most of the time when he was at home. Since his kidneys were now working at only one-third capacity, the swelling in his legs increased and spread through his whole body. He lost muscle because his kidneys excreted most of the protein he ate. We bought a half a cow, and I served high-protein meals every day. Bill was given diuretics to get rid of the fluid, and a heart medication for his arrhythmia. More tests would be done to determine the extent of amyloid deposits found in his heart. His heart rate was very fast, and he was short of breath with minimal exertion.

Bill decided to talk to Tariq and Tore to tell them the truth, but Daniel was another problem since we felt he was too young to know. That might have been a big mistake. Bill had an emotional talk with Tariq and Tore, telling them that he expected them to get a college education and to help me out as much as they could.

For things to go more smoothly for me after he was gone, Bill settled his affairs and made a will.

We lived in a daily nightmare, and I cried while I spackled and painted the basement walls. I had been given Valium by my doctor since I had a hard time coping. Before Bill came home from work, I would take a Valium, so he couldn't see that I had been crying.

At one point, I became very angry and said to myself, "I refuse to take part in this horrible play. I have done this before, and I can't do it again! If Bill wants to die, he can do it on his own!"

I realized that I was terrified to face the incredible pain of grief again. It was such an indescribable pain—it had burned through my entire being for years. I didn't want to do it again.

The minute, after this thought entered my mind, I recognized how selfish it was. I was not the one dying. At that moment, I knew, that I needed to support Bill and help him die, peacefully. I also needed to make him believe that I was strong and that we would be okay after he died. This was my gift of love to him, even though it was killing me on the inside.

I needed to know more about death and dying and what happens to everyone involved. I started reading Elisabeth Kübler-Ross's book *On Death and Dying* and learned about the five stages of grief—denial, anger, bargaining, depression, and acceptance. I finally gained an understanding of what I had been through in the past, and what was happening to Bill. My attitude changed in an instant, and from that day on, I became Bill's support and strength. That was all I had to give, besides my undying love for him. I started living for the moment, relishing all the beautiful moments with Bill.

One afternoon, Bill came home even earlier than usual because he was so exhausted. The boys were still in school. We were sitting in the dining room talking when we suddenly heard the radio playing the chorus to a song by Dan Hill:

And sometimes when we touch
The honesty's too much
And I have to close my eyes
And hide
I want to hold you till I die
Till we both break down and cry
I want to hold you till the fear in me subsides

We looked at each other with tears in our eyes. We embraced passionately and desperately, and then we cried. There was nothing to say, as our emotions said everything. It was a beautiful moment full of love and sadness for what might come, and I knew I would never forget that day.

Later that evening, Bill wanted to make love, which surprised me since he was so fatigued. His whole body was edematous and he looked very pale. I looked at his sweet face with the warm, loving eyes and my heart filled with an aching sad feeling, knowing that this would probably be the last time, we would ever make love. I remembered one of his letters where he had written:

> *It's like magic, a very special magic and we make love to each other with more than our bodies, which makes me feel so good and whole.*

It didn't matter to me what he looked like because I loved him with my whole heart and soul. We made love slowly and tenderly while an all-encompassing sadness filled the room.

Chapter 34

Death never comes at the right time,
despite what mortals believe.
Death always comes as a thief.
—Christopher Pike

We needed to tell Bill's parents the terrible news. I made the call, and I told them that I thought they should come for a visit as soon as possible. An ominous feeling brewed in me that this would go much faster than the doctor had predicted because Bill's condition was deteriorating fast. I told Tariq and Tore that I didn't think Bill would live out the year.

At the end of May, Bill's immediate family came for a visit—his parents, his sister and brother with their spouses, and Rachel's baby girl. I was anxious about the visit and how Bill's mother would behave.

When I found someone crying in a corner from the sadness and grief, I was the one comforting them. Some days I felt detached because I had to cope with so much, and at other times I would break down crying when I was alone in my bedroom. Bill was quiet, pale, and lethargic. I would look at his ashen face and wonder how he felt. For the first day or so, it felt comforting to have Bill's family around, but after a few days, it became overwhelming and stressful.

One night, we were invited out to dinner by Bill's family to the Japanese Steakhouse. It was a treat for me, and I got a little tipsy on my piña colada. On the way home, we stopped off at the store for some groceries, and I bought Bill three red roses.

When I gave him the roses, I said, "*Jeg elsker dig,*" which means "I love you" in Danish.

Bill thought I was wasting money. I was a little hurt, but this was a normal reaction from him. He had difficulty accepting a gift or just saying, "Thank you."

When the kids and I had given him a watch for his birthday, he had said, "It's too good for work and it is too expensive."

He could have just thanked us. Later, he complained that the watch didn't have a second hand. He did recognize the fact that the watch was beautiful, though, so he kept it. I knew that he didn't want much for himself and that he sacrificed everything for us. Even though he was grumpy about receiving gifts, I knew what was in his heart.

During the next couple of days, Bill's brother and brother-in-law erected the paneling in the family room. Bill supervised and made sure that everything had been done right, but he was unable to do anything himself.

The girls and I spent an afternoon in town, relaxing and talking about Bill. They gave me all sorts of advice, but I felt nobody understood my difficult situation. Their lives would not change in any practical way, but mine would. I knew what was coming, with no income, heavy medical bills, kid's educational expenses, and handling it all alone. How would I manage financially? These were practical things to think about but impossible to deal with ahead of time. I was told to be strong and to not give up hope. But what if I couldn't be as strong as they wanted me to be? Would I then be condemned to the agony of feeling guilty for the rest of my life? I was afraid that I would be blamed in the end, just as I had been in Africa.

From personal experience, I knew the family would need a scapegoat for their grief and anger, and I feared the day I would have to face Bill's family alone.

How could this happen again? I thought that I had paid my dues. Living without Bill was inconceivable. I wanted to be strong, cheerful, hopeful, loving, and kind, but that was hard when my insides were in a knot, full of pain, anger, and despair.

Bill's mother kept needling me during her stay, and one day I finally blew up and told her off. Etta kept telling me that I was killing Bill and that it was all my fault. When she and my father-in-law got back to Brooklyn, she called and apologized to Bill for leaving in anger, and then she asked to talk to me. She couldn't apologize to me, so I did it for her. I told her that we were both unhappy about what was happening to Bill, that I was under so much stress, and that was the reason I had lost my cool. I apologized to her and told her to come for a visit anytime.

While Bill's family was still visiting, my friend Helle arrived for a visit with her two boys. Spending some time with her helped my troubled mind. It was good to unload and to have a listening ear, rather than being told what to do all the time.

I also started seeing a therapist. The first therapist could not handle listening to my woes, so he dismissed me after a couple of weeks. I finally found another therapist, a psychologist, who was calm and thoughtful, and talking to him was comforting. He wanted me to see a psychiatrist as well because I needed another prescription for anxiety so that I could better handle my difficult situation.

Bill seemed more relaxed after everyone had left, and I realized that I needed to keep the visits to a minimum.

Atif and Mahnoor had also planned a visit, but they were calm, comforting people to have around. It helped a lot to talk to Mahnoor over the weekend. Meanwhile, Bill was getting increasingly worse.

During their visit, I asked Mahnoor, "Why does God have to take Bill? Why can't he take a bum on the street instead, since Bill has so much to give society?"

Mahnoor answered curtly, "So what?"

Her brutal answer was shocking, but I understood what she meant. Life is cruel and unfair at times, and there is no reason why.

By the middle of June, Bill had deteriorated so badly that he had to start dialysis. I hoped that would make him feel better.

Tariq was feeling guilty one weekend because there was a dance at his high school, and he thought that he should stay with his papa at the dialysis center. I told him that his job was to be a teenager and to go and enjoy himself and that nothing would change if he didn't attend the dance. I drove him to the dance and then went to spend the evening with Bill during dialysis.

A few days later, Bill ended up in the hospital due to uremia from kidney failure, and the doctors started him on Solu-Medrol. Solu-Medrol is a brand name and a synthetic form of methylprednisolone sodium succinate (a cortico-steroid produced by the adrenal gland) which is used to treat various medical conditions to control inflammation.

When Bill's family would call, I had to console them, and I had to be cheerful and optimistic with Bill to keep his hopes up. There was no time to think of myself. I was merely existing, running back and forth to the hospital. I knew that everyone in my family was relying on me. I had lost ten pounds since Bill got sick and hadn't even noticed until a friend commented on it. She was envious, but I offered to take her problems if she would take mine, and that shut her up.

I spent most of my time every day in the hospital taking care of Bill.

One morning when I was bathing him, he looked at himself in the mirror and saw his own gaunt face, and said,

"Oh, how terrible I look! My eyes just stare. Who is that man in the mirror? This is not me at all. I am just a shadow of what I used to be!"

After dialysis, he looked like a prisoner from a concentration camp, because of his emaciated face and body. His face and body had sunk in after all the fluid was gone, and I could see the deterioration of all his muscles. He looked like a dying man, and I felt a dread of what might come.

As he lay back on the bed, Bill took my hand gently and looked lovingly at me. "I am so surprised how strong you are, Maud," he said. "You are a good woman! Will you be okay?"

I blinked back the tears that were always there behind my eyelids and nodded.

Then he said, "I love you so much, and I am only living for you now."

When I mentioned how important his work was to him, he said, "No, you are the most important thing in my life."

He apologized several times for giving me such a hard time and not spending enough time with me. I told him that now he needed to lean on me instead, and he did. I spent at least twelve hours a day with him at the hospital, walking him, bathing him, and shaving him. The kids had to take care of themselves somehow.

After a week in the hospital, I felt it was time for the boys to go to see their papa, as he was getting worse. Just before we were going to leave in the morning, the nurse called and said that Bill was not up to seeing the kids because he was too tired. The boys were sitting on the couch ready to go when I told them what the nurse had said. They looked so utterly disappointed that I decided to take them anyway.

When we arrived at the hospital, I left the boys in the waiting room while I went in to talk to Bill. I was again shocked to see how bad he looked. Every day he was looking a little worse. Bill gave in and promised to see the boys for a short while.

As I walked down the hallway with the kids in tow, I noticed all the nurses looking at us with pity in their eyes. My heart was heavy because I was afraid that this would be the last time the boys would see their father. Bill was our rock and stability, and now we had to be his comfort for as long as it lasted.

The boys looked shocked to see their father so sick, but they handled it amazingly well. How much Daniel understood was probably limited, as we had not told him much, poor boy. I had to assure Bill that we would be alright after he was gone so that he could die in peace. I believe I did that.

When I visited again on June 26, 1979, I thought Bill looked a little better. He appeared alert and questioned the nurses about the infusion he was getting. He wanted to know everything about the medications and treatment and seemed to be his sharp, usual self. Solu-Medrol had caused problems with bleeding from all orifices, so it had been stopped. The doctors had ordered a blood thinner instead because of his amyloid-affected heart, to prevent blood clots.

While I was in the room, Bill went into congestive heart failure, and I immediately called the nurse. Shortly thereafter, the code team arrived, and I was told to leave the room. As I was walking down the hall with an overwhelming fear consuming me, Carol, a doctor friend, who used to be our neighbor at the faculty housing, came over to me and put her arms around me. She had heard over the intercom about the code and knew it was Bill. Bill was intubated and put in the ICU. He was unconscious.

Carol talked me into coming to her house to get some sleep. There was nothing I could do anyway, she said. She gave me a Valium and put me to bed and then checked up on my boys.

When I woke up the next morning, Carol informed me that Bill had died during the night.

I screamed in pain and cried out, "I should have been there! Why wasn't I there when he needed me the most?"

I was inconsolable. Bill was gone, and I had let him down during the last hours of his life. I secretly blamed Carol, but mostly I blamed myself for giving in to her plea to think of myself rather than Bill. My guilt was heavy, and I felt my life was over, but I had to hold on for my boys' sake.

After a couple of days, we had a funeral service at the temple, and then Bill's body was shipped to New York City to be buried according to the family traditions. It didn't matter to me where he was because he was still in my heart.

When I saw Bill in the casket with his serene, beautiful face, I felt like jumping in there with him. I refused to wear black to the service. I wore white instead. I thought that was more fitting.

The day Bill died, Daniel said several times, "This is the worst day of my life!"

My little seven-year old boy lost his father so young, and Tariq and Tore had now lost a second father. Life can be so cruel.

One of my neighbors spent the night with me for the first two nights, and I will be forever grateful to her for that. I was petrified of being alone; the pain was indescribable.

For the next few days, the house was full of people who came to show their respect. Everybody brought food and tried to help out with various things.

After the funeral service, and while people were still there, I went into the bedroom to be by myself. I was crying when Daniel found me.

He sat down next to me on the bed and said, "Mom, it's not good for you to sit here all by yourself like this. You need to get out of here and be with other people."

I told him that I was missing his papa, and then he said, "But, Mom, he is still here, you know!"

Then we hugged and cried together.

Chapter 35

Without you in my arms, I feel an emptiness in my soul.
I find myself searching the crowds for your face—
I know it is an impossibility, but I cannot help myself.
—Nicholas Sparks

My parents arrived a few days after Bill's death; we needed them desperately. To the outside world, it looked like I was holding up well because I would put on a happy, smiling face. My mother's first observation, when she and Pappa arrived, was that I looked thin and pale.

For the first two weeks, I was very busy taking care of practical things. I had legal papers to file, including insurance, and electrical and plumbing work to be finished in the basement.

There would be no more paychecks after Bill's death, and therefore no money, so I had to file for a widow's pension and make sure I received the small life insurance Bill had. I didn't know how we would make it financially in America on our own without Bill.

The boys were acting out in different ways. Tariq was becoming bossy because he felt he had to fill Bill's shoes. I had to explain to him that he was not the dad but still a kid. Tore was having headaches every day and worrying that I would fall apart emotionally. Daniel could not fall asleep at night, and he would frequently remain awake until his brothers went to bed. When he did sleep, he had nightmares.

I sat down with the boys one day and talked to them about our situation. I wanted them to know that we would be all right. I think I relieved some of their worries about me because they seemed more relaxed the next day.

We were all barely hanging on, though, so my parents became the stabilizing factor for us for a few weeks. Bill had been our rock, stability, and strength, and without him, life as we knew it would drastically change.

My beautiful, loving, kind, unselfish husband was gone, but I felt him in the house and would speak to him at night in our bedroom. When I went into town, I would sometimes see him in the crowd, or I thought I saw him. It was an eerie, unsettling feeling, and it always made me cry.

Because so many things reminded me of Bill, I had a hard time accepting that he was indeed gone. I felt part of me was gone, too. At the same time, I felt Bill would never be completely gone. How could he be gone if I still loved him? I knew I would always love him; the hard part would be missing him forever.

Regardless of all my ups and downs, we had been happy. At least that's what Bill told me before he died. Bill said that he had always loved me and that he had been happy with me despite my depression. When I was good, I was so incredibly good that it made up for all the bad, and we never wavered in our love. In between my depressive periods, I was a happy, charismatic, and fun person. Bill had made my life worth living.

I was a good housekeeper, and Bill appreciated my efforts and hard work. He came up with a joke one day about my neatness.

He told some friends, "Maud is so neat that when I get up at night to go to the bathroom, the bed is already made when I come back."

I was afraid that I would not be strong enough for the boys. I was familiar with the incredible pain we would have to live with for a long, long time to come. The pain of grief was unbearable at times, but to see my boys suffer was even harder. I couldn't do much about it, and that was the worst part. I used all my strength to hold on, and there didn't seem to be enough time or energy to be there for the kids as much as I wanted to be. I still had to appear strong for them, at all costs.

Thank God for my parents. My mother had to get back to work after three weeks, but my father stayed for another three weeks.

For the first two weeks, I barely cried; I was afraid to open the floodgates. The only thing that helped was staying busy, and I had plenty to do on a daily basis. It was at night that I would break down and cry when I was alone in my room. The bed seemed too big and empty, and I felt excruciatingly lonely.

My Love Is Gone

When your love is gone
and you are all alone
and you need someone to hold
What do you do?
You can read a book
make a cup of tea
squeeze your kids
pet your dog
or watch some TV

When nothing helps
you take out the pictures
and the old letters
then you cry and cry
but you smile in between

Then you get angry
and you curse the Almighty
for such an unfair thing
but then you feel guilty
cause that's part of it all

But you survive,
because you can't stop breathing
you try not to think
about the pain
then you remove all the pictures
letters and everything

—Maud Steinberg

The kids started school, and Daniel began playing soccer for the first time. My father would bring Daniel to soccer practice and help him in practical ways. Pappa spent much time with Daniel, which was great for me. They would also go fishing together, and I bought a tackle box and other fishing supplies for Daniel.

On the last day of the soccer clinic, Daniel played well, but then he had a bad fall at the end. He got upset and said that he had amnesia and wanted to go home. Pappa would not hear of it since a game with the parents versus the coaches was coming up. Tariq, Pappa, and I played on the parents' team, and we had a great time. I was the only woman on the team, and I played with enthusiasm and energy. I desperately needed the physical outlet.

Pappa was the goalie, but he injured his right leg during the game. He refused to go to the doctor or the hospital because he had a deep fear of both. I gave him some Valium for sleep, so he could calm down and some ibuprofen for the pain.

The next morning, his ankle had swelled up quite a bit, and I knew he needed to get that leg looked at, but he still refused. In desperation, I called Carol, the doctor who had helped us in the past. I thought my father would probably listen to her, as he knew her. Pappa agreed to see Carol for an evaluation, and he had the ankle x-rayed. There were no broken bones, just a bad sprain. Pappa had a cast put on his entire lower leg, and he recovered after a few weeks. A couple of weeks later, Pappa left to go back to Denmark and work.

Six weeks after Bill's death, his mother, sister, and brother arrived for a visit. Bill's mother seemed to be holding up well, but his father stayed behind in Brooklyn.

While Bill's family was visiting, we were supposed to go to the Busch Gardens theme park in Williamsburg with the kids on a Saturday. I had gone into town for some grocery shopping in the morning, and when I arrived home, Bill's mother and siblings had left. The kids looked upset, and they had been crying. Tariq told me that Etta had said that I had killed Bill.

He became angry with her and said, "You have no right to say something like that about our mother behind her back."

After that verbal exchange, Tariq had asked them to leave, as he and his brothers no longer had any desire to go to Busch Gardens with them.

It was shocking to hear this, but I was not surprised, as I knew how grief could bring out the worst in people. I had been accused of killing a husband for the second time, and I felt sad that people could be so ugly. But, I had to let the anger toward them go, for my own sake.

Bill and I had borrowed a few thousand dollars from his parents for the down payment on our house in 1975. Bill's mother had promised that we could deduct a thousand dollars from the debt if we had someone finish the basement, which we did. Bill and I had discussed this money problem before he died, and Bill believed that his parents would forgive the debt under the circumstances. I had my doubts.

It didn't take too many days after Bill's death before Etta demanded that I pay back the loan. She wanted a thousand dollars more, and she had added interest. Bill's father wanted the diamond watch that he had given Bill when he earned his PhD. I was disappointed and hurt by their demands. I considered giving the watch back, but then I talked to my mother, and she made me see how wrong that was. Bill had promised Daniel that watch, and I felt I needed to save it for him. So, in the end, I refused to give back the watch but paid Bill's parents a little more than Bill had suggested. The Steinberg family never did anything to help us after Bill died, and we never saw or heard from them again.

I wanted to leave the States and go back to Denmark after Bill died. I felt I needed my family for support. In the States, I had nobody. But when I talked to the kids about it, they became quite upset. Tariq and Tore wanted to finish high school in America, and they pleaded with me to stay, so I gave in.

At the beginning of our marriage, Bill had wanted me to convert to Judaism, but I had no desire to do that again. I didn't believe that my particular religion mattered. After getting married, Bill became more religious and wanted to celebrate several Jewish holidays, which was fine with me. I told him that he would have to take charge of that himself, and I would help him make it work.

However, Bill refused to let us have a Christmas tree, and he didn't want us to celebrate Christmas, either. I had celebrated Christmas with Tariq and Tore while we lived in Denmark, and I didn't' want to deprive them of that. I adhered to Bill's rule of no Christmas tree, but on Christmas Eve, I would always make a big Scandinavian Christmas dinner with all the trimmings and dessert. Then I would give the kids a couple of presents, which Bill accepted. During the week of Chanukah, which happens around Christmas, the kids would receive more presents. We had managed to compromise. We sort of celebrated both holidays and I agreed that the kids could go to Hebrew school since that had been so important to Bill.

We didn't go to the temple often, but we usually attended services on Rosh Hashanah (Jewish New Year), Yom

Kippur (Day of Atonement), and Passover. Bill would follow the Jewish traditions regarding these holidays, and I would help make the food. These celebrations were always a very close, comforting family time for us all. After Bill died, the Jewish traditions fell by the wayside, as they were not my traditions.

The boys had been going to the temple for Hebrew lessons during the last few years. I asked them if they wanted to continue those studies. None of them did, and I was relieved, as I had enough to attend to; moreover, we couldn't afford it. The kids were very grateful that I had asked their opinion about it.

After my father left, we were all trying to cope. We were all having emotional problems in one form or another. Only time would take care of that, but in the meantime, we had to grin and bear it and try to do the best we could.

Grief

I am dancing in a misty cloud
of tears running down my face
My legs and arms are moving,
but my heart is heavy and holding me down

Like slow motion in space
Move, move into a faster spin
Let the vibrations fill my heart
and give it wings
I need to fly and stay in midair for a while
I want to hear the bluebirds sing

I want to love, I want to live
I want to feel happiness again
So, let me dance my tears away
Let me fly around the world one time
Leave me high, leave me sane
or all this crying will get me down

—Maud Steinberg

Chapter 36

We must welcome the future, remembering that soon
it will be the past; and we must respect the past,
remembering that it was once all that was humanly possible.
—George Santayana

The first few months after Bill's death were incredibly difficult. I just wanted to stay in bed, but I had three kids to take care of. I needed to figure out how to survive—not only emotionally but also financially. There was no time for a pity party, as there was much work to be done.

I continued therapy to help me with the grief. Tariq and Tore refused therapy, and I couldn't force them to go. They were too old (fifteen and thirteen) and too big to be dragged anywhere.

Daniel, on the other hand, was only eight years old and was expressing his anger at school in various ways. I was able to take him to see the child psychologist, I had found. Daniel didn't want to go, but I forced him into the doctor's office. That's all I could do. Daniel refused to see the doctor, and he walked out of the office as soon as we got there. He walked around the neighborhood for the entire hour, and I paid ninety dollars each time. This happened once a week for many weeks.

When Daniel finally gave up and stayed for the therapy session, he blew up with explosive rage, cussed out the doctor, and was quite rude and uncontrollable. The doctor told me later that he had to physically sit on him to calm him down. Daniel stayed in therapy for at least a year and it was very helpful. My poor children were grief-stricken about losing their father.

One day, Daniel said to me, "Well, I guess I have to do it all by myself now."

He shared his father's love of science and knew I could not help him.

My older boys were dealing with their own emotional problems and with being teenagers. I felt a heavy responsibility for those boys, and I worried constantly that they would get into trouble, and they did a few times.

One late-fall evening in 1979, I went to the theater with a friend. When I came home, I noticed that our second car was missing from the driveway. The boys looked quite nervous when I walked into the house. I asked what was wrong and where the car was.

Tariq, as the oldest, took control and said, "Mom, you better sit down, as we have something to tell you."

I replied, "The hell I will. You better tell me right now what is going on."

I noticed that the boys' pants looked kind of bulky. The boys had padded their pants with a couple of books. They thought I would give them a beating after they told me what they had done. Tariq finally started telling their story.

After I had left that evening, the boys had decided to take the car for a little joyride, but neither had a driver's license. Tariq sat behind the wheel and drove out of the neighborhood, down a small gravel road. He lost control of the car and drove up a bank. Then, the car rolled over and ended up back on the gravel road, upside down. My boys were sitting upside down inside the car, staring at the ceiling in shock.

Daniel was in the backseat, and he hollered, "We better get out of this car. It might blow up."

Daniel kicked out the back window and crawled out, and then Tariq and Tore followed. It amazed me how well my boys handled the situation. They did all the right things after that. Tariq walked home and called the police, while Tore and Daniel stayed with the car. By the time I came home, the car had been towed away. It was completely totaled.

After I heard their story, all I thought about was that I could have lost all my kids that night. I didn't care about the car.

I was so upset that all I could say was, "I am so angry with you right now that I don't even want to look at you or even speak to you. Just go to bed, and we will talk in the morning."

I cried all night, thinking how that evening I could have lost them all. Tariq told me later that that was the harshest punishment he had ever gotten: my refusal to even talk to him.

My car insurance was canceled, as I was now a real liability with two teenagers prone to joyrides without a driver's license. It took many tries and quite a lot of money to get car insurance coverage again.

We had planned to go to Denmark for the Christmas holidays to see my parents. Being without Bill for the holidays would have been too difficult for all of us. The trip almost didn't happen, due to lack of car insurance. Just a few days before the date of the scheduled trip, I managed to acquire insurance at a high cost. The kids and I drove to Dulles Airport and parked the car there while we were in Denmark. My boys learned a big lesson from that car accident.

After doing some research on how to invest in real estate, I developed a long-term plan. I enrolled in a tax class at the community college. I knew I couldn't afford help with the taxes, so I needed to learn how to do them before tax time. Bill was the one who had done the taxes each year, but I was the one who had gotten all the numbers together, so I had some knowledge of what was needed. I was also trying to figure out a way to get the kids through college.

The life insurance money was not enough to put all the kids through college. After paying off the loan from my in-laws and using some of the insurance money for the first few months before the widow's pension kicked in, I had thousands less. I also had many medical bills and bills for the work in the basement.

By investing in real estate, I would incur many tax-deductible expenses related to the properties. The deductions would decrease my taxable income substantially, and my kids would be able to get financial help for college with Pell Grants, student loans, and scholarships. Besides, I would also make some money. I wanted to test this plan out in class and then put it into action. The tax course served me in several ways.

So, in 1980, I invested the remaining insurance money in a dilapidated house in a predominantly black neighborhood in downtown Charlottesville. Everyone said I was crazy to buy a house in the black part of town, but that didn't bother me.

Since this broken-down house needed to be refurbished, I had to ask the bank for a loan. The house was not livable in its current condition, and it had no heat. I had no work history because I had been a stay-at-home mom, so getting the loan was complicated. I wrote up a business proposal for the bank about my plan and laid out what the estimated expenses and potential income would be for the property. The loan officers were impressed and gave me a loan.

I turned the house into a rooming house with eight bedrooms, one efficiency, three bathrooms, a common living room, a kitchen, and laundry facilities. After the tenants moved in, I had positive cash flow of hundreds of dollars every month. I bought a second house a year later, and I was approved for another loan. I had proved myself.

During this time, I worked at least twelve hours a day and was rarely home. I hired a man for the heavy-duty restoration work of the house, but I did all the cleaning, spackling, and painting myself.

When I first advertised the rooms for rent, I found out that everyone wanted furnished rooms. I immediately ran out, bought furniture from a second-hand store, and furnished the whole house for $1200. When all the furnished rooms were rented out, I maintained and cleaned the common areas every week, which included the living room, kitchen, and bathrooms. I knew nobody would take on that responsibility, and it needed to be done to keep up the quality of the rental. I collected rent every Friday evening when people received their paychecks.

My mother quit her job in Copenhagen and came to stay with us for nine months that year. She was never able to get another good job again due to her age. Mamma sacrificed a lot for me, and I was awed and grateful. Her heart had always been in the right place, even though she had had a hard time showing her feelings toward me. I realized she had always loved me. It was comforting to have her with us during this adjustment period after Bill's death. She cooked dinner for the kids and greeted them when they came home from school.

Occasionally, I would go dancing in the evening after working all day. I started going to a "singles club" on Wednesday evenings. After the club meetings, I would gather a group of friends to go dancing afterward. Dancing was helpful in dealing with my grief, and it kept me sane.

I had told my boys that they needed to get all A's to gain admission to UVA or another state college, as out-of-state colleges and universities would be too expensive.

The real estate plan worked, and my two older boys were able to graduate with four-year degrees from UVA without any debt attached. Of course, they'd had to work part-time to earn spending money. I was very proud of them.

I continued college and received a Bachelor of Arts degree from Mary Baldwin College. I realized that a BA wasn't going to get me anywhere, so I applied to a new "second-degree program" in nursing at UVA. I had been out of nursing for so long, and I needed to get a registered nurse license in Virginia. This was a competitive new program for people who already had a degree.

Before making this decision, I had volunteered with Hospice for a couple of years, taking care of patients who were dying. I wanted to make sure that I could handle it emotionally. I found that my fear of death and dying was gone, which gave me the courage to pursue nursing again.

To my delight, I was accepted, and I was the second-oldest person in the two-year program to get a Bachelor of Science in Nursing. After graduation, I was granted membership in the Golden Key National Honor Society as recognition of my outstanding scholastic achievement.

Tore and I graduated the same year from UVA, so I couldn't attend Tore's entire graduation, as I had my own to attend. Tariq had graduated a year earlier from UVA and had gone to work for Merrill Lynch in New York City.

After five years I sold the houses. I did very well on the first house, doubling my money, and my second house sold with a small profit.

I wanted to continue to study for a master's in nursing and then become a nurse practitioner, but I had to stop my studies, as I needed to make money to help put Daniel through college. After I sold the houses and started working as an RN at UVA hospital, Daniel could not get the same breaks for financial assistance as his brothers had, so I had to help him out monthly. Daniel graduated from Virginia Polytechnic Institute and State University and became an inventor and entrepreneur. All my boys are entrepreneurs in one form or another.

We had our struggles after Bill died, but we made it. My brother told me recently, "I could never have done what you did—living with such uncertainty and fighting for survival every day."

When I look back, I don't understand how I did it either.

It had been five years since I visited Momma and she had had another stroke. I had kept the correspondence going as I had done all my life, but now it was Britt who answered the letters for her as Momma was paralyzed, bedridden, and could not speak.

I had heard from Mamma that Momma had almost died a few times. Intuitively, I knew that Momma needed to see me before she died, and I wanted to show her that I was okay. So, in the summer of 1983, I traveled to Copenhagen to visit my parents and home to Undersåker to see Momma, Dagmar, and Britt. Britt had remained in the family home to help out with Dagmar, but Momma had to be placed in a nursing home after her last stroke.

Momma could not speak a word and had trouble swallowing, but she laughed until her eyes filled with tears. I didn't know if she was really laughing or maybe she was crying. I sang some songs for her, held her hand, and kissed her pale cheek, but without communication, it was painful to see her like this. The visit was emotional and saying goodbye was even harder, as I knew it would be the last time, I would see Momma.

About a week after my return to Charlottesville, the phone rang one early morning as it did so many times during the day. As soon as I heard the ring, I knew Momma had died. I picked up the phone, and it was my mother. I had been right; Momma was gone. My heart ached from the grief, but I felt relief that Momma did not have to suffer anymore. Momma had loved God and Jesus and had been a faithful Christian all her life, but being a good, religious, and god-fearing person did not save her from suffering.

Missing Bill and Momma have been part of my daily life, but the pain has subsided over time. I will always love them and miss them. I hope to see everyone when I die—God willing.

It has been almost fifty years since I moved to America from the Land of the Midnight Sun, and it has been an educational experience. America can be a harsh country to live in, as there is no safety net for the misfortunate like in Scandinavia. America can be cruel, unjust, and prejudiced, but it can also be beautiful, friendly, and provide opportunities for success. America is not for the faint of heart but for the strong who has courage and determination to succeed.

I have enjoyed America's culture and nature and made many interesting friends. However, I wish I had gone back to Denmark after Bill died as my life would have been easier, with more support, and less stress. I will always miss Sweden and Denmark, but I doubt that I will ever go back. It's too late.

When I discussed this subject with my brother, he made this surprising comment, "Maud, it would be hard for you to move back to Denmark because you are an American now."

I realized that he was right.

Death Sacrifice

My heart was crushed, my veins were dry
The torment came out in a desperate cry
Can you understand my enormous grief
Of death that came as a cruel thief

My tender heart and innocent soul
Cried out for a silent death as a goal
But I couldn't give in to this crushing pain
That wishful thinking was forever in vain.

I was not alone, I could not be free
I had to think of thee, thee, and thee
I had to fight to stay above ground
To save the children to whom I was bound.

I survived it all, the pain and the death
I close my eyes and cherish my breath
I live on forever, though scarred and broken
I haven't been beaten, but I have spoken

— Maud Steinberg

Epilogue

Writing this book healed me in many ways. During the process of writing my story, I realized that I had suffered from post-traumatic stress disorder as well as a reactive depression after Afzal's sudden tragic death. Due to my youth and lack of experience, I did not fully comprehend that my depression and PTSD had been caused by the traumatic events in Africa.

PTSD was recognized by the American Psychiatric Association in 1980 but was never addressed in my case even though I had all the symptoms: nightmares, flashbacks, insomnia, irritability, anger, and suicidal thoughts. It's not just war veterans who suffer from PTSD. It can happen to anyone who has experienced a traumatic situation, such as mental, physical or sexual abuse.

I thought the depression and PTSD were due to my own shortcomings, so I criticized myself for not being good enough, strong enough, or smart enough. I felt that whatever happened to me was all my fault, and I felt ashamed. Adequate psychiatric help was lacking, and I was often mistreated by healthcare professionals which enforced my feelings of inadequacy and insecurity.

After suffering from depression and PTSD for twenty years, I decided in 1988 that I had had enough. I went to my family doctor and demanded an antidepressant to get me out of the hole. The doctor prescribed imipramine which I took for two years. It felt as if a veil lifted from my mind. I have not needed anti-depressants since.

My resilience, strength, and overall optimistic personality helped me survive the traumas and tragedies that happened. However, we have to accept that people react and cope differently to life's challenges.

Life's Lessons

I have learned that love lives on after death
And my heart can be open and free
My power is within my own silent breath
And I don't need a you and me

I have learned to be happy on my own
And my happiness comes from within
This is how I see that I have grown
And it also shows where I have been

I have learned that life can be a mess
And it matters how I learn from mistakes
And what I do and what I confess
And how I deal with my many aches

I have learned that no one will save me
And it's up to me to take control
To believe in the infinite me that I see
And to find my truth is the ultimate goal

—Maud Steinberg

Made in the USA
Columbia, SC
25 September 2019